# THE SECRETS
# OF CREATING

The Junior League of Rochester took the name of their cookbook from a lucky slip of the tongue, but the success of *Applehood and Motherpie* (60,000 copies sold in three months) was the result of a great concept, winning design, and delicious recipes. Arline Isaacs collected recipes from her California neighbors, interspersed them with local history and photographs, biographies of the cooks and anecdotes about cooking, and came up with the very successful *Who's Cooking in Laguna Beach*. *Bayou Cuisine*, published by St. Stephen's Episcopal Church in Indianola, Mississippi, contains so much history and lore that it is sometimes shelved with history in the library. And the idea for *A Man's Taste* originated with two husbands who thought a book of recipes by and for men would be a winner—and it was! Now, for all who have dreamed of writing a cookbook, this knowledgeable and easy-to-follow guide gives you the secrets for creating a classic of your own.

# HOW TO WRITE
# AND PUBLISH
# A CLASSIC COOKBOOK

HAYS, ROLFES & ASSOCIATES, founded by Helen Hays and Ellen Rolfes, is the foremost consulting firm specializing in community cookbooks. They created the distributorship, The Collection, Inc., a network for cookbook publishers nationwide, which makes available such bestselling, best-loved titles as *River Road Recipes*, *The Cotton County Collection*, and over 250 other successful titles.

# HOW TO WRITE AND PUBLISH A CLASSIC COOKBOOK

——— BY ———

Hays, Rolfes & Associates
with
Perre Magness

*Illustrated by*
*Michelle Dent*

A PLUME BOOK

**NEW AMERICAN LIBRARY**

NEW YORK AND SCARBOROUGH, ONTARIO

PLUME TRADEMARK REG. U.S. PAT. OFF. AND FOREIGN COUNTRIES
REG. TRADEMARK—MARCA REGISTRADA
HECHO EN HARRISONBURG, VA., U.S.A.

SIGNET, SIGNET CLASSIC, MENTOR, PLUME, MERIDIAN
and NAL BOOKS are published *in the United States* by
New American Library, 1633 Broadway, New York, New York 10019,
*in Canada* by The New American Library of Canada, Limited,
81 Mack Avenue, Scarborough, Ontario M1L 1M8.

**Library of Congress Cataloging-in-Publication Data**
Main entry under title:

How to write and publish a classic cookbook.

   Includes index.
   1. Cookery—Authorship.  I. Magness, Perre, 1940–
II. Hays, Rolfes & Associates.
TX 644.H69  1986    808′. 066641    85-21613
ISBN 0-452-25732-8

First Printing, February, 1986

  2 3 4 5 6 7 8 9

PRINTED IN THE UNITED STATES OF AMERICA

# Dedication

To the Junior League of Memphis, Inc.
who trained us;

To the *thousands* of volunteers and self-
publishers who trusted our guidance
and shared their enthusiasm, experiences,
and information;

To our children, Walker, Lauri, Amy, and
Ellie, who are our "associates";

But most of all to our husbands, Walker
and Barney, whose support, love,
encouragement, help, and patience have
allowed us to reach this point.

# Contents

# Authors' Note

HAYS-ROLFES had its beginnings through volunteer jobs. In 1976 we found ourselves as chairman and vice-chairman of the cookbook committee of the Junior League of Memphis, which at that time had two very successful cookbooks on the market, *The Memphis Cookbook* (published in 1952) and the *Party Potpourri* (1971). It quickly became apparent that what had first seemed like just another volunteer placement was actually the opportunity to learn the national publishing business—a free education in cookbooks, marketing, and office systems. And we *loved* it.

Besides running the League's cookbook business, we were spending many hours answering letters and phone calls. The Memphis books were so successful and widely respected that people from all over the country wanted advice and information. We soon realized the need for sharing information and exchanging ideas about cookbooks; a network was needed. Thus, the first Hays-Rolfes Community Cookbook Seminar was born. In the years since, we have conducted seminars and private consultations in literally all parts of the country.

As we became even more familiar with the cookbook world, we realized other voids existed—and our cookbook world expanded. In 1979 we created *The Collection*. Originally an invitation-only cooperative advertising catalog for self-publishing organizations, it developed into a community network that became the largest wholesale distribution company in the country. Even though we sold the company in 1983, it was another education—in shipping books, supply and demand, customer service, sales and marketing. It also gave us our first introduction to the annual American Booksellers Convention—a national "book event" to which we return every year as exhibitors of community cookbooks.

We later founded and were part owners of a printing company that specialized in cookbooks—yet another education in the appreciation of a specialized part of the book industry. We are presently working as consultants to Grolier, Inc., in developing a community cookbook club for its mail order series.

In May, 1985, we formed Goodlett Press, Inc., a publishing company designed to fill another void. The company provides information and materials needed by self-publishers to direct them through the many facets of publishing.

We have had a unique experience as volunteers, cookbook chairmen, cookbook creators, seminar instructors, trade show exhibitors, distributors, printers, publisher's consultants, and self-publishers. *We've been there!* And we have developed a strong philosophy about classic cookbooks and an incredible belief in the people who create them. Our knowledge and experience, for all they are worth, are now yours.

We would like to thank our friend and associate, Perre Magness. She is a gifted writer and good friend, filled with wit and the incredible ability to pull together our muddled thoughts and reams of paper. Perre turned our experiences and beliefs into a book; we frankly could not have done it without her.

*Helen Hays    Ellen Rolfes*
HAYS, ROLFES & ASSOCIATES

# Introduction

THE FIRST RECIPE was probably exchanged shortly after man discovered fire. While we won't claim quite as long a history for cookbooks, we would like to make a point: where there is a market for food, there is a market for cookbooks.

Just what is this phenomenon? Why are cookbooks so successful? We think we have come up with some of the answers.

For nearly ten years, we have been involved in the cookbook field. We began as volunteers working on a charity cookbook, and became cookbook chairmen. We have been self-publishers and cookbook writers and editors. We have been involved with cookbooks as the owners of a printing company, as distributors, as entrepreneurs, as trade-show exhibitors, and as publishers' consultants. Our motto is "Ask a thousand questions." That's how we learned, by asking about anything and everything that we did not completely understand. We will recommend the motto to you throughout this book. We have worked with over 1,500 cookbooks, teaching techniques, systems, publishing, and marketing. Wherever you are in the cookbook field, we've been there! And we are the greatest believers in the enduring value of cookbooks.

There are over 4,000 cookbooks on the market today, meeting with all degrees of success and failure. Some are failures because of poor execution, lack of care in the planning, or poor marketing. Many of them are successes. And about 500 are what we consider Classics.

In this book we will give you all the information we can to help make your book a Classic Cookbook.

# A BRIEF HISTORY OF COOKBOOKS

The first cookbook in English was probably written by one Alexander Neckham in the twelfth century. By the fourteenth century, there were several books of cookery and "bokes of kervynge," detailing how to carve up a peacock and serve a heron, as well as how to prepare whale, porpoise, seal, swan, sturgeon, and other delicacies. These cookbooks are more than just curiosities; they give an unparalleled glimpse into the lives of people long ago. The gargantuan feasts of hundreds of dishes seem impossibly remote, but the love of color—saffron and parsley—and the concern for the appearance of the dishes seem quite "nouvelle cuisine."

As early as 1747 a cookbook became a best-seller. *The Art of Cookery Made Plain and Simple* by Hannah Glass sold for almost one hundred years. Talk about shelf life! Of course, the prejudice against women made many people claim that a man had written it, and Hannah Glass's name did not appear on the book until after her death, but it illustrates a point: a good cookbook will sell on and on and on.

Food and its preparation have played an important part in the history of the United States. After all, the discovery of the New World was a byproduct of European appetites. Christopher Columbus was sent on his voyage because of the hunger for spices from the Orient. The New World sent many delicacies to the old—corn and potatoes among others. Taste was taken seriously. The British taxes on the colonists' tea and molasses provoked more than a mild complaint.

Cookbooks reflect both the time and the place. The pioneer wife on the westward trek learned to cope with buffalo tongue and beaver tail. She made do with buffalo dung for fuel and baked bread in ovens dug into hillsides or made of piled rocks. She even discovered her own labor-saving devices: butter could be churned by the rocking of a covered wagon.

Changes in life-styles, advances in technology, and new products can be charted through cookbooks. Today's working women want recipes for the microwave and the food processor, but it was not so long ago that cookbooks were explaining the advantages of the new powdered gelatin over isinglass and ground calves' feet. Lydia Pinkham, maker of tonics, wrote a popular cookbook aimed at helping women's ailments. But in today's nutrition-conscious world, some of the lengthy menus from the past make us shudder.

It was through cookbooks that women exchanged information about how to make soap and starch, how to preserve and pickle, how to get rid of insects and pests, how to make cures and lotions and perfumes. To read these records of hearth and home is to admire the ingenuity and creativity of our grandmothers. Cookbooks were a means of self-expression as well as a practical guide, and served as a link with other women in the days before mass communications. The importance of cookbooks in history has been recognized by the collections at Radcliffe College, the Smithsonian, and the Longone Collection in Ann Arbor, Michigan.

# WHO WRITES COOKBOOKS?

We hope we have made our point about the enduring importance of cookbooks. But who is publishing cookbooks today, and what kind of books are they publishing? The list is as long and as varied as an Edwardian banquet menu.

Probably the most famous writers of cookbooks are those professional cooks, members of the "food establishment," who have a wide following eager for whatever they write: Julia Child with her television series, Craig Claiborne through his *New York Times* articles, the late James Beard through his syndicated columns. There are scores of others with a local or regional reputation, or a reputation for a particular talent such as entertaining or ethnic cooking. The professionals, published and marketed by major publishing houses, always find a large market of fans eager to buy their latest effort.

Then there are the celebrity cooks, people who make their names in another field and then write a cookbook. The folksy, down-home comments in Dinah Shore's cookbook, the menus and recipes from elegant restaurants compiled by Vincent Price, the Italian heritage in Robert Alda's Italian cookbook—all make salable items. The dustjacket's picture of a favorite star in the kitchen doesn't hurt sales either.

Of course, there are many less well-known individuals who write cookbooks. They range from the home economics editor of *The Atlanta Journal*, Mrs. S. R. Dull, who published *Southern Cooking* in 1928 (it can still be found on the shelves), to Mary Ann Pickard. Her husband's illness led her to changes in her family's diet, the outgrowth of which was *Feasting Naturally*; its success led to two subsequent volumes. Sometimes a cook just wants to type up her own much-loved recipes, staple them together, and give them to her children and friends. The owner of a restaurant in Louisiana, whose local fans kept asking for her secrets, found that her cookbook, *The Best of Southern Louisiana Cooking*, spread her fame and was the best possible advertisement for her restaurant.

Then there is the fortunate discovery, like that of Barbara Dalia Jasmin, who found in a trunk the journal and recipes of a nineteenth-century New England sea captain's wife, and edited them into *The Captain's Lady Cookbook*. Jean Durkee, whose microwave cookbooks have sold 400,000 copies, says, a book is successful if "the author finds a need and fills it, shares her treasured recipes, teaches the readers, and adds a pinch of her personality."

Somewhat more impersonal, but no less popular, are the compilations of recipes published by major magazines or publishing companies. *The Better Homes & Garden Cook-*

*book* and *Joy of Cooking* are so comprehensive that they are culinary bibles in most kitchens and the first presents for many new brides. *Southern Living, Gourmet,* and other magizines have published volumes of recipes from their pages. *The New York Times* series embraces microwave, vegetarian, and all sorts of cooking. The *Time-Life* series of lavishly illustrated ethnic-heritage cookbooks are another series. Betty Crocker, the trademark name used by the General Mills company, is on a series of books published by Random House that cover everything from beginning basics to Chinese cooking.

Another whole category of cookbooks are those books written for a special product or food. They are published by individuals or publishing companies for one specific appliance: microwaves, crockpots, food processors, or blenders. They can be as small as the booklet that comes with the machine or as large as the Litton Industries series of volumes on microwave cookery. Companies like Campbell's publish *Cooking with Soup* and *Diet Simply with Soup*.

Then there are the cookbooks aimed at promoting a specific idea, such as a wild game cookbook published by a hunting association, or geared to a special program, like the Weight Watchers® cookbooks.

Finally, there are the community cookbooks: books published by charitable organizations as fund-raisers and to promote a special cause. Again, the range is great: from *River Road Recipes*, published in 1959 by the Junior League of Baton Rouge, Louisiana, which has sold one million copies, to a mimeographed pamphlet put out by a church circle which raised just enough money for new carpeting in the sanctuary.

Community cookbooks are a particularly American phenomenon, and the groups that compile them are particularly American institutions. The pioneer society gave rise to women getting together in quilting bees, husking parties, or sewing circles, which combined useful work with socializing. Women had experience in preparing church suppers, so the next step was a logical one. If the church needed a new roof why not collect recipes and sell them to raise the money?

It is said that the earliest of these charity cookbooks was published during the Civil War to raise money for the Sanitary Commissions and battlefield relief. The practice spread quickly, and soon regional cookbooks sprang up all over the country. The tradition was established. Even *Joy of Cooking* was first created and sold to benefit a church in St. Louis.

# WHY SHOULD YOU WRITE A COOKBOOK?

With all of these different types of people, corporations, and organizations publishing cookbooks, the question, of course, is why should you write a cookbook?

The answer: for the very same reasons all the rest of them do!

The first of these reasons is the *profit motive*. Cookbooks do sell.

Julianne Belote, author of three books, has been writing, editing, and doing public relations in the food field for ten years. She says, "Cookbooks have long been the dependables for booksellers and publishers alike. Although they represent only one or two percent of the books published each year, twenty-five percent of all books sold are cookbooks."

Some cookbooks have a net profit of from $150,000 to $200,000 a year. We think there are several reasons why they do so well.

1. There is an established market. By conservative estimates there are over 300,000 collectors of cookbooks in the United States today, and more coming on every year. They buy books to cook from, to read, and just to have. They collect them the way other people collect stamps or coins.
2. Cookbooks know no season. They are the perfect

gift for any occasion and any person. Food is a common denominator for all people. Cookbooks are given for Christmas, house-warmings, thank-yous, showers, weddings, Mother's Day, birthday presents. No one ever has too many cookbooks.

3. A good cookbook goes on forever, unlike most books. Fannie Farmer published 3,000 copies of her *Boston Cooking School Cookbook* at her own expense in 1896. By its tenth revised edition in 1959, over three million copies had been sold—a gold mine for Little, Brown and Company, who bought the rights.

4. The market for cookbooks is expanding. There is an increased interest in food today. The number of gourmet shops, specialty markets, and cooking schools is growing by leaps and bounds, and so is the number of people who will buy cookbooks.

Second, there is *ego satisfaction*. If you enjoy cooking and are a good cook, you want to share your pleasure with others. It is a wonderful feeling to see your name on the finished product, something that is so personally and particularly yours.

Third, there is the *public relations motive*.

1. A cookbook is a "traveling chamber of commerce" for your town, region, or company. Banks and businesses are beginning to underwrite cookbooks for this very reason; they realize the value of the image that a good cookbook promotes.

2. A cookbook is more than just a series of recipes; it is a record of a place and a time. Cookbooks can be read for much more than the food contained in them. You don't have to like *lutefisj* to be interested in the customs and traditions of the Norwegian settlers in Minnesota.

3. A cookbook promotes your business, or your product, or your restaurant, or your cause—and on and on. Look at the groups publishing cookbooks: symphony leagues, museum guilds, cancer societies, associations for the promotion of this or that. Their

message is seen every time someone opens the book. Unlike a pamphlet or a matchbook that gets thrown away, a cookbook is not only kept, but used.

Organizations publish cookbooks for all of the reasons above, plus a few more. As a project, a cookbook has stability. Once the machinery is in place, it is not a parasite on an organization, and it can provide a regular source of budgeted money for an unlimited future. A cookbook has the futher advantage that you are offering the public something—not asking for a donation. Then there is the career development motive. Putting together, printing, and marketing a cookbook provides training for people with a variety of interests: design, layout, artwork, research, publishing, office systems, bookkeeping and marketing. Volunteers today are eager for skills that will help them in a paid or unpaid career, and a cookbook committee offers invaluable training.

And, of course, there is one more reason for both groups and individuals—*fun!* Some of the best friends you will ever make come through working on a shared goal. The esprit de corps generated on such a project can have lasting effects on an organization. When an individual publishes a cookbook, all the family, friends, and neighbors can get involved, and share the pride in the finished product.

Well, if cookbooks are so terrific that everybody's writing them, isn't the market glutted? A good question. We don't think it is. Look at some statistics. After fifty years, *The Better Homes & Gardens Cookbook* is second only to the Bible in sales. *Joy of Cooking* is going strong with 8.5 million copies in print. *Charleston Receipts*, the grandmother of all community cookbooks, published by the Junior League of Charleston, South Carolina, in 1950, continues to sell well. *Applehood and Motherpie*, from the Junior League of Rochester, New York, sold 60,000 copies in just three months.

Craig Claiborne and Julia Child continue to break records with new and old books, while a whole new galaxy of stars is developing. Martha Stewart and Maida Heatter had phenomenal successes with their first books, and have followed up with other strong sellers.

If the product is good enough, there is a market for it, and it will be a success.

And, after all, success is how you define it. For Julia Child, a success may mean that the new book outsells the old, or it may mean that she is able to explore a new idea, as she has done with her emphasis on American regional foods.

Not every group wants to have a *River Road Recipes*, selling a million copies. Success may mean raising just enough money for a particular project. Success may mean being able to compile your family's recipes and print just enough to pass on to grandchildren and a few friends. Success for a company may have less to do with the sales of the cookbook than with the successful promotion of a product and the positive image created.

Your success is determined by what you need and want from your effort, and cannot be measured in anyone else's terms. A book can be a success whether it sells 100,000 copies or 500 copies. It is what you want it to be.

In our work with over 1,500 cookbook publishers across the country we have seen all sorts of definitions of success. Some cookbooks satisfy their creator's dreams and are never heard from again. And some go on to become Classics, continually being reprinted and selling for years and years. We hope that we've given you some reasons why *you* should write a cookbook. Now we are going to tell you how to make your book a Classic.

# CHAPTER 1

# Creating a Classic Cookbook

So YOU WANT to write a cookbook—one that is special, wonderful, and surely to be a Classic.

Perhaps the idea came first; you've looked everywhere for a certain type of cookbook and you just can't find it, so you've decided to write it yourself. Perhaps you've become an expert in a certain type of ethnic cooking, or developed a marvelous new diet, or thought of two hundred wonderful things to do with your new microwave. Perhaps your friends are constantly begging for your recipes, and you've already started collecting and standardizing them.

Or perhaps you—or your organization—need money, and you see the burgeoning cookbook market as a golden opportunity. Maybe you haven't got an idea about the type of book yet, but you are intrigued by the possibility of making a profit.

No matter what the inspiration or ambition for wanting to write a cookbook, the first step is its creation. But how do you start? We're going to help you.

Remember our definition of a Classic Cookbook—one that enjoys continual reprinting because of ongoing consumer demand. Each Classic is also an authentic example of a culture, an expression of the taste, style, and habits of a particular people at a particular time. Each book reflects the uniqueness of the writer(s). Whether your Classic is aimed at a huge nationwide market or at success in a smaller sphere, it will have certain characteristics.

• *A Classic Cookbook must have a unique theme development.* It needs to have a continuity that holds the book to-

11

gether whether it is based on a personality, an ethnic tradition, a particular food, or a certain idea.

* *A Classic Cookbook has tested recipes.* The buyer knows that she can trust the book, that the recipes work.

* *A Classic Cookbook has a professional-looking design concept.* It has visual appeal—it looks good.

As you create your cookbook, you will want to pay close attention to these ideas. Let's look at each one carefully.

# THEME DEVELOPMENT

The theme is the idea that holds the book together. It provides continuity and should be reflected in the title, the text, the choice of recipes, the cover, the artwork, the color scheme—in how the book looks and reads. The theme can be based on a personality, a city or region, a worthy cause, a life-style, a diet, a food, a method of cooking, or a way of entertaining. Whatever the theme, it should be both unique and unifying.

Yes, we know that some of the old-time best-sellers do very well without a theme; you have only to look at the success of *River Road Recipes*, which recently sold its one millionth copy. But books like this sell on their established reputations, and a cookbook published today has to make a place for itself in an increasingly sophisticated market.

## Your Personality and Taste

How do you go about selecting the theme that is going to make your book stand out? Perhaps *you* are the secret. Maybe you are an undiscovered Julia Child. The personality and the taste of the writer may be all that is needed for a book. Martha Stewart had a reputation in Connecticut for giving and catering fabulous parties. When she combined her recipes and party ideas into the beautifully photographed *Martha Stewart Entertains*, people across the country were just as enthusiastic as her friends and neighbors had been.

Bootsie John Landry combines the cooking of her Lebanese ancestors with that of the Cajun country where she lives. Her experience of thirty years in the restaurant business led her to package some of her products as "Bootsie's Mixes," and then to write *The Best of South Louisiana Cooking*. The unique style that had delighted her customers made for a successful cookbook.

The Charlotte, North Carolina, Symphony Women's Association created a personality for their cookbook *First Chair Gourmet*. It features clever cartoons of Herb, a violinist who is equally at home in the orchestra or in the kitchen. Throughout the book we see Herb putting down his violin, cooking, tasting, and eating—and getting fatter and fatter.

Whether you are a "down-home" cook or a sophisticated hostess, your personality can become the theme of the book. After all, it's your taste and your way of doing things that you are writing about. Your own way of saying things is better than an imitation of someone else.

## A Regional Identity

If you are lucky enough to have a regional cuisine, landmark, customs, or identity that can be developed in a new way, use it. Regional cookbooks are some of the all-time best-sellers. People in the area love to read about it, and visitors and would-be visitors want the book to tell them about the place. Ann Paulson, a former volunteer cookbook chairman in Kalamazoo, Michigan, who now owns a public relations company says, "Long before American cooking became chic, these cookbooks were promoting and preserving the glorious diversity of our regional cuisines. Their recipes are loved, used, and recommended. The joy of these cookbooks is their absolute devotion to region! They contain *the best* and *most authentic* regional American recipes available."

Lila Gault used the abundance of fish, game, and fresh fruits and vegetables around her home in Seattle for *The Northwest Cookbook*, featuring recipes using the fresh, natural products of the region. Arline Isaacs collected recipes from an assortment of her California neighbors, interspersed them with local history and photographs, biographies of the cooks, and anecdotes about cooking, and came up with *Who's Cooking in Laguna Beach*.

*Mountain Measures* by the Junior League of Charleston, West Virginia, has an Appalachian quilt on the cover. The preface talks about the culinary heritage of the mountain folk; photographs and excerpts from the writings of residents of the mountains are used throughout. Each section is indicated by a different quilt pattern, and all through the book tiny quilt symbols mark recipes for particularly regional dishes, like Sassafras Tea, Ramp Salad, Venison Stew, and Black Walnut Pound Cake.

*Fiesta* from the Junior League of Corpus Christi emphasizes the Mexican heritage of south Texas. There is a special section of Mexican recipes, a bright orange and yellow cover, and drawings of Mexican crafts, pottery, tiles, and flowers. The Junior League of Colorado Springs calls their cookbook *Nuggets: Recipes Good as Gold*, and uses the divider pages between sections to tell the history of the gold rush country. Throughout the book a miniature miner's pick identifies "Picks," recipes that take less than fifteen minutes to prepare.

If there is a local event such as Mardi Gras, a strawberry festival, or a bowl game, capitalize on it. *Tea-Time at the Masters* by the Junior League of Augusta, Georgia, is built on the famous golf tournament held there every spring, from the pun in the title through the color scheme based on the green of the coveted winner's jacket. The artwork uses golf balls and clubs, a tee symbol sets off certain instructions, and famous golfers' wives have contributed recipes. Every year the book finds a whole new audience in the new spectators at the tournament.

The Junior League of Shreveport, Louisiana, calls their cookbook *Revel*, after the Red River Revel, an annual arts festival. Building on the theme of revelry, the book includes color-coded sections of menus for such seasonal revels as spring's Easter Egg Hunt and Kentucky Derby Party, summer's picnics and bridal parties, fall's tailgate picnic and Oktoberfest, and winter's Christmas parties and New Year's supper.

Cookbooks can be read like travel books, too. *The Flavor of Spain* by William H. Emery is a guide to the history and customs of the various regions of Spain as well as to regional dishes. *Gourmet* magazine's *Old Vienna Cookbook* makes you want to go there as well as to make a Sachertorte. *Recipes from Great American Inns*, published by Benson & Hedges, features fifty-four inns from Vermont and Virginia to Wisconsin and Wyoming. There is a picture and description of each inn, as well as one of their special recipes. It is cookbook and a guidebook to good eating, too.

## A Worthy Cause

If the proceeds from your cookbook will benefit a worthy cause, perhaps that cause can provide a theme. The ladies of the Polk Memorial Auxiliary in Columbia, Tennessee, used photographs and menus from the home of the eleventh president in *The James K. Polk Cookbook*, and donate the profits for the upkeep of this historic home. Museums and art galleries frequently use their collections for illustrations, providing double appeal: a handsome cookbook and a marvelous souvenir of the museum. *Private Collections: A Culinary Treasure* from the Walters Art Gallery in Baltimore is a good example.

The League of the Dallas Museum of Art staffs a lunchroom at the museum, and has collected dozens of recipes for the soups served there in *Gallery Buffet Soup Cookbook*, illustrated with ten full-color reproductions of portraits in the museum. *Winterthur's Culinary Collection* makes use of the collection of American antiques and decorative objects in the Delaware museum. The dishes in the recipes are photographed amid settings of rare china, silver, and furniture, and there are also line drawings of beautiful tankards, compotes, tureens, and bowls.

Musical themes have provided symphony and opera guilds with outstanding cookbooks. *Cooking with the Santa Fe Opera* has ten chapters, each tied to one of their productions. "Cio-Cio San's Delicacies" features Japanese menus and recipes and illustrations of *Madame Butterfly*. "Italy à la Verdi" features Italian food and *La Traviata*. "Backstage in Santa Fe" spotlights New Mexican cuisine and backstage photographs.

The Junior Committee of the Cleveland Orchestra uses a play on words that combines both music and menus. The book contains menus and recipes for picnic and patio entertaining and is called *Bach's Lunch*. The sections have musical names: "preludes" for appetizers, "main themes" for meat, seafood, and poultry, and "suites" for desserts. The book has been so successful that they have published two additional books: *Bach for More* and *Bach for an Encore*.

## History and Literature

Unusual themes can come from history or literature. The four authors of *The Thirteen Colonies Cookbook* did a masterful job of research and selected one woman from each of the original thirteen colonies. By telling something of her history, home, and customs and giving recipes typical of her colony, they have created a vivid picture of life in eighteenth-century America. The Women's National Book Association of Nashville, Tennessee, published *The Literary Allusions Cookbook*, which is sure to delight book lovers. It is full of quotations about food, drawings of famous authors, and essays about such subjects as the uses of cooking in feminist literature, the role of afternoon tea in favorite British novels, and food as weapons in mystery stories, all complete with bibliographies.

## Life-Styles and Food Styles

Life-styles and hobbies can provide all sorts of possibilities. Skiers and hikers will like *Red Checkered Picnics* by

Holly Elliott and Betsy Robinson, full of take-it-with-you recipes and hints. Hunters and fishermen (and their wives) will be interested in *The L.L. Bean Game and Fish Cookbook*, or *Quail Country* from the Junior League of Albany, Georgia, an area noted for its hunting. Sailors will want *The Boatcook*, by Donna Marxer, with dishes to be cooked while afloat, tested under ship's galley conditions. And campers, sailors, and RV owners will use *Two Burners and an Ice Chest*, by Phyllis Bultmann, which tells how to buy, pack, and cook with limited facilities.

The editor-in-chief of *The Cook's Magazine*, Judith Hill, says, "Considered more practically as a how-to guide, cookbooks should be, quite simply, on a needed subject, and it's surprising how many such topics are left to languish. Years into the second barbecue craze in this country, there is still no complete serious hardback on the subject. One of the major publishing houses is in the process of bringing one out, but it could have been selling like hotcakes for years."

Of course, any type of food can provide a theme. Sharon Kay Alexander assembled recipes using strawberries and published the very successful *From the Strawberry Patch*, a pink and red cookbook shaped like a giant strawberry, promoted it into a national success, and has gone on to do similar books—apples, and so on. There have been dozens of books about chocolate and pasta, and almost as many on avocados, tomatoes, and zucchini.

A look on the shelves of any bookstore will show you the popularity of health-related cookbooks. There are cookbooks written to cover every type of vegetarian preference. The physical fitness boom has made diet the hottest subject in the cookbook market. There are books for diabetics, heart patients, and people with all types of allergies, as well as for low-salt diets and high-fiber diets. There are books specializing in sugar-free desserts, whole-grain breads, no-salt dinners. Famous chefs have written their own versions of special diets.

"I am fascinated with how perceptions of food have changed. Our heightened food awareness has really made nutrition THE food story of the 80's," says Julianne Belote, author of an article on the Nitty Gritty Press cookbook survey. "In California, what began as our preoccupation with ingredients that are fresh and colorful turned into a full-blown food revolution. Once it was considered trendy, but now you see it reflected in restaurants, cookbooks, and buying habits across the country."

Think about using a special method of cooking as a theme. Jean Durkee adapted French and Creole recipes for the microwave in *Tout de Suite I & II*. Food processors, convection ovens, grills, woks, crock pots—any appliance or gadget can be your inspiration. So can the way you like to do things: cooking for two, cooking for a family, cooking for large crowds, casserole cooking, cooking with wine, cooking with herbs.

Time- and effort-saving methods offer many ideas. Pierre Franey's *The New York Times Sixty-Minute Gourmet*, outlining meals prepared in less than one hour, had great success. You might concentrate on recipes that can be prepared in advance, simple versions of classic dishes, or meals that can be frozen. *The everyday gourmet* from the Junior League of Northern Westchester codes all its recipes with symbols according to difficulty: one small chef's hat means easy, two means average, and three indicates a complicated recipe.

If you are heir to an ethnic tradition (or have learned one), use it. The enduring popularity of books on Chinese, Indian, or Italian cooking shows how eager people are to try new and different things. Louisiana cooking, that combination of French, African, Latin, Cajun, and Creole traditions, practically rates a chapter to itself for its appeal, as witness *La Bonne Cuisine* from All Saints Episcopal Church in New Orleans and *Talk About Good* from Lafayette, Louisiana.

The Reynolds Wrap company sponsored a contest for traditional Black family recipes and printed the results in *The Way Mama Cooked It*. Waddad Habeeb Buttross of Natchez, Mississippi, published the family favorites in *Waddad's Kitchen: Lebanese Zest, Southern Best*. The Junior Welfare League of Holland, Michigan, published *Eet Smakelijk*. The title is a Dutch phrase meaning "Eat well and with taste." The theme of Dutch heritage is carried out in the blue and white cover, reminiscent of Dutch tiles, the illustrations of traditionally costumed boys and girls, and in many recipes with names like "banket staven" and "saucijzen broodjes."

Ways of entertaining are a gold mine of themes. *Party Potpourri* from the Junior League of Memphis covers all kinds of parties from the most elaborate formal dinner to a child's birthday party, from a bridal luncheon to a casual picnic. The "potpourri" in the title refers to the rich mixture of ideas: table settings, menus, decorations, invitations, garnishes, flower arrangements. The Rockdale Temple Sisterhood in Cincinnati took a more specialized approach and has had a long-running success with *In the Beginning*, a book of hors d'oeuvres and appetizers. The book is even available in Braille.

Think of all the possibilities in entertaining—brunches, buffets, teas, holiday food, casual dining, children's parties—and you may find your theme.

*Beyond Parsley*, a lavish book by the Junior League of Kansas City, focuses on the presentation of beautiful as well as tasty food. In the recipes and in the full-color photographs the writers illustrate how to go far beyond the usual instruction, "Garnish with a sprig of parsley," suggesting ways to enhance both the visual appeal and the taste appeal of food.

## Don't Despair!

If you still aren't sure about a theme that is just right for you, invent one! Get some friends or a committee to help you. Take a good look at what makes you or your community different, and be willing to capitalize on it. Be introspective. What do you really like? What do you do best? What hobbies and interests do you have? How do you and your friends entertain each other? What is it that makes your way of life and your way of doing things special and worth sharing? You can find that special flavor that is yours alone. In marketing, this is called product differentiation. You look for what separates your book from all its competition and build upon that specialness.

When the cookbook committee of the Peoria Junior League tried to decide on a theme, they were hard pressed to think of something really special. They tried variations on the saying "If it'll play in Peoria," like "It'll cook in Peoria," but couldn't get a solution. They analyzed their city, a manufacturing town that prides itself on being the "test capital of the country." They realized that their recipes were undergoing thorough testing and were good enough to serve anywhere, so they decided on *The Pride of Peoria* and hit exactly the right note of civic enthusiasm to get the whole community behind them.

The Junior League of Rochester didn't have a theme, but, as the apple recipes flowed in, the committee kept coming back to the fact that apples are a major product of upstate New York. They tried to resist it, but apples *were* Rochester. The name was an accident, a lucky slip of the tongue, but the success of *Applehood & Motherpie* is not: 60,000 copies were sold in three months and the apple theme keeps right on rolling—into notecards, aprons, pins, and so on.

The idea for *A Man's Taste* originated with two husbands who thought a book of recipes by and for men would be just as good as the cookbooks they had heard their wives talking about. That idea came first, the recipes later.

But if you still don't have a theme, don't despair. Go ahead and start collecting recipes. As you go along, ideas will come to you, and what you collect may determine your theme.

We've been asked, "Can a theme be dated?" Yes, perhaps it can. Certain celebrities or restaurants may lose their luster. A new appliance will replace an old one. Photographs may look less stylish in a few years. But if a book is a good one, you can always update a later edition, and good recipes last forever. Try to avoid dating your book too much because you want your sales to go on for years.

## Title

Obviously a big part of theme selection involves the title. The title should be short, easy to say, easy to spell, and easy to remember. And, of course, it should convey the theme of the book.

Remember that most cookbooks sell by word of mouth, and you want your title to do some selling for you. The majority of good cookbook titles seem to be three words long (give or take a word):

*Joy of Cooking*
*Southern Sideboards*
*Jacksonville & Company*
*The everyday gourmet*
*America Discovers Columbus*

If you can't say everything you want to say in three short, snappy words, consider a subtitle:

*Applehood & Motherpie: Handpicked Recipes*
   *from Upstate New York*
*La Bonne Cuisine: Cooking New Orleans Style*
*Simply Simpatico: A Taste of New Mexico*
*Bach's Lunch: Picnic & Patio Classics*
*Perennials: A Southern Celebration of Foods & Flavors*

To get ideas for titles, go to bookstores and libraries and look at other cookbooks. Look at billboards and advertisements. Notice what catches your eye. Look at menus in restaurants (sandwich and drink titles are great). You might have a contest to name the book, with the prize a delicious meal prepared straight from its pages.

You may want the author's name in the title if that will help sell cookbooks:

*Paul Bocuse in Your Kitchen*
*Martha Stewart Entertains*
*Beard on Bread*

The same rule applies for the name of the restaurant, product, or cause you are promoting. If including the author's (or authors') name in the title will help, consider putting it in the subtitle, or at the bottom of the cover.

Sometimes the title sells the book—like *The Enchanted Broccoli Forest* by Mollie Katzen, or *The Best Little Cookbook in Texas* by the Junior League of Abilene. Beware: there is a very fine line between simply terrific and disastrously cutesy. Sometimes a title can be so original and clever that it completely obscures what the book is about. Remember what you are aiming for: a title that is memorable and expresses what your book is about.

## Content

A terrific title will sell a book once, but the contents will resell it again and again.

Obviously the recipes are the major portion of the content, and the recipes will make the difference between a good book and an excellent book. We'll go into recipe collecting, organizing, and testing in detail in a minute, but before we get to recipes, let's talk about some of the other text you may choose to include because it is appropriate to your theme. Not all people who buy cookbooks are cooks. Some may never pick up a pot, but just find reading cookbooks enjoyable. Cookbooks are frequently read at night, right before bed, by people who fantasize about entertaining or food.

Some people will buy cookbooks to find out about a region's culinary heritage and history. *Guten Appetit!* from the Sophienburg Museum tells the story of the German families who settled New Braunfels, Texas, and includes a section of pioneer folk remedies. *Bayou Cuisine*, published by St. Stephen's Episcopal Church in Indianola, Mississippi, contains so much history and lore of the Mississippi Delta that it is sometimes shelved with history in the library. It tells stories of the many peoples who have inhabited the land—the Indians, Spanish, French, and English—and gives recipes from each culture, then traces the history of the region from the days of the Mississippi

Territory through the War Between the States to modern times.

The Symphony League of Jackson, Mississippi, published *The Jackson Cookbook*, which contains a charming essay by Eudora Welty called "The Flavor of Jackson" that tells of her childhood and recalls what it was like for a child to help make mayonnaise on a summer's day. Leonie Samuel-Hool's *To All My Grandchildren: Lessons in Indonesian Cooking* is full of stories about her Indonesian childhood, legends of the rice god, and accounts of her grandmother's methods, as well as recipes adapted to modern kitchens.

Barbara Dalia Jasmin discovered the journal of a New England sea captain's wife from the mid-nineteenth century, which included recipes and household lore. She published *The Captain's Lady Cookbook*, with excerpts from the journal, shopping and cargo lists, poems, letters, and recipes to give a vivid picture of a way of life long ago. *Pirate's Pantry* by the Junior League of Lake Charles, Louisiana, recounts the legend of Jean Lafitte, a pirate whose spirit still haunts the rivers and bayous of southwest Louisiana.

Perla Meyer's *The Seasonal Kitchen* has information about seasonal shopping for the freshest herbs, vegetables, fruits, and cheeses, plus gardening and storage information and menu planning for each time of the year, using the best available ingredients.

Many cookbooks contain an introduction explaining why the book was written or how the theme was chosen: why the writer believes in a certain diet, why a particular gadget can change your life, why the writer wants to share her talents, what is special or traditional in her area. *Recipe Jubilee!* by the Junior League of Mobile, Alabama, includes this brief but expressive preface:

> A unique phenomenon occurs on the eastern shore of Mobile Bay. Natives of the area know the signs to watch for—in the moon, the tide, and the winds. Shrimps, crabs, and fish race to the water's edge and the cry of JUBILEE! rings up and down the beach. With buckets, baskets, and

nets in tow, visitors and natives alike gather a bounty of fresh seafood.

Perhaps you don't think that writing is your greatest strength. You might ask another person—a local celebrity, a well-known cook or writer—to contribute a foreword. Frank X. Tolbert, a columnist for the *Dallas Morning News*, wrote a colorful history of Texas cooking for *The Texas Experience* by the Richardson Women's Club. Doyenne of food writers M.F.K. Fisher wrote the introduction to *California Fresh*, published by the Junior League of Oakland–East Bay.

James Beard wrote an introduction to the Walters Art Gallery's *Private Collections*. An introduction or contribution from another person may add to the special flavor of your book and may broaden the audience of potential buyers.

You may decide to include helpful hints, poems about food, quotations, or serving suggestions. The general list of possible cookbook inclusions given in the "Format" section of this chapter is only a sample of the ideas that can be included in your book. It is your decision as to what carries out your theme development.

# RECIPES

To make a bad pun, it is the recipes that are the meat of the book. To have appeal, a recipe must read as if it tastes good. Many people, cookbook collectors especially, buy cookbooks as much to read as to use in the kitchen, so the recipes and instructions must sound good. We don't have to tell you what too many cans of mushroom soup can do to a cookbook. So now let's talk about the recipes themselves.

An important factor in making a cookbook a Classic is that it can be trusted. The buyer knows that the recipes will work because they have been thoroughly tested. You may have cooked an old favorite so many times that it is second nature to you; the trick is to get it across to the reader so that she can get the same wonderful results. When a prospective buyer looks through a book, she should say, "I can do that. This book looks like something that I can use and understand." Once she buys the book and uses its recipes, the word will spread among her friends.

"Recipe development is an art that hides within every cook. It is a creative expression that is limited only by the cook's imagination. Be it challenging or uncomplicated, a recipe that entices is built on fine and fresh ingredients. A beautiful, delicious dish is a melding of many things— creative thoughts and foods that are fresh, simple, and nutritious," is the opinion of food communications specialist Nancy K. Wall.

As you begin to pull all your recipes together in their final form, there is something important you must consider: the copyright question. There is a fine line between theft and adaptation. There are too many horror stories out there for anyone to take this subject lightly.

A recipe is considered an idea or system, and that cannot be copyrighted. However, what *you* do with the recipe is what makes it individual, and what you *can* copyright is your way of expressing the idea.

So be careful, and be honest. Do not take recipes from other books. Make sure you know the source of your recipes, and if they aren't yours, in your own words, give credit where credit is due. The threat of a lawsuit can complicate and sour the pleasure of publishing a cookbook as several Kentucky cookbook authors found when they discovered that the recipe they printed for Derby Pie belonged to a Louisville restaurant, which had trademarked the title.

Remember that individuality will help make your cookbook a success; nothing is worse than a collection of recipes clipped from newspapers with no originality, and that happens all too frequently. (Of course, you'll want to protect your work too. We'll go into that a little later.)

## Recipe Writing and Collection

Whether you are collecting recipes from friends, restaurateurs, members of an organization, or are assembling your own creations, you will want a clear, concise recipe format. Here are the points to consider.

## INGREDIENTS

List in order of use
Spell out all measurements—*no* abbreviations!
Give exact measurements—size of can, package, etc.
Decide whether or not to use brand names
Supply specifics—are herbs fresh or dried, are onions chopped, is garlic minced, are fruits and vegetables peeled, etc.

## COOKING DIRECTIONS

Decide whether to write in paragraph form, in numbered steps, in outline form, etc.
Define terms (be consistent—do you use "whip" or "beat"?)
Give size and shape of pans, molds, casseroles
Provide adaptation to microwave or other appliances
Give directions for unmolding or other procedures
Supply time of preparation and cooking time
Give oven temperature
Give number of servings

## OTHER OPTIONS

| | |
|---|---|
| Degree of difficulty | Cost |
| Will freeze | Metric conversions |
| Can be doubled or halved | High altitude conversions |
| Can be prepared ahead | History, anecdotes |
| How to garnish, serve | Comments |
| Menu suggestions | Contributor's name |
| What wine to serve | Source of recipe |

Obviously, if you included all these things, the recipe would be too long and hard to read. The theme and style of your cookbook will determine what you ask for. The important thing is to be consistent. As you collect recipes from various sources make sure that the form works for what you want to do and that all the recipes are written the same way.

If you are requesting that recipes be sent to you by friends or outside sources, you will find that the response is much better if you send a form that is a self-mailer, or send a stamped, self-addressed envelope for return.

Recipe collection forms come in all styles. (We heard of one that was three pages long! We wonder how much luck that group had in getting all the recipes they needed.) If all recipe collection forms looked alike, so would all cookbooks. You will want to design your own format, one that works for you and covers all the information you want.

To give you ideas, two examples follow, one short and simple, the other more involved.

---

### RECIPE FORM: #1

Recipe title: _____

Contributor's name: _____

Source: _____

Ingredients (list in order of use): _____

_____

_____

Method of preparation: _____

_____

_____

_____

Number of servings: _____

Time of preparation: _____

Cost: _____

Comments: _____

_____

## RECIPE FORM: #2

Recipe name:                              Category:

Please read the entire form before filling out. Be brief but complete. Please sign the release on the back. Please type or write in black ink. Use no abbreviations. If the recipe is adaptable to microwave or convection oven, please state and give exact directions.

Yield:                    Can be doubled:          Halved:

Preparation time:            Cooking time:

Approximate cost:

Special containers or utensils:

Can be prepared ahead:              Frozen:

List ingredients and
quantities in order of use:


Directions:



Comments:



Suggestions for serving or garnishing:

Accompanying wine:

Preparation hints:

Source of recipe:

History or interesting facts about recipe:


PLEASE RETURN THIS FORM BY _____

Now let's take an actual recipe, something you might have cooked a hundred times, or something your next-door neighbor gave you, and work it into something suitable for inclusion in a Classic Cookbook.

## Hamburger Casserole

1 lb. ground beef
2 T. butter
1 pkg. noodles
1 teaspoon garlic
1 teaspoon salt
Pepper to taste
Large onion
1 pkg. Philadelphia cream cheese
1 T. sugar
1 cup sour cream
1 ½ cups Cheddar cheese, grated
2 small cans Contadina tomato sauce

Mix the first 8 ingredients in a skillet and cook.
Add other ingredients.
Bake at 350 till hot and bubbly.

The dish may turn out to be wonderful, but the recipe isn't there yet, is it? First we need to get the exact amount of every ingredient, the size of the packages of noodles and cream cheese, the size of the cans of tomato sauce. Then we need clear instructions. In this example several key instructions were left out; for example, are the noodles supposed to be cooked or uncooked? What form are the garlic and onion in? It sounds as if you are supposed to add a large *whole* onion! Some of the measurements are abbreviated. The ingredients are not listed in order of use. Let's go back to the contributor, get some more specific information, and try again.

Here's the result after some of those questions have been answered.

## Hamburger Casserole

2 tablespoons butter or margarine
1 pound ground beef or chuck
1 teaspoon instant minced garlic seasoning
1 teaspoon salt
Pepper to taste
1 tablespoon sugar
1 large onion, finely chopped
1 package (5 ounces) egg noodles, uncooked
1 package (3 ounces) Philadelphia cream cheese
1 cup sour cream
1½ cups grated Cheddar cheese
2 cans (8-ounce size) Contadina tomato sauce

Melt the butter in a skillet, brown the beef. Add the next six ingredients and stir occasionally while they cook. Add the last four, then put in a casserole and bake at 350° about 30 minutes.

That's better, isn't it? At least we know what to do with the noodles and how long it takes to cook the dish. You will notice that the package sizes are given, abbreviations are eliminated, the ingredients are listed in the order of use, and the instructions are clearer. After all, there is a big difference between 1½ cups of grated cheese and 1½ cups of cheese, grated.

But it's still not quite good enough. It needs more editing. If you've decided not to use brand names, those have to go. How many people does it serve? Let's edit a little more and also give it a better title.

The result after a little more fine-tuning appears on the next page.

# Helen's Hearty Hamburger Casserole

2 tablespoons butter or margarine
1 pound ground beef or chuck
1 teaspoon minced garlic
1 teaspoon salt
Pepper to taste
1 tablespoon sugar
1 large onion, finely chopped
1 package (5 ounces) egg noodles, uncooked
1 package (3 ounces) cream cheese
1 cup sour cream
1½ cups grated Cheddar cheese
2 cans (8 ounce size) tomato sauce

Melt the butter or margarine in a large skillet; add the ground beef and brown. Add the seasonings, the chopped onion, and the uncooked noodles, and simmer for about 15 minutes, stirring occasionally. Then add the cream cheese, sour cream, Cheddar cheese, and tomato sauce, mixing well. Pour into a greased 2-quart casserole and bake, uncovered, in a 350 oven until hot and bubbly (about 30 minutes).

Serves four, and makes a delicious meal with a green salad and French bread.

This casserole freezes beautifully. Cook the casserole for 20 minutes, wrap tightly in foil and freeze. Take it straight from the freezer, and cook, uncovered for one hour, or until center is done.

Now we're cooking! Notice how much more precise and easy to follow the instructions are in this version. Anyone should be able to make this dish and get good results.

How you decide to write the recipes can be very important. You may decide to write them in paragraph form with a chatty commentary, as if you were telling a friend how to do it. You may use descriptive phrases, like "Mix till it is the color of cafe au lait," or "Use a lump of butter the size of a walnut." You may opt for numbered steps and an impersonal form with no comments. You may intersperse your comments throughout the recipe, or give them only at the beginning.

*Sunset* magazine food and wine editor Jerry DiVecchio says, "Many cookbooks are ridiculously dependent on French terminology, often used incorrectly, to describe methods best explained in simple direct English. The use of French is either an elitist device, or one used to cover the inability of the author to express a concept clearly."

To get an idea of the varieties of recipe writing, once again go to the shelves. Try looking up one basic recipe— an omelet, puff pastry, or a sauce—that is likely to appear in many cookbooks. You will see how different writers treat the same subject. You don't want to imitate other cooks, only to see in how many different ways one recipe can be written. Not all recipes are just lists of ingredients and simplified steps of preparation. And not all recipe writers can or should write lengthy descriptions of their methods. The reason that Julia Child's books are so successful is that she really has something to say. What she does is unique, and that makes it valuable. The important thing is to find your own voice, to write a recipe in the way that comes naturally to you. Then it will be truly your own.

If you are writing a step-saver cookbook, the recipes should *look* quick and easy. The buyer who is looking for a time-saving cookbook should know immediately that this is it. Here's an example:

# Rosy Pears

4 ripe pears
Sugar to taste

1 cup red wine
½ cup slivered almonds

Peel, core, and quarter pears. Sprinkle with sugar.
Marinate in wine for 1 hour before serving.
Garnish with slivered almonds.

If you are writing a book about an ethnic cuisine, you will need to spend some time defining terms and outlining methods. You will need to talk about the typical foods and seasonings used, and should offer possible substitutions that can be found in most grocery stores. Even if you don't include stories and lore, the book should have a style that reflects its subject. Although the recipes are obviously going to be different, a Chinese cookbook shouldn't look or sound like an Italian cookbook.

In a regional cookbook, the way the recipes are written can give the flavor of the region in the same way that the choice of recipes does, as the following recipe demonstrates.

## *Ambrosia*

This is a traditional Southern Christmas dessert that is as much a part of the holiday menu as boiled custard and fruit cake, or country ham and beaten biscuits. I've never seen it served except during the holidays, but no Christmas table would be complete without a sparkling bowl of Ambrosia.

*5 or 6 large seedless oranges*
*1 coconut*
*Sugar to taste*

Peel the oranges carefully so that no white filbers cling to the pieces, and divide them into sections.

Punch a hole in the "eye" end of the coconut with an ice pick, and let the milk drain out. Crack the coconut all over with a hammer, then shell it. Grate the meat with a fine grater. Fresh coconut is essential to the goodness of Ambrosia.

Layer the orange sections and the finely grated coconut in a glass bowl and sprinkle each layer with sugar, repeating until the bowl is full. Cover the bowl and put it in the refrigerator overnight, so that the flavors will mingle.

If your personality is integral to the theme of the cookbook, the recipes need to read as if you are talking to a good friend. The ways of doing things that you have developed need to come across as particularly your own. Everything that you say should reflect your personality. If the book is to be a gourmet cookbook for advanced cooks, the recipes will reflect that in the use of foreign terms, sophisticated methods, and specialized equipment. If you are writing a special occasion or party cookbook, the recipes need to sound pretty and rich. If there is a special way the dish is to look, you will need to describe that in more detail than you would if you were making a basic hamburger. An example follows.

# Italian Festival Bombe

*For this spectacular and colorful dessert, you need a chilled two-quart mold. But don't worry—a bundt pan works perfectly and even a two-quart Pyrex mixing bowl will do—just be sure you chill it first.*

    1 quart vanilla ice cream
    Green food coloring
    1 package (16 ounces) chocolate wafers
    1 quart chocolate chip ice cream
    1 quart *pink* peppermint ice cream
    1 can (3 ounces) chocolate syrup
    Red and green maraschino cherries

1. First, soften the vanilla ice cream in a mixing bowl and add drops of green food coloring, mixing well, until you get a lovely shade of green. Then, line the chilled mold with the green ice cream so that you have a layer about an inch or an inch and a half thick covering the entire mold. Put the mold back into the freezer to harden for about 20 minutes.

2. While the first layer is hardening, put the chocolate chip ice cream out to soften. Put half the chocolate wafers in a plastic bag and crush them evenly with a rolling pin. (Of course, you can use a food processor for this step if you want to.) When the first layer of ice cream is moderately

hardened, press the chocolate wafers over it in an even but thin layer, and return the mold to the freezer for another 15 minutes.

3. The next step is to add a second ice cream layer over the chocolate wafer crumbs, using the softened chocolate chip ice cream. Return the mold to the freezer for another 20 minutes or so. While that layer is hardening, allow the pink peppermint ice cream to soften, and crush the rest of the chocolate wafers.

4. Add another layer of chocolate wafer crumbs when the chocolate chip layer has hardened, and put it back in the freezer. When that has firmed up, fill in the center of the bombe with the pink peppermint ice cream. When the mold is full, level it off with a knife so that the surface is flat, cover it with plastic wrap, and return it to the freezer for several hours until it is good and hard.

5. A couple of hours before serving the dessert, take the mold from the freezer. Have a chilled serving plate or silver tray ready. I find the best way to unmold the bombe is to invert the mold over the chilled platter and quickly put a dish towel wrung out in warm water over it. If it doesn't unmold in a minute, try another warm towel. With a knife, smooth the surface and clean up any dribbles that have fallen on the platter with paper towels, then put it back into the freezer quickly so that it will stay nice and firm.

6. Punch a small hole in the top of the chocolate syrup can. Remove the mold from the freezer again, and, working quickly, drizzle chocolate over the surface in a lacy design, then pop it back into the freezer so the chocolate can harden.

7. When you are ready to serve, garnish it with the red and green maraschino cherries. When you bring it to the table, be prepared for "ohs" and "ahs." Slice it into pie-shaped pieces with a sharp knife.

———— ♦ ————

*I call this Italian Festival Bombe because it is the colors of the Italian flag. Of course, it is a spectacular Christmas dessert, but it seems a pity to serve something so good only at Christmas time.*

Some cookbooks give metric conversions beside each ingredient. Some give serving suggestions, ways to garnish or decorate a dish, what to serve with it, what wine to use. Some include symbols for the degree of difficulty or the time required for preparation. Instructions for freezing or preparing ahead, instructions for high altitude cooking, instructions for doubling or halving a recipe can also be given. What you do with the recipe is what makes it your own. Your own way of writing it is better than an imitation of someone else's style, provided that your way is clear and correct. Your own voice is what is important, for that is what makes your cookbook unique.

You must decide on a time frame for recipe collection, and stick to your deadline. If you are asking a large group of people for recipes, a clearly stated turn-in date printed on the form and a self-mailer will help. You may need incentives to get the recipes pouring in. A restaurateur might contribute meal tickets for the mention of his restaurant in the book. You might have a party for those friends whom you want to contribute recipes. An organization might divide into teams with a prize for the team that submits the most recipes. Even your family and friends will need a little prodding now and then.

Your deadline arrives. Of course, you have either too many or too few recipes. Too many is easy; they will be weeded out in the testing stage. Too few (or too few in one category) is more likely. Now you have to get on the phone and call some of the best cooks you know. Remember that cooks have egos; tell them you are calling for their help because you know they are fabulous cooks.

The chances are that you will find that you are short in one or more categories. Go back through your own collection; perhaps you can vary some of the recipes you already have, or beg and plead for more to fill in the gaps. Perhaps you can combine categories: for example, meat, poultry, and fish into "entrées," or appetizers and soups into "first courses." The theme of your book will determine what you need—and what you get may determine the theme.

## *Recipe Testing*

Testing takes a year's time on the average, but, of course, this depends on the size and scope of your book. Now is the time to involve your friends or your membership. Each recipe needs a minimum of two testings. If there is any doubt, or if there are conflicting opinions, send the recipe back for a third testing, possibly by a "super tester," one of the best cooks you know.

If you are publishing your own recipes developed over many years, testing by someone else is highly recommended. You need to have practiced the recipe and recorded it so carefully that anyone who cooks it will get the same results. You may know what "a little salt" or "stir till well mixed" means to you, but you have to communicate that *exactly* to your readers. Enlist your friends and your family to help test, both to see if they get the same results that you do and to tell you if your directions are clear and complete. For your cookbook to be worth money to someone else, you have to able to communicate verbally what you know by instinct.

Richard H. Graff, chairman of The American Institute of Wine and Food in San Francisco, gives this good advice: "The directions for the preparation of whatever-it-is should be complete and easy to follow, but equally important, in my opinion, tested, not by an expert who already knows all about cooking and can thus automatically make up for any deficiencies in the instructions, but by an amateur who has never attempted the dish. Nothing is more annoying than a set of directions which is vague or incomplete or which assumes knowledge without reference."

Make certain that all the recipes to be tested are standardized and on paper that will reproduce. You should have at least three copies of each recipe whether you are using family, friends, or members of an organization as testers. Never throw anything away. Keep the original in a file, and when in doubt, go back to the original. This is the only copy that should have the contributor's name on it. The other copies, without the name, are given to the testers. After all, you don't want to prejudice the people testing!

Making all these copies—and copies of the evaluation forms that you will be using—will cost money. The food to be tested will cost, too. Be sure you figure these expenses into your budget plans from the beginning.

Now the testing starts. This is one of the most important ingredients in the success of a cookbook. One reason that community cookbooks by nonprofit organizations sell so well is that they are *trusted*. Unless you are a very famous chef, the buyer needs to know that you can be trusted, too, and testing is the only way you can assure that. We saw one commercial cookbook that printed a disclaimer on the first page. Can you imagine buying a cookbook that told you right up front that it was not to be trusted?

General Mills tested the 1,600 recipes in *The Betty Crocker Cookbook* in their test kitchens for three years before they sent them out for another round of testing by over a thousand homemakers around the country. A large publishing company may have its own test kitchens, or employ independent testers, but most do not. In any case, it is your responsibility to know that what you have written will work before you turn over the manuscript.

Some printing companies (the company you pay to print your book if you decide to self-publish) also have their own test kitchens and may offer to test for you in order to get your printing business. *Be wary of this*. It may be a lure to get your printing contract and you may have no control over the testing process or the tester's decisions.

Each recipe needs to be tested at least twice to rule out flukes, and each tester needs to fill out an evaluation form. As far as possible, let the testers choose their recipes— the cook should *want* to try that particular dish. Try to assign as few recipes as possible. Testing is a wonderful opportunity to build friendships and create an interest in the new book. You might consider testing teas or luncheons, pot-luck suppers or dessert parties, and get a group evaluation of the recipes. For your own long-suffering children, who face the tenth version of hamburger casserole, larger bribes may be in order.

Sometimes the evaluation form can be so complex that it scares the tester. When you design your evaluation form, decide what *you* want to know from the testing. You may want a strict rating on a scale of one to ten, or you may want conversational comments and rave reviews (save these; you'll find other uses for them). You can ask for additional information on a supplementary form. Just keep in mind the point of the testing process: to make sure that everything that you write will work for someone else.

Your testers may want to get together to share opinions or at least to report back to you regularly. If there is a borderline recipe, test it again.

Just as all recipe collection forms should not look alike, neither should evaluation forms. Here are some of the things you need to consider in writing your own recipe evaluation form.

- Were the ingredients listed in order?
- Were measurements given correctly?
- Were the instructions clear?
- Were container sizes given?
- Were procedures clearly outlined?
- Were temperatures given?
- How many servings did it make?
- Was time of cooking clear?
- How long did it take you to prepare this dish?
- Were there any terms you did not understand?
- Have you ever seen this recipe before?
  Where?
  How is it different?
- Do you have any suggestions for improvement? For variations?
- Would you serve this dish to family? To company? To neither?
- How would you serve this dish? Garnish it?
- What menus might include this dish?
- Should this dish be included in the book?

• Rate this dish according to:

TASTE

Excellent ＿＿ Good ＿＿ Average ＿＿ Poor ＿＿

APPEARANCE

Excellent ＿＿ Good ＿＿ Average ＿＿ Poor ＿＿

DEGREE OF DIFFICULTY

Easy ＿＿ Average ＿＿ Difficult ＿＿

• Give any comments or criticisms you have.

Here are some sample testing forms to help you design your own.

---

### RECIPE TESTING FORM
#### (Please type or print)

Name of recipe: ＿＿＿＿＿＿＿＿＿＿＿＿＿＿＿＿＿＿＿＿＿＿

Tester's name: ＿＿＿＿＿＿＿＿＿＿＿＿＿＿＿＿＿＿＿＿＿＿

Please rate this recipe:

| | According to taste | According to appearance |
|---|---|---|
| Excellent | ＿＿ | ＿＿ |
| Good | ＿＿ | ＿＿ |
| Average | ＿＿ | ＿＿ |
| Poor | ＿＿ | ＿＿ |

Please answer the following questions:

Were the ingredients listed in order of use?

Were the measurements correct?

Were the instructions clear?

How long did it take you to prepare this dish?

Was this dish easy to prepare? ＿＿ Average? ＿＿ Difficult? ＿＿

Would you serve this dish again? ＿＿ To company? ＿＿ To family? ＿＿

Should this dish be included in the cookbook?

Comments and criticisms or suggestions for improvement:

＿＿＿＿＿＿＿＿＿＿＿＿＿＿＿＿＿＿＿＿＿＿＿＿＿＿＿＿＿

＿＿＿＿＿＿＿＿＿＿＿＿＿＿＿＿＿＿＿＿＿＿＿＿＿＿＿＿＿

## RECIPE EVALUATION FORM

Please type or print the following answers and return by _____

Name of recipe: _____

1. Were the ingredients listed in order? _____
2. Were measurements clear and correct? _____
3. Were instructions easy to follow? _____
4. Were any special procedures required?
   Were they clear? _____
5. Were container sizes given? _____
6. Was time of cooking correct? _____
7. Were special terms defined clearly? _____
8. Were serving instructions clear? _____
9. How many people did it serve? _____
10. What would you serve with this dish? _____
11. What wine? _____
12. How would you garnish this dish? _____
13. Could a beginning cook or a child of 10 make this dish?
    _____
14. Can it be prepared ahead? _____
15. Can it be frozen? _____
16. Can it be reheated successfully? _____
17. Can it be turned into leftovers? _____
18. How would you improve this dish? _____
19. What comments did you receive? _____
20. Would this dish photograph well? _____

Rate this dish: ____ Superior ____ Outstanding
                ____ Average ____ Poor

Rate degree of difficulty: ____ Very easy ____
                          ____ Easy
                          ____ Average
                          ____ Fairly hard
                          ____ Extremely difficult

Rename this dish to suit the theme of the cookbook ____
_____

Tester's name: _____

As the testing proceeds, pay attention to the names of the recipes. Who wants to cook one more "Hamburger Casserole"? "Harry's Hamburger Heaven," or "No Leftovers Hamburger Casserole," or "Quick and Easy Hamburger Supper," or "Before-the-Game Beef Casserole" has more appeal. The theme of the cookbook may help with the names; a symphony cookbook might have "Haydn's Hamburgers." You should tell the contributors that their recipes may be retitled; this will prevent hurt feelings and unpleasant surprises. Here again there is a fine line between being clever and being too cutesy—the titles in one book we saw were *so* clever that they became ridiculous, and the result was a complete turn-off on the book.

Once again, we want to emphasize the importance of the recipe selection and testing. Your cookbook must contain good, proven, tested, and evaluated recipes if you want large sales and long shelf life. Remember, *the contents will determine continued sales*.

## Indexing

A clever name may make a dish more appealing, but it can also make it hard to find and hard to remember for future use. Every dish needs to be listed several different ways to make it easy to find in the index. The index, an alphabetical listing of recipe titles and recipe categories at the back of the book, makes it easy to use your cookbook by making it easy to find a particular dish.

An index can make or break a cookbook. Reviewers and food writers often mention the index when reviewing a cookbook. Prospective buyers often flip to the index before they buy. A strong, well-developed index can even be a marketing tool: you can advertise it as a strength of your cookbook with phrases like "usable," "fully referenced," or "carefully indexed" that let the buyer know this cookbook will be a pleasure to use.

The first edition of one of our favorite cookbooks had a weak index. The publishers felt that the book was so superior in quality that the poor index was a problem, so they redeveloped the entire index for the second edition. That expenditure of money and time paid off, for the book has gone on to be a best-seller.

The index needs to be clear, complete, and easy to use. Indexing is a technical, systematic process that cannot be completed until all the recipes are collected, tested, and chosen. In the interim, study all the indexes you can find to see what kind appeals to you. You can also ask your friends what they find most useful and which cookbook they think has the best indexing system. You could give your helpers a list of all the recipe titles and ask them to write beside each one the various ways they might look for it in the index. This could be included on the evaluation form.

We suggest these guidelines: recipes should be listed alphabetically by title and cross-referenced at least once. Beyond that, the possibilities are endless. Let's take an example: Aunt Sue's Raisin and Pecan Casserole. You could list that under:

| | |
|---|---|
| Recipe title | Pecans |
| Casserole | Accompaniments |
| Raisins | etc., etc., etc. |

Of course, some restraint is in order to keep the index from running longer than the book. Indexing can be creative and varied, according to the taste of the individual. There is no need for all cookbook indexes to be alike, but we cannot repeat too often: *a good index is a necessity for a Classic Cookbook*.

Several pointers:

• Have a group of cookbook "users" advise you on the best system for your book and on the categories; it is then easier for one person (at most, two) to actually put the index together.

• The indexer should be a "detail person" who is meticulous, systematic, and careful.

• If you have a computer, the index is the perfect place to put it to work.

- If you don't have a computer, the easiest way to start indexing is to use 3"×5" or 5"×7" index cards; they give you the flexibility of adding and discarding them and moving them around.
- When the index is typed for the manuscript, page numbers cannot be put in until the printer or publisher has typeset the book, numbered the pages, and sent back the proofs. At that point, you go back through the proofs and add the correct page numbers to the index.

Here's a way to begin your index. As you finish each section of the cookbook and the final selections are made, type an index card for each recipe, using the recipe title, and file them alphabetically. When you have all the recipes in the book listed on cards and alphabetized, you have a list of the basic contents of the book ready to be typed.

On the file card write the categories under which the recipe will be cross-indexed, like this:

---

HELEN'S HEARTY HAMBURGER CASSEROLE

    Beef
    Casserole
    Hamburger
    Main courses

---

You may want to color-code each card: assign a color to each section in the book and use magic markers on the margins of the cards. Do the same thing for food categories like beef. This makes it easy to sort quickly. If a recipe appears several times, make a new card for it under each heading.

You will also need to make cards for the headings you will use, like "beef" or "casserole," such inclusions as menus, measurements, freezing information, wine chart, and whatever. You may need *cross-index* cards, like "appetizers: *see* hors d'oeuvres."

Now, go through all the cards and categorize them, making sure you have a card for every time you want a dish to be listed. Alphabetize the cards. When you have got it in the order in which you want it, you are ready to type the list. As we mentioned before, you cannot add the page numbers at this time, but must wait until the proofs of the book are in final form.

Some publishers use free-lance indexers. You will still want to have some say in the way the index is done. If you are self-publishing and don't want to do your own index, ask for the names of professional indexers from a printer or publisher in your area. Some printers now offer to index books for self-publishers on their computers. This is fine if you like their system and don't mind your index looking like every other one they print.

To see if your index is a "normal" length, compare it to the index in a similar book. This will give you an idea of the number of pages it will take.

An index is a necessity for a Classic Cookbook. Choose the system you like best but be sure it is complete and easy to understand and use.

# DESIGN CONSIDERATIONS

How your book looks will definitely affect its sales, but remember that best-sellers come in all shapes, colors, and sizes. Any subject can be treated in any number of ways. Be creative—and keep in mind your theme as you think about the book's design. Debra M. Cordell, owner of Food for Thought in Denver, says, "The sales of all books, and more especially cookbooks, depends on how attractive the book is. A book with an unusual or attractive cover will sell much more readily than one which looks like a dull text. An attractive text, as well as illustrations, is important. A beautiful illustration not only sharpens the appetite, but entices the buyer."

## *Who Designs Your Book?*

If your book is to be published by a publishing company, you may have little to say about the design. When you turn in the manuscript, the publisher's art and production departments will take over. Many publishers will consider your suggestions, but the final decisions are theirs to make.

If you are planning to sell your book to a publisher either on your own or through an agent, the more complete the concept is, the more salable the book will be. You may want to present the whole package: contents, artwork and all. Smaller publishing companies may be more open to your suggestions than large ones.

If you decide to self-publish, you will be involved in every step of the design process and will make all the final decisions. Chances are that your main creative interest is cooking, not designing. If so, you need help. Your best friend may be just dying to help you. Or, if you are the chairman of a cookbook committee, you may have ten members who suddenly jump in and say, "I was an art major. I've always wanted to do something like this. I just know I can do it."

Watch out! If you let a friend or a volunteer stay up nights designing your book, how are you going to tell her that you hate it? You can't fire a volunteer or tell a friend that her work is awful and not at all what you want. And of course, artists have egos, which makes things even more difficult.

You get what you pay for. If you have a businesslike arrangement from the beginning, you can say, "This is not exactly what I had in mind; please try again." You can pay a designer, and it is probably worth it in the hurt feelings avoided. If you do use a friend or a volunteer, set the requirements and the timetable at the very beginning. Ask the volunteer to submit a portfolio and suggestions, just as you would expect a professional to do.

Make sure that it is very clear at the start who has the final authority over every decision.

As author and owner, *you* have the final authority. After all, the book is going into the world bearing your name. In an organization, the design committee, with the cookbook chairman as leader, has the final authority, and here we have another warning. We know one group who put the artist on the design committee. Have they got trouble! They can't even talk about the book design in front of her. She is unable to critique or change her own work. The relationship with the designer/artist should be totally professional and as removed from personal considerations as you can make it.

There are places to look for help: a professional graphic designer or artist if you can afford it (and there are plenty of good free-lancers who are not expensive). If not, try an art school or applied art classes at a university or college. There are many students who would love the challenge and work very hard. *Beware*: a printing company may offer you the services of their designer. It sounds good, but you may find that all the books they print look alike, and that is not what you want for your book's special identity.

We suggest that you interview several people and look at samples of their work. Give them an idea of what you want (but don't give all your secrets away) and see what they come up with. Be clear about your requirements, deadline, and authority. When you chose the person to design your book, have an agreement in writing that spells out those things. We know of one cookbook publisher whose designer demanded a percentage of each book sold *after* the book had been published. They had only a verbal agreement about payment. Verbal agreements don't stand up. Get your requirements, deadlines, and authority in writing in a professional manner.

## Number of Pages and Paper Stock

A Classic Cookbook can be as big as *Bayou Cuisine* (over 400 pages of oversized paper measuring 7" × 10") or as small as *Fanny Pierson Crane: Her Receipts* (50 pages, measuring 5½" × 8½"). Most books fall somewhere in between. Obviously, the size of a book makes a big difference in its cost, appearance, and storage. However, big is not necessarily better. One of the first community cookbooks to be nominated for the prestigious Tastemaker Award was the delightful, small *A Private Collection* by the Junior League of Palo Alto, California, which contains only 110 carefully selected recipes with beautiful line drawings and measures 6" × 9".

The type of paper you use and the size of the book (number of pages and trim size) are important because they will directly affect the final cost of the book. The cost of paper can be as much as one third the cost of the entire book. If your book is accepted by a publisher, the type of paper and number of pages will be dictated by the publishing house production staff. Cost of production and possible selling price are "bottom line" factors to them and they operate on budgets and past experience.

As a self-publisher, you can have anything you want and can afford. Look at books that you admire and get estimates from printers on the size and weight of paper that you like; then you can make up your budget. Self-publishers are always looking at costs and savings. Here we must warn you again to beware. Something that self-publishers hear all too frequently is, "I know where you can get a great deal on paper." Watch out! One lady thought she had discovered a real bargain. The price was unbelievably low, and she had seen the paper and it was a special color that would make her book truly unusual. Then she found out why the price was so low. The paper was the last of a lot that would never be made again because the dye faded. Fortunately she found out in time and didn't get stuck with a stack of fading books that could never be reprinted in the same color.

You may have to be flexible about cutting recipes or adding some when the final number of pages is decided. Sheets of paper come in sizes that will cut into multiples of 8 pages, standard size, because that is the size that will fit on the average printing press. Any book that has pages headed "For Your Favorite Recipes" or "Notes" had extra pages left over when it was put together.

## Trim Size

There are several "standard" sizes for cookbooks. The first is 6″ × 9″ or 5½″ × 8″. The next is 7″ × 10″ or 7½″ × 10¼″. This is because standard paper comes in these sizes and these pages will fit on standard printing equipment. However, you can print any size or shape book that you or your publisher choose. Just look at the variety in any bookstore.

*La Bonne Cuisine* is tall and thin, 6″ × 10½″. The *Minnesota Heritage Cookbook* is square, 8½″ × 8½″. *The Artist in the Kitchen* is 9″ long by 6″ high—actually standard paper bound in an unusual way. *Mastering the Art of French Cooking* is 7″ × 10″. Novelty cookbooks like *The Little Green Avocado Book* fit in the palm of your hand.

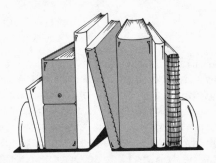

Also notice that on some cookbooks the cover trim size and the paper trim size are the same. On others, notably hardback books and books with tab dividers, the trim size of the cover is slightly larger than the trim size of the paper. An unusual size or shape may cost more, but if it adds to the interest and the unique quality of your book, it may be worth it.

## Type Style and Size

There are few things in the world as confusing as a typesetter's style book. There are literally thousands of typefaces to choose from, and pretty soon they will all begin to look alike to you. Look at *lots* of cookbooks. Choose a book you like to help you choose the look you want. In choosing type, keep these things in mind:

It must be readable: large enough and not too fancy.
The type face should be available in various fonts like bold face, italic, shadow, etc., to provide some variety in the book.
In the last analysis, clarity is the main concern.

Of course, you can be as original as you want to be here, too. *The Enchanted Broccoli Forest* reproduces hand-lettering. Other books have used calligraphy very effectively. The type chart on page 51 gives an idea of some of the many typefaces available.

## Color

This is important from start to finish; the cover, the divider pages, the content paper, the ink, the illustrations—all may be in the colors of your choice.

The colors should suit your theme, of course. *Applehood & Motherpie* uses apple colors: a green cover with red and white apples and, on the inside, red and green ink on white paper. The Junior League of South Bend, Indiana, publishes *Nutbread and Nostalgia* using pale tan paper and nutmeg-colored ink to carry out the old-fashioned look. *Simply Simpatico* uses the colors of the desert, beige and

715 Brookhaven Circle West • Memphis, TN 38117 • 901-682-7601

Helvetica HE 45 ZOROASTRIANISM: Religious system of the Persians

Helvetica HE 55 ZOROASTRIANISM: Religious system of the Persians

*Helvetica HE 56 ZOROASTRIANISM: Religious system of the Persians*

**Helvetica HE 65 ZOROASTRIANISM: Religious system of the Persians**

***Helvetica HE 66 ZOROASTRIANISM: Religious system of the Persians***

**Helvetica HE 85 ZOROASTRIANISM: Religious system of the Persians**

Helvetica HE 57 ZOROASTRIANISM: Religious system of the Persians

**Helvetica HE 67 ZOROASTRIANISM: Religious system of the Persians**

Century Textbook CS 55 ZOROASTRIANISM: Religious system of the Persians

**Century Textbook CS 65 ZOROASTRIANISM: Religious system of the Persians**

*Itek Bookface IB 56 ZOROASTRIANISM: Religious system of the Persians*

Times Roman TR 56 ZOROASTRIANISM: Religious system of the Persians

Tiffany TY 65 ZOROASTRIANISM: Religious system of the Persians

Optima OP 55 ZOROASTRIANISM: Religious system of the Persians

*Optima OP 56 ZOROASTRIANISM: Religious system of the Persians*

**Optima OP 65 ZOROASTRIANISM: Religious system of the Persians**

Souvenir SV 45 ZOROASTRIANISM: Religious system of the Persians

**Souvenir SV 55 ZOROASTRIANISM: Religious system of the Persians**

*Souvenir SV 56 ZOROASTRIANISM: Religious system of the Persians*

Bauhaus BH 45 ZOROASTRIANISM: Religious system of the Persians

Bauhaus BH 55 ZOROASTRIANISM: Religious system of the Persians

Friz Quadrata FZ 55 ZOROASTRIANISM: Religious system of the Persians

Bodoni BO 70 ZOROASTRIANISM: Religious system of the Persians

*Zeph Chancery ZC 56 ZOROASTRIANISM: Religious system of the Persians*

*Roundhand RH 55 ZOROASTRIANISM: Religious system of the Persians*

*Park Avenue PA 56 ZOROASTRIANISM: Religious system of the Pe*

**Brush BR 75 ZOROASTRIANISM: Religious system of the Persians**

Wedding Text WT 75 ZOROASTRIANISM: Religious system of the Persians

rust and black with a bright turquoise cover, to recall the part of the country it comes from—New Mexico. *Soupçon*, from the Junior League of Chicago, uses bright green, yellow, orange, white, and red pages, each color denoting a different section. And of course, many people think good old black ink on white paper is the easiest to read.

You can achieve a variety of effects by using color in different ways: one color, two colors, one-color ink on another color paper, full-color illustrations, color on the cover or divider pages only—whatever suits your taste and your budget. A good designer can help you get the effect you want by different combinations of paper and ink.

Make sure that the color of the ink is strong enough to be legible on the paper. Light brown ink on beige paper will be hard to read, and you might lose an entire audience of older cooks who cannot see the words. There is no "right" color for cookbooks today—only what is right for you and your theme.

## Art

There are as many different types of cookbook art as there are cookbook titles. *The Better Homes & Gardens Cookbook* uses full-color photographs to show you how the food can look, and black and white photographs to show you how to prepare it step by step. James Beard, in *Beard on Bread*, chose line drawings to illustrate how to knead the dough and braid the challah.

Some illustrations are purely decorative. *Savoring the Southwest* by the Symphony Guild of Roswell, New Mexico, has full-color reproductions of paintings by such well-known southwestern artists as Peter Hurd and Henriette Wyeth. *Quail Country* uses line drawings of wildlife printed in brown ink on beige paper in section headings as well as throughout the pages.

Some cookbooks use art only on the divider pages between sections. *Bach's Lunch* uses the same black and white drawing of Bach for the cover and the divider pages; the only difference is that on the cover there is one spot of bright red—the wine in the glass that he is holding—which matches the red plastic binding. *Perennials*, by the Junior Service League of Gainesville, Georgia, uses twelve beautiful botanical drawings of colorful wildflowers as dividers, and two more on the front and back covers. *Southern Sideboards*, by the Junior League of Jackson, Mississippi, carries out their theme of southern hospitality by using as section headings unusually screened photographs of every kind of sideboard, from a formal Sheraton one set with candelabra and silver dishes, to a picnic served on a patio table, to a breakfast tray set with dainty china. The photographs are reproduced in such a way that they have the effect of drawings.

Other books use illustrations throughout, sometimes to illustrate a particular technique or show how the finished dish is supposed to look, sometimes as a filler on a page. Camille Glenn's *The Fine Art of Delectable Desserts* uses a different small engraving at the bottom of each page: fruits, utensils, herbs, a serving tureen. The Junior League of Chattanooga built the theme of its cookbook around the city's railroad heritage and the popular song, "Chattanooga Choo Choo." The book is called *Dinner on the Diner*. The bright red cover and frontispiece use an Art Deco style drawing of a stylish couple seen through a dining-car window. The book is given unity by the black silhouette of a train across the bottom of each page, with a stylized engine design decorating the menu pages.

You can use art only on the cover, on the divider pages, interspersed throughout the recipes, or on every page. The aesthetic decision is up to you. Of course, twenty full-color reproductions of famous paintings like those in *The High Museum of Art Recipe Collection* will cost more to print than one reproduction of your child's black and white drawing (lots more).

If you are not an artist and don't have a museum full of fine paintings right at hand, there are several things you can do. Again, we suggest trying a nearby art school or art department for a young artist who would love to add a credit to his résumé for a reasonable price. The public library has files of old photographs or prints that can be reproduced with permission, like those in *Nutbread and Nostalgia*. Libraries also have books of "public domain" art that can be used. Printers and graphic designers also have large supplies of "pull" or "clip" art, designs that can be combined in a variety of ways with excellent results. Maybe there is a certain charm to your Aunt Martha's sketches of her kitchen. (Maybe not!)

## Dividers

Once again, the choice is yours. Most cookbooks have some differentiation between chapters or sections because it makes it easier to find recipes and categories, but this depends on the arrangement of your recipes. Perla Meyers in *The Seasonal Kitchen* has the headings—Summer Desserts, Fall Menus, Winter Vegetables—in bold type running parallel to the spine in the outside margin of each page.

If you choose to have pages dividing the sections, they can range from a page of the same weight and color paper with a simple title—"Soups"—to a page of larger size, different color, heavier or coated paper with a colorful illustration and divider tabs.

*Applehood & Motherpie* uses the same paper as the text printed in a different-color ink, with plastic-coated divider tabs. *The Better Homes & Gardens Cookbook* has larger, heavier, tabbed dividers, with the contents of each section printed on the divider page. *Soupçon* divides the sections by printing all of the recipes in each seasonal section on different-colored paper—green for spring, yellow for summer, orange for fall, and white for winter. Some books use the same paper as the text, only in a different color, with or without artwork.

Cost is certainly a factor here, as is your taste and the theme of your book.

## Binding

As you know from looking at cookbooks, they come in all sorts of bindings. If your book is to be published by a publishing company, it will probably be either hardback or perfect-bound (like a paperback), or if you are lucky and have big sales, an edition of each. However, if you decide to self-publish, you have a wide choice of bindings. Why? Because while the big publishing houses are set up to do one or two types of things and cannot economically branch into all sorts of novelty binding (except for some of the "novelty" publishers), there are printing and binding companies across the country that can offer you a variety of options at all different prices.

Let's look at some of the many types of bindings that are available today:

*Hardback or Casebound*—The standard binding found in most published books. Most of these books have dust covers, the paper jacket wrapping around the book that can be removed. Authors like Julia Child and Craig Claiborne are usually published first in hardback. Many self-publishers use hardback now, as it can be done affordably. Also, hardback books can now be bound so that they will lie flat when open on the counter.

*Perfect Bound*—Used in popular paperback books, this method utilizes adhesive glue and can handle from 60 to 500 pages. Frequently, bestsellers come out first in hardback, then in a less expensive perfect-bound edition.

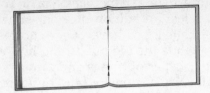

*Saddle-stitched*—A fancy name for stapled. The pages are held through the center fold with staples. The limitation is size; this method can only hold up to approximately 60 pages, but it is good for a small, pamphletlike cookbook.

*Spiral Bound*—There are two basic types of spiral binding:

 *Comb Bound*—Holes are punched in the pages and in the cover, and the book is bound on a plastic comb. This has been popular for cookbooks because it allows the book to lie flat when open. Many community cookbooks, both large and small, have been published this way. The title can be printed on the comb, and some books have even printed metric conversions or measurements on the inside of the rings so that they can be read at each page when the book is used.

Caution: the plastic comb has to be large enough to allow the pages to be turned easily. Too-small combs are a common problem.

 *Wire or Wire-O*—Plastic-coated or metal wire rings that resemble a larger version of your old school composition book, but much more sophisticated, can now replace the plastic comb. The rings are available in different colors, but the disadvantage is that the title cannot appear on the spine of the book.

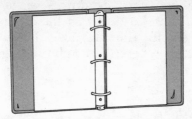

*Notebook (Ring Binder)*—Actually a three-ring notebook. Holes are punched into pages and pages are inserted in the ring binder. This style lies flat and allows for additions and/or rearrangement. *The Better Homes & Gardens Cookbook* is the grandmother of these, but self-publishers are now using them, too. A few books of this type have plastic rings that cannot be opened.

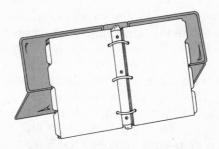

A variation of this is the *Easel-back or Bent-back Notebook*. This is a three-ring binder, the bottom half of which bends backward to form an easel, so that the book is self-standing. *Applehood & Motherpie* was the first self-published book to use this; others have followed.

These are some of the most commonly found, or "standard" cookbook bindings, but there are many variations and combinations. We might mention:

*Singleboard or Stepdown*—Imagine a combination of hardback and comb or wire-o binding. This means that the front and back covers are hard boards, joined by either a plastic comb or wire-o. This combines the strength and durability of a hardback and the convenience of spiral bound. A variation is the "stepdown" version, which looks very much the same, except that the covers are made of two boards of slightly different sizes that give a recessed, or "gutter," effect where the comb binding is inserted.

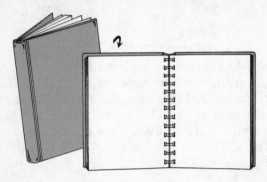

*Wrap-around*—A wire-o binding inside a wrap-around hard cover. From the outside, this looks like a hardback book, with either a flat or a rounded spine—with the added advantage of the title printed on the spine. When it is open, it has a wire-o binding attached to the cover.

Then there are variations on any of these. *Vin et Fromage*, a cookbook featuring recipes from the Sonoma Valley wine country, is a standard size 5¼″ × 8½″ comb-bound book, but the type is set parallel to the longest side of the page, like a calendar.

For years, cookbooks were either hardback or comb bound. Combs were popular, particularly among self-publishers, because they were inexpensive and allowed the book to lie flat. Now hardbacks can be made to lie flat, and plastic combs, because they are petroleum products, have become more expensive. If you have decided to self-publish, take an assortment of bindings that you like to various printers and get estimates before you make up your mind. Remember that the more sophisticated the binding, the higher the cost. Companies that specialize in cookbooks may offer more different bindings than the local all-service printer. You should explore all the options, but remember that the expense of the binding does not determine the quality of the book. You may lust after the most expensive type of binding, but be realistic about your budget.

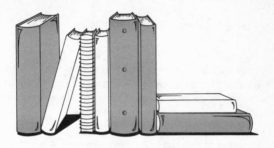

## Format

This is how the book is actually set up cover to cover—you will determine whether you have a foreword, an introduction, recipes divided by category, by season, by national origin, or by food type; whether you have additional text at the beginning of each chapter or section, where you put the credits, whether you include quotations, helpful hints, poems, wine charts, herb charts, or any other sort of information.

Again, the decision is yours. Just remember that a cook wants to be able to *use* a cookbook. It can be different and interesting, but if you make it too gimmicky and tricky, you may make it hard to use.

On the next page we provide an outline for one possible format; the list on page 61 offers other possible inclusions. The lists could go on and on, determined only by what you think adds to the appeal and theme of your book. This is simply a guide; your cookbook will combine the elements that you want.

## BASIC COOKBOOK COMPONENTS

1. *Cover*
2. *Title page*—a right-hand page that gives the title, author, and/or publisher.
3. *Title page verso*—the back of the title page and very important. It contains the copyright notice, name and address of the publisher (organization or individual), list of printings, identification and registration numbers (ISBN, LCCN, etc.), and other information.
4. *Dedication page*—a right-hand page. The word "to" and the name of the person, place, group, etc., to whom the book is dedicated (your choice).
5. *Acknowledgments*—list of individuals, companies, organizations, etc., to which public appreciation should be expressed.
6. *Foreword*—written and signed by either the individual or organization. Should be brief.
7. *Table of contents*—begins on a right-hand page and lists sections or chapters with the beginning page numbers.

TRADITIONAL CONTENTS

| | |
|---|---|
| Appetizers & Canapés | Sauces & Accompaniments |
| Soups | |
| Cheese & Eggs | Breads |
| Seafood | Desserts |
| Game & Poultry | Cookies & Candies |
| Meat | Beverages |
| Vegetables | Miscellaneous |
| Salads & Dressings | |

This can obviously be expanded, combined, or changed.
8. *Text pages*—actual body of the book (text and recipes).
9. *Extras*—dividers, photographs, drawings, hints, charts, etc.
10. *Index*—begins on a right-hand page and contains alphabetical listing and cross-references of items in the book with corresponding page numbers.
11. *Coupon pages*—multiple coupons for direct orders. Usually found only in self-published books.

## EXTRA COOKBOOK INCLUSIONS

Weights and measures
Equivalents or conversions
Wine chart
Ingredient substitutions
Herb guide
Menu suggestions
Suggestions for complementary dishes
Timetable for fish and meat cooking
Ways to utilize leftovers
Quantities for large groups
Calorie and/or carbohydrate chart
Freezing information
Metric conversion table
Consumer hints (cooking and/or household)
Buying guide for fruits, vegetables, meats, etc.
Candy and frosting chart
Microwave timetable
Food processor guide
Party planners
Table settings
Temperature conversion tables
Content volume of baking pans
Meat chart (various cuts)
Glossary of basic cooking terms
Recipes for children
Holiday suggestions
Extra pages for buyer's recipes
Degree of recipe complexity (easy to gourmet)
Budget meals
Quick and easy meals
Natural food recipes

## Layout

Layout refers to the way in which each page is arranged for use and for eye appeal. You can have one recipe to a page—or three. You can print the ingredients at the top, on the side, in different sizes or styles of type, in paragraph form. You can use boxes or borders. Each page can have an illustration or a heading. You can put helpful hints or comments or quotations on every page, only occasionally, or at the beginning or ending of chapters.

You can have several columns of print to a page. *The Silver Palate Cookbook* by Julee Russo and Sheila Lukins, owners of the New York gourmet shop of the same name, has pages of three-column width. On most pages the recipes run across two columns printed in black ink; the third column has serving suggestions, interesting tidbits, or menus printed in red. Instructional or decorative line drawings can appear in any column throughout the book.

Where you place illustrations, and how frequently, is important. Even such a small thing as where the page number is placed—at the top, at the bottom, inside or outside the margin—is important. Whether each page has a chapter heading or only a recipe title matters.

Look at every book you can find. Ask cookbook users what they like and dislike, what they find useful and appealing, what makes them *not* like a cookbook. You and your designer must choose the best elements from each style to suit your taste and fit your theme. Here are a few basic principles to help you:

• The simpler the better.
• Pay attention to page spread. A pair of facing pages will be taken in by the reader at a single glance.
• The "white space"—the blank areas on a page—is very important.
• Recipes should not run onto the next page as a continuation unless the recipe is exceptionally long and detailed and will not fit on one page. In any case, the cook should *never* have to turn the page in the midst of cooking.

Let's look at several possible recipe layouts. There are a number of ways to lay out recipes. Several possibilities appear on pages 63–64. You can also look at various cookbooks for ideas.

# Scrumptious Shrimp Spread

3 7-ounce-size
   cans shrimp
1 8-ounce package
   cream cheese
2 tablespoons
   minced onion
⅔ cup mayonnaise

*Wash, mince, and drain the shrimp. When the cream cheese is softened, mix all the ingredients together and let stand in the refrigerator for 24 hours. Serve with crackers.*

# Spinach-Sausage Casserole

2  frozen spinach souf-
   flés
1  pound smoked sau-
   sage
½ cup finely chopped
   onion

1 cup Cheese Sauce (be-
   low)
1 can crisp fried onion
   rings

## Cheese Sauce

2 tablespoons butter
2 tablespoons flour
1 cup milk
½ cup grated Cheddar cheese

Grease a 2-quart casserole dish. Partially thaw spin-ach soufflés. Chop sausage into half-inch pieces. Mix sausage, onion, and cheese sauce with spinach and pour into casserole. Top with onion rings and bake at 350° for 45 minutes to one hour.

Serves four.

# Mini-Pizzas

This recipe was given to me by a dear old lady with many years experience pleasing young people. Children love to get these out of the freezer to fix their own lunches. Teen-agers positively adore them, and they make a nice appetizer for adult cocktail parties, too.

1 pound hot sausage, cooked, drained, and crumbled
1 pound sharp Cheddar cheese, grated
1 11-ounce can tomato soup
Garlic salt, oregano, and pepper to taste
2 loaves sliced party rye bread
1 ½ cups Parmesan cheese, grated

Preheat oven to 350 degrees. Mix the sausage, Cheddar cheese, tomato soup, and seasonings and spread on slices of bread. Sprinkle each slice with Parmesan cheese. Arrange the slices on a cookie sheet and bake for 7 minutes. At this point, you can cool and freeze them on the cookie sheet, then pop them into plastic bags and store them in the freezer. Take out as many as you need at one time, and bake until bubbly.

## Cover

What can we say? When your book is on the shelf in a store, it has a split second to catch the buyer's eye. Your cover *must* have "shelf appeal"! Put your money on the cover, even if you have to save someplace else. Although the reputation of the cookbook will sell it the second time, those first sales often depend on the cover. Since this is true, this may be the place where you are most in need of professional help. The cover presents the theme for the first time and makes the buyer want to open the book. It has to look good.

Although most publishing companies prefer hardback books with dust jackets, we feel that the ideal cookbook cover is cleanable and water resistant. Cookbooks get more use than most books; look in your kitchen and see which kinds of covers have worn well. Cover stock comes in many varieties: plastic coating on heavy paper, hard covers, vinyls, plastics. Shop around to see what you like and ask your friends what they find durable and practical. If you decide on a dust jacket, think of it more as an added decoration than as protection for the cover.

Don't forget the back cover and the spine of the book. The spine should have the title on it, for this may be the only part of the book the buyer sees on the shelf.

One reason for an attractive cover is the important gift market. This is a big part of cookbook sales because cookbooks make such wonderful gifts for all occasions. A good-looking cover is a necessity to attract this market.

Finally, if you are working with a group, give the all-important final decision on the cover to a small steering committee. An organization we know hired an artist to design a new logo. The artist's three proposals were presented at a board meeting with much fanfare. Every one of the thirty women present had strong, purely subjective opinions. The arguments got so violent that the meeting might still be going on if the chairman had not withdrawn the suggestions and started all over again, giving the final decision to a group of five people this time.

Moral: You can't please all the people all the time and there is no accounting for tastes.

# PLANNING AHEAD: CALENDARS AND BUDGETS

Now you know what is involved in creating your own Classic Cookbook. Let's talk for a moment about how to plan for the creation. How long is it going to take and how much is it going to cost you?

One of the questions we are asked most frequently is,

"How long does it take to produce a cookbook?" The answer, of course, depends on many things: the type and scope of your book, whether you are doing it entirely on your own or with an organization (then, how large is the organization and how much support can you expect from them), and what other commitments will occupy your time while you are working on the book? The record time that we know of for producing a nationally successful cookbook was five months—an incredible feat! We also know of one that was seven years in the making. You may feel that your cookbook is the work of an entire lifetime. It took Julia Child and her collaborators about ten years to complete *Mastering the Art of French Cooking*.

The average time is two to three years, start to finish. Today, thanks to seminars and improved communications, cookbook publishing is getting more sophisticated and less trial and error. Better planning saves time and headaches. If you choose to submit your book to a publishing company, the one factor you will have no control over is the time you spend waiting for a response, but you can plan the rest of the stages, and self-publishers should plan for the whole process.

When you begin to plan a cookbook, assess all the variables that will affect you or your organization. How many recipes do you already have? How many people will help test? How long will it take you to decide on a theme or do you already have one? Will it take long to assemble the artwork or any extra written material? Who is going to type the manuscript? Are you thinking of self-publishing? How large a book are you planning, and what type is it? You can think of many more questions like these.

Make an educated guess about the time you will need, then set up a calendar—and stick to it! (See example, page 68.) Be reasonable, but make it a little on the short side to push yourself. If you are self-publishing, start by setting the publication date (the date the book will actually go on sale, six to eight weeks after you receive the books from the printer). Remember that you have already edited it when the manuscript goes to the printer. When he sends your proofs back, you will only be checking for errors. If your book is to be published by a company, the target date is the date you submit the completed manuscript. Thereafter, the schedule will be dictated by the publisher, who will notify you when you will receive and return the edited manuscript, when to expect galleys and when they must be returned. Allow six to eight months for this process. Work backward from the date that you set.

If your book is being done by a publisher, the schedule will vary, depending on how long it takes to sell your idea and come to contract, how long it takes the publisher to decide to accept the finished manuscript, when they want to publish the book, how much editing they want to do on it, how long the copyediting takes, etc. Much of this is out of your control, but a well-done, carefully thought-out, proofread manuscript can help speed up the process, and that is *very much* in your hands. You should figure on anywhere from a year to two years from the time that you submit your contracted manuscript until the time the book is published.

As you can see, a cookbook is going to cost you a lot of time. It's going to cost some money, too. We will talk about budgets for self-publishers in a later chapter. There are going to be some costs involved in the creation stages for you, whether you self-publish or sell your book to a publishing company, and it is wise to plan ahead from the very beginning.

The most obvious early expense is that of the food for experimenting and testing. You may absorb this into your household budget, but you may find yourself spending more—buying another sirloin strip just to make sure you've got it right. Don't let a big bill slip up and surprise you.

You will also have some expenses for photocopying and typing the recipes, then for typing the manuscript unless you are skilled enough to make a perfect copy yourself. Where are you going to get artwork if you decide to use it? Do you need to pay an artist? Do you need to pay the costs of a photographer and photographic processing? Are you going to need money to pay a designer? You may

## COOKBOOK PRODUCTION CALENDAR
## FOR SELF-PUBLISHING

**1985**

| September | October | November |
|---|---|---|
| *Idea!* | *Research* | *Start collecting & Testing Recipes* |
| December | January | February |
| | | |
| March | April | May |
| | | |
| June | July | August |
| | *Recipes Finished* | *Proofing* |

1986

**1986**

| September | October | November |
|---|---|---|
| *Artwork & Design Done* | *Manuscript Finished* | *Bids (self-pub.)* |
| December | January | February |
| *Manuscript to Printer* | | *Proofing Stages* |
| March | April | May |
| | | |
| June | July | August |
| *Books Received* | | *Publication Date!* |

1987

have costs involved in correspondence and research, too. It will cost to mail that manuscript, especially if you have to do it several times.

You need to make a budget, getting estimates on all "cost" facets, estimating how much you will need for all the things involved in the creation stage. You also need to keep careful records of how much you spend. It might be well worth the cost to get the advice of a good accountant to help you plan. If you have "advance money" from a publisher, you may want to allocate some of it for business expenses.

# THE BIRTH OF A COOKBOOK: A TRUE STORY

Let us tell you a true story about the creation of a cookbook. After having served as chairman of publications for the Memphis Junior League, Helen had experience in marketing the League's two cookbooks, *The Memphis Cookbook*, first published in 1952, and *Party Potpourri*, published in 1970. Then, in 1979, Helen found herself chairman of a committee to create a new cookbook, something she'd never thought about.

It happened this way. The husbands of two League members had been hearing about the League's cookbooks and came up with an idea: why not a cookbook for and by men? They were convinced the idea had potential as a money-maker for their wives' organization. The membership liked the idea and Helen was asked to chair the committee to put it all together.

The theme had come first in this case, a men's cookbook. This saved time, as did the fact that the League already had the business systems in operation. A small committee was formed, including the two husbands and several League members. Two women were put in charge of collecting and testing recipes. The committee purposely decided not to have a standard recipe collection form because they wanted the recipes in the men's own words. The co-chairmen began to contact men who were known to be good cooks. All the men contacted were flattered and thought it was a wonderful idea, but it took quite a bit of prodding from wives and friends to get the recipes actually written down.

Instead of forming a special testing committee, volunteers from the membership were asked to test. An evaluation form was prepared and each recipe was tested twice. Two "super cooks" agreed to test any questionable recipes; because they were gourmets who knew what they were doing, their decisions were accepted as final on any controversial recipes. Another expert was called in to check spellings and terms, particularly French words.

Each tester paid for her own ingredients except in a few special cases, like the lady who asked to be reimbursed for a six-pound sirloin strip, saying she had never served anything like that to her family before. Helen recalls that probably less than one hundred dollars was spent by the organization on testing to reimburse testers, including the printing of evaluations forms.

The committee's biggest decision was not to edit the recipes because they wanted to preserve the style and humor of the men's descriptions of what to do. For most cookbooks, editing to make sure all the recipes read alike would be an important process, but since the style of men's cooking was to be the theme of the book, only two policies were used: ingredients would be listed first, in order of use, and almost no brand names would be used.

The recipe co-chairmen were responsible for calling the contributors for clarification, making sure the recipes were legibly typed, collecting the evaluations, and making the final decisions about what was to be included. As expected, plenty of game, fish, and barbecue recipes were submitted, as well as plenty of bread and dessert recipes. One of the co-chairmen remembers that vegetable recipes were hard to come by. The ones that did come in were largely zucchini recipes, making the committee wonder whether men liked zucchini a lot, or whether it was the only vegetable they know how to cook. It took some work to solicit more vegetable recipes.

While the testing was going on, the design process was begun. A volunteer who was a professional graphic artist was chosen. She submitted three entirely different design concepts, then left the meeting so that the committee could discuss the ideas freely (an ideal situation).

At first, the concept had been to publish a small, inexpensive book to complement the League's two larger cookbooks and give a third price category. However, the men had definite ideas about what they liked, and they insisted on a format with only one or two recipes to a page and lots of "white space." This meant that the book was growing into a regular-sized book, and so the price increased, all of which had to be resubmitted to the membership for approval.

Because Helen had had experience with reprinting the other two books, she knew how to prepare a spec sheet to present for different printers' bids. First she called in a printer who did other work for the League but who didn't have the equipment to print a book. He was able to answer questions and give unbiased advice. When four bids were received, the final decision was made by the executive committee.

To choose a title the League held a contest, with dinner for two at a top restaurant as the prize. Helen remembers that some of the titles were really awful. She recalls that it took several meetings to pick a title, and that holding the meetings at night with plenty of wine helped the process. The final title, *A Man's Taste*, wasn't the first choice of any committee member, but it was the phrase that recurred in everyone's reasoning about the book. Finally someone said, "Look, we keep talking about a man's taste. That will have to be the title."

Of course, there were delays and unexpected happenings that were funny in retrospect. One wife on the committee looked at her husband's recipes and said, "Oh, that will never work. I don't know why he said that," and sat down and rewrote them. Then there was the volunteer typist who, when asked when she'd have the typing finished, replied, "Oh, I'll have to find somebody to do it. I don't type. I just signed up because it sounded like an easy job."

The book took only a year to complete because the theme had already been chosen, fewer recipes were required, and the design and testing went on simultaneously. *A Man's Taste* made its debut to the delight of all the men who contributed.

We tell you this story to show that a successful cookbook can be created by a few people in a short time, and that they can have fun doing it.

Creating a Classic Cookbook can be great fun and a wonderful learning experience. You can make it fun and save yourself headaches by planning ahead—making schedules and budgets for yourself. Remember that your cookbook should be an expression of your unique qualities, an authentic reflection of your time and place and way of life. To accomplish this, keep in mind what makes a Classic: a theme development that is both unique and unifying; tested recipes that are easy to understand and use and can be trusted to produce good results; and a good-looking design concept that expresses the theme and will have "shelf appeal."

# CHAPTER 2

# Publishing a Cookbook

PUBLICATION is the stage that takes your book from manuscript form to the finished product: a bound, printed, illustrated book, ready to hit the market. Before that exciting moment when you hold a shiny new book in your hands, there are a good many things you have to consider.

There is a difference in "printing" and "publishing." Printing is the process that manufactures books; it includes typesetting, printing, binding, and boxing the books. Publishing is the larger process of editing, printing, promoting, and distributing the book.

If you sell your book to a publisher, they own the book and pay you, the author, royalties. The publisher takes over the design and the distribution and promotion as well as the manufacture of the book.

If you decide to self-publish, you are responsible for all of this, as well as for financing the project. As for profit, in the first instance you and the publisher share the profit; you are paid a percentage from the sales of the book as royalty. In the case of self-publishing, the profit is 100 percent yours—but so are the risks and the work.

Let's explore the first option, publication by a publishing company. There are all sorts of publishers: big companies with famous names like Doubleday and Random House; smaller companies of all descriptions; regional and local publishers; specialty firms. One of these may be right for your book.

# FINDING A PUBLISHER

How are you going to find a publisher? Of course, the ideal would be for a publisher to find you, to offer you a fabulous contract to record your favorite recipes. It can happen, particularly if you have some claim to fame, if you are a well-known cooking teacher, restaurateur, or personality. If you have ever published anything before, the odds of your getting into print the second time are much greater, and many people who have self-published one book can find a publisher for the next one.

But let's assume this is your first effort, and no publisher knows who you are—yet. There are two ways to proceed with your book idea: Submit it yourself or use an agent.

## *Submitting It Yourself*

**Step 1:** *Learn all that you can about getting published.*
In your public library you will find dozens of books about writing and selling books, enough to make you think that every other person that you meet is a secret author with manuscripts hidden in every drawer. There are books that deal with fiction, with nonfiction, with magazine writing. One that we have found to be particularly useful is *How to Get Happily Published*, by Judith Appelbaum and Nancy Evans. Use what applies from any sources that you can, but remember that what might help you if you've written a novel may not have much to do with cookbooks.

**Step 2:** *Make a list of possible publishers.*
Not every publisher publishes cookbooks, and there is no point in submitting your book to a company that prints only the encyclopedia or teen-age romances. So the first step is to identify the possibilities: those companies that publish cookbooks or how-to books. Check the public

library and your local bookstore to find out what companies have published books similar to the one you have in mind—or have published other cookbooks and might be interested in yours because it adds something different to their list. If yours is a health food or diet book, you will find companies that specialize in those. If you envision a large-format, lavishly illustrated book with banquet menus, you can probably identify who might be interested and who might not. If one company has just issued a series of ethnic cookbooks, they are probably not going to be interested in another Italian cookbook right now, but one of their competitors might be. Ask your local bookstore owner what is new and selling best. Look on the shelf to see what is recent, and also look in *Books in Print* for both hardbacks and paperbacks. We have included an appendix listing some known publishers of cookbooks, but the list changes often.

Another invaluable resource in preparing a list of possible publishers is *Literary Market Place (LMP)*. This is the directory of the trade, listing everything and everybody connected with publishing, and your library will have a copy. *LMP* has an alphabetical listing of publishers that covers one hundred pages of very small print. It also lists publishers according to fields of activity, like mass market paperbacks, general trade books, reference books, and so on. Even more helpful is the breakdown by geographic region and by subject matter, such as "Cookbooks, Food, Beverages," "Health, Nutrition," and "House and Home."

The most recent issues of *Publishers Weekly* (a trade magazine) can be a help, too, with current information about who is publishing what. It can also be found in your library. *The Book Publisher's Directory* is another resource. All of these will give you names and addresses. If you send off your book addressed merely to "Editor, Doubleday & Company," you've lost it in the "slush pile," and its chances of being noticed are delayed, if not killed. You want to address any communication to a specific person, preferably the person in charge of buying cookbook manuscripts. Before you send anything off, it is wise to use your telephone. If you call to make sure that person is still at that address, you may get closer to sending it to the person who can do you the most good.

### Step 3: Use your contacts.

Another approach is the "who do you know" angle. Here, don't be afraid to dredge up any connection, however distant, that might introduce you to someone currently active in publishing. Your sister's college roommate works for a publisher of history books in New York. Chances are she knows somebody who could help you. The food editor of the local paper regularly reviews cookbooks and goes to meetings of editors around the country. There's a possible connection. You met a lady in Florida who'd written a couple of cookbooks? Call her; she might be flattered by your interest in how she did it.

Look for your regional publishers' association and attend trade shows of booksellers and publishers. Attend writers' seminars at a local college. Talk to your bookseller. Use any connections that you can think of that will help you get your foot in the door or that will at least get you the name of an editor of publisher who might read your book and buy it.

### Step 4: Develop a proposal.

Assuming that you now have a name and an address, what are you going to send? Almost no publisher wants your complete manuscript to arrive unannounced. This almost guarantees you a form letter saying, "We regret that we are unable to accept unsolicited manuscripts," and besides, it's expensive to mail the whole thing.

You need to write a letter telling enough about your book to sell the idea and make the editor want to see more. You will tell:

- What your cookbook is, including approximate length.
- Why this is unique and worth his/her interest.
- What audience the book will appeal to.
- Who you are—including all your qualifications as a cook and writer.
- A complete outline, sample chapter, and sample recipes.

It goes without saying that the proposed must be grammatical, correctly spelled, and neatly typed. Enclose a stamped, self-addressed envelope for the reply. Of course, you keep a copy of the proposal and a record of the date you mailed it.

The following sample proposal was developed by first-time cookbook writers Jan Brink and Melinda Ramm, whose book *S.N.A.C.K.S.: Speedy, Nutritious and Cheap Kids' Snacks* was later published by New American Library.

---

## S.N.A.C.K.S. PROPOSAL

Dear Editor:

We want to open your eyes and minds to the advantages of wholesome, natural snacks that you can make yourself.

That's what we do now, and you can too! The idea for this book started one Halloween when we were faced with the problem of "treating" a neighborhood full of ghosts and goblins. Junk food was out; we don't eat it, we don't believe in it, so we refuse to serve it. The local grocery store had only the usual assortment of overprocessed, oversugared, and nutritionally empty snacks. The "health-food" store had plenty to choose from, all of it too expensive. Even our many cookbooks did not have ideas for fast, economical, and yet healthy treats.

So industrious resourceful women that we are, we decided to write a book ourselves; a book to which parents could go to find ideas and ways to give their kids healthful snacks that are fast, easy, and economical.

In *S.N.A.C.K.S.*, we'd like to show you how you can have wholesome snacks on hand for your family, spend your food dollars more effectively, and how with just a little planning and organization you can make your own life a whole lot simpler, and still keep the smiles on those healthy kids of yours.

Read and enjoy! We look forward to hearing from you.

Sincerely,
Jan Brink and Melinda Romm

## SAMPLE OUTLINE

Preface

Introduction—"Snacks Can Make the Difference"

Chapter 1   "Getting It All Together"—The purpose of this chapter is to help parents save time by becoming more organized in three main areas: their foods, their kitchens, and their basic approach to each recipe.

Chapter 2   "Smart Shopping"—This chapter tells readers how, what, and where to buy the wholesome ingredients used to make the recipes in S.N.A.C.K.S.

Chapter 3   "Back to Basics"—"B to B" gives a brief explanation of why we have chosen the main ingredients used in this book. It also describes some ingredients the average reader may not be familiar with and some which should be avoided.

Chapter 4   "Absolutely Instant"—Contained in this chapter are ideas for snacks that require virtually no preparation time, can be kept on hand, and are delicious. Because these snacks are such timesavers, we feel this chapter is one of the major selling points of the book. (Approx. 75 recipes)

Chapter 5   "Quick and Easy"—This chapter contains snacks that require a little more preparation— but just a little! They can all be made in five minutes or under. (Approx. 110 recipes)

Chapter 6   "Drinks"—In "Drinks," parents can find recipes for beverages which can be high in protein, high in vitamins, use fresh fruits, or be used as substitutes for soda or chocolate drinks. Both hot and cold beverages are included. (Approx. 38 recipes)

Chapter 7  "Breads and Muffins"—All of our breads are non-yeast breads so they can be made quickly. The recipes in this chapter produce easy baked goods using high-quality ingredients, fruits, and nuts. (Approx. 20 recipes)

Chapter 8  "Cookies"—Our cookie recipes are new and traditional. We have included chewy, crunchy, big, small—something to please everyone. Many are old standbys that we have changed to be more wholesome but still delicious. (Approx. 20 recipes)

Chapter 9  "Pies and Cakes"—Since pies and cakes are perennial favorites with kids, we've found recipes which are fast yet still wholesome. Included are basic cakes, fruit pies, "special occasion" cakes, and others. (Approx. 20 recipes)

Chapter 10  "Candy, Nuts, and Seeds"—Parents can find ideas that appeal to any sweet tooth and still have lots of high-protein treats in this chapter. This is where we've put recipes for candies which are raw and cooked, and all snacks made with nuts and seeds. (Approx. 35 recipes)

Chapter 11  "Eggs and Cheese"—Parents of kids who don't eat enough protein at meals have but to turn to this chapter to find lots of ideas for high-protein snacks. (Approx. 20 recipes)

Chapter 12  "Fruits and Vegetables"—Recipes and ideas in this chapter show parents a variety of ways to make both fruits and vegetables appealing to kids. (Approx. 35 recipes)

Chapter 13  "Milk and Yogurt"—Milk and yogurt are good foods for kids. This chapter shows parents ways to serve both to make them real treats. (Approx. 20 recipes)

Chapter 14 "Sandwich Fillings"—Our sandwich recipes will give parents ideas for lots of new and exciting sandwich treats. Again, we've included ways of increasing the nutritional value of old standbys. (Approx. 20 recipes)

Chapter 15 "Lists of Lists"—We have included this chapter as a guide to parents to help them choose which recipes in *S.N.A.C.K.S.* are the most appropriate for specific occasions.

List of Sources

Index

[In addition, the authors provided a copy of their introduction to give an idea of their writing style plus some sample recipes to give an idea of their culinary style.]

---

After you submit a proposal, you wait. Of course you are impatient, but remember that editors go on vacation, pass your proposal around to other editors, or just plain may not get to it for a while. After four weeks you can send a polite letter of inquiry, and if that gets no response, you can call in two more weeks.

What about sending the proposal off to several publishers at a time? Publishers usually frown on multiple submissions. If your letter is rejected by the first publisher you write to, try the second one on your list, keeping a careful record of all your correspondence.

## Using an Agent

If finding a publisher by yourself sounds uncertain and time-consuming, you may consider finding an agent to sell the book for you. By being in constant contact with the people in the publishing business an agent knows what is selling and to whom. A good agent knows what publishing company is most likely to be interested in your type of book and what editor to present it to. An agent can smooth the way for you, for in many cases an editor will look at an agent's submission more quickly than at a letter from an unknown writer.

An agent works on commission, usually 10 to 15 percent of an author's gross earnings. Therefore, the agent has a stake in seeing that you get the most favorable terms and in selling your book for the highest price. An agent knows about contracts and will negotiate for your benefit. Most agents are located in the centers of publishing—New York or California—but there may be a literary agent in your city (try the yellow pages or the Chamber of Commerce's business directory) who will take an interest in your work.

As always, a personal recommendation is the best introduction. Think of anyone you know who has written any kind of book and ask for the name of his or her agent. That at least puts you in touch with someone who can refer you to an agent who handles cookbooks.

How else can you find an agent? Some of the same rules and questions about finding a publisher will apply. Again, *Literary Market Place* is invaluable, with a listing of agents and the types of books they handle. In nine pages of agents (again very small print), only *two* specifically mention cookbooks, although many specify nonfiction, how-to books, or women's interests. You will find that many say "No unsolicited manuscripts, query first with SASE (self-addressed, stamped envelope)."

Other resources are the Society of Authors' Representatives and the Independent Literary Agents Association. *Writers' Market* (available in your library) lists agents with descriptions of services and the type of material handled. *Literary Agents* is a publication of Poets & Writers, Inc., which outlines working with an agent and lists many addresses.

Remember, cookbooks are different and agents are, too. The person who negotiated a million-dollar deal for Norman Mailer or Judith Krantz may not know one thing about cookbooks. You want someone who knows the specialized cookbook field. Look for the name of someone who represents nonfiction, how-to books, or home and garden books. Call or write to see if he or she will consider representing your book. If that agent doesn't handle cookbooks, perhaps he will put you in touch with someone who does.

An agent needs to be sold on your book, too. He or she is not going to accept a client unless he thinks the client's book will sell. You need to approach an agent in the same way you would approach a publisher—by sending a query letter and a proposal. Tell the agent who you are and why you have written this book, why your book is unique and who the potential audience will be. If you have ever published anything before—magazine or newspaper articles, contributions to other books—you will have a better chance of getting a hearing. Use any connections that you can think of here, too.

Be prepared for rejection; you may have to try several times. Not all cookbook agents handle all types of cookbooks. But agents are always on the lookout for something special. Elise Simon Goodman, of Goodman Associates in New York, says, "I look for an authentic voice, someone who has a personal connection to a particular region (grew up in Albania or has grandmother's recipes from Czechoslovakia or was raised in the Mississippi delta by a family of cooks, etc.) or a particular style or method of cooking. I like lots of anecdotes with my recipes, and I find suggestions for what to serve with each particular dish very useful."

Once an agent accepts your book, he will try to get the best deal possible for you, but the agent has to believe in the book, too.

When you make contact with an agent who shows interest, it is time for some frank discussion. Ask questions. What publishing companies does he have in mind and why? If you've done your homework, you'll know some of the possibilities, too. What other cookbooks has he represented? What time frame are you talking about? If he doesn't sell the book within a certain period of time, what happens? Some agents don't think it is worth their while to deal with small presses. Find out. Ask what his commission is and find out who pays for such expenses as postage, telephone calls and copying, and how much this could amount to. Find out how he sees your book— hardcover, paperback, etc.—and how he plans to proceed. If you don't sign a contract with the agent (frequently you don't), have a clear agreement as to what you can expect.

Agents who want to be paid a fee in advance are looked upon with suspicion in the book trade. Be careful. If someone wants money on the front end, get in writing exactly what you get for the fee.

## MANUSCRIPT PREPARATION

Once you have aroused some interest either in an agent or a publisher, you will be asked to submit a detailed proposal—an outline, chapter titles, approximate length, sample text, and sample recipes—or the entire manuscript.

You want your work to look professional and appealing. A sloppy, careless manuscript is not going to inspire confidence in you as a careful cook or writer, and may keep the work from being read at all. If you are not a really good typist, this is one place you will need to spend money. Here are some guidelines for manuscript preparation:

1. Text should be typed and double-spaced on one side of white, unlined, 8½″×11″ standard bond paper.
2. Have at least a one-inch margin on all four sides.
3. Place all text and recipes in exact order for the final book. Type one recipe to a page (with the exception of an extra-long or complicated recipe that won't fit on one page).
4. Number pages in sequence in the upper right-hand corner. (The number will have nothing to do with the final printed numbering of pages.) This cannot be done until everything is in final order,

so it should be the last step before you hand the manuscript over, as there might be last-minute additions or deletions. You can number the pages by hand, neatly, if necessary.

5. Put the title in the upper left-hand corner of each page. This is for product identification only and has nothing to do with the final copy.

6. When typing *text* (not recipes), keep approximately the same number of lines on each page.

7. Keep at least two copies of the manuscript: one for yourself, and one for the publisher or printer. Often a publishing company will request *two* copies.

8. There should be no staples, binders, or paper clips on the manuscript.

9. Never paste or clip artwork or photographs in the manuscript. Keep this separate and indicate its location in the book by giving a description in the appropriate place in the manuscript. Put the page number and explanation on the corresponding piece of art or illustration.

10. If there are captions accompanying the artwork, they should be typed in the manuscript in the appropriate place and should be numbered to correspond with the illustration.

## REJECTION—BE PREPARED

Before we move into the details of clinching the sale, we must say a word about rejection. It happens to everybody—even to Julia Child in the beginning. Sometimes it can be a healthy thing. An editor—or an agent—may tell you why he or she is rejecting your book: the subject has limited appeal, there are too many similar titles, your organization or format is not appealing, the concept is too broad. Pay attention! With a little work you may be able to try again—and have a better product. If you get the same comments more than once, you know you've got a problem, but that doesn't mean you can't fix it.

There are all sorts of reasons for rejection. Maybe the editor had a bad day. Maybe that company has a similar book already in the works. Maybe you didn't approach the right person. Maybe your idea needs refocusing toward a different audience. If you believe in your book, keep trying. Only you can tell when to stop. If you have tried and tried and keep getting rejection slips from publishers, you can still believe in your book—just skip the next few pages and go straight to the chapters on "Self-Publishing." Maybe once you've got a book that you've published yourself to be proud of, the publishers will come looking for your next one.

# WHEN YOUR BOOK IS ACCEPTED

When your book is accepted—well, you certainly deserve a celebration dinner out! But there are some more steps to follow carefully before you can expect to cash your first royalty check or to have the checker at the supermarket ask for your autograph. The big one is the contract.

## Contracts

A contract is the legal agreement between two parties, the author and the publisher, which spells out the commitments and responsibilities of each, and the financial terms of the arrangement. If you have an agent, the agent will do most of the negotiating for you (some people think that this is the best reason to have an agent). However, you must understand the contract thoroughly before you sign it. Now is the time to get a lawyer to represent your interests and to clarify all the issues.

The "standard contract" varies from publisher to publisher and book to book, but it will always include the following:

- You, the author, promise to provide by a certain date two copies of a satisfactory manuscript of a certain description and approximate length. Your responsibility may or may not include charts, diagrams, and illustrations.

- You, the author, will guarantee that you own the work, that it does not infringe upon anyone's copyright, that it has not been published before, that use with general care will not result in injury, that it is not obscene, libelous, or unlawful.

- You grant to the publisher the exclusive rights to publish, print, and sell the work within a certain territory (the United States, the United States and Canada, etc.).

- The publisher will apply for copyright either in the author's name or the publisher's name. RED FLAG! You want the copyright in your name. Be firm.

- The publisher should agree to publish the work within a certain period, say twelve or eighteen months.

- The publisher agrees to pay the author a percentage of the retail price based on the number of copies sold. For example, for a hardcover, 10 percent up to the first 5,000 copies, 15 percent thereafter. For paperbacks the percentage is usually lower, say 6 to 7 percent. You want to know the schedule of payments and the projected number of copies in the first printing, the projected retail price, and if there are any exceptions to the percentage. Exceptions might include mail order sales, serial rights, and book club sales.

- The publisher gets the right to promote and distribute the book as he sees fit.

- Subsidiary rights will be assigned. This means paperback reprint, book clubs, publication of excerpts in magazines, anthologies, etc., foreign rights.

- The publisher reserves the right to make editorial changes. The publisher agrees to furnish galley proofs and the author agrees to proofread the galleys within a specified time. Responsibility and costs of author's alterations are set out.

* The publisher has the right to institute legal proceedings against infringement of copyright.
* Advance payment is agreed upon. You may request an advance against income—probably paid in installments, so much on signing the contract, so much on delivery of the manuscript, so much on publication. This will be subtracted from your royalties.
* Agreement should be reached on what happens when the book goes out of print or when the publisher fails to reprint. Do you have the option to buy the rights and find another publisher?
* The publisher may want an option to publish your next work. The terms of any subsequent publication will be decided at that time.

The contract can even spell out such things as number of author's free copies, author's right to buy additional copies at a discount, disposition of the publishing plates, use of material from the book in promotion, author's role in promotion, foreign rights. You or your agent may retain some of the subsidiary rights to negotiate independent of the publisher. We haven't heard of a cookbook being made into a movie yet, but there is always hope.

## Fine-Tuning the Book

If all goes well, you complete the manuscript on time and the book enters the production stage. Under "Design Considerations" in Chapter 1, we said that if you sell your book to a publisher you will have little to say about how the book finally looks. A publisher has a professional staff trained to make books look attractive to buyers. A small publisher may be more open to your design suggestions than a large one, and may have more flexibility than a company that is set up to turn out great numbers of books with little variation. The designer works with an eye to the overall cost of printing the book. To make the book economical the designer must figure out how many pages, how many recipes to a page, how much "white space," and so on. You may say what you'd like to have, but basically these decisions are out of your hands. The cover, whether it is hard or soft, the price, and the design are all the province of the publisher. If some design element is crucial to the concept of your book, include this in the contract. Then you won't be unpleasantly surprised at someone else's idea of your book.

*Recipe testing* is another function that a publisher may assume, but the majority won't. Some companies that specialize in cookbooks may have their own test kitchens or employ independent testers. Most publishers will not, however. We stand by our statement in Chapter 1: no matter how many times the recipes are tested, the responsibility for their accuracy is up to you. You have to have had your own testing system before the manuscript leaves your hands.

*Indexing* follows the same pattern. A publisher may hire a professional indexer to do it. If you have strong opinions about the kind of index you like to use (and most cooks do), you'd better do it yourself, or come to an agreement with your editor on the format to be used for the index.

All of this brings us to your final responsibilities for the manuscript: *checking the editing* and *proofing the galleys*.

*Editing* can make the difference between a so-so book and a great book. The person who buys your book may be your editor or pass the job along to someone else. The editor may be one or several people. The editor will clarify what you have to say, will suggest additions or deletions, may make major structural changes, and may want you to revise or rewrite a lot or a little. Your feelings may be hurt if the editor wants to rewrite the whole thing, but remember, the editor knows the audience and can make your work more appealing. You both have the same goal in mind: a book that sells lots of copies.

Your editor can be your best friend. In any case, you want to have a good relationship with this person. The better prepared and more professional you are, the better your chances are for a happy working relationship. If you realize that the goal of editing is a better book, you will be able to keep your sense of proportion when your death-less prose comes back full of blue lines.

Once the editor has gone over your manuscript and you have agreed on the changes, it goes to the *copy editor*. The copy editor's function is to make sure that all the copy and the recipes will "read" the same way. The goal here is conformity of style and format. This includes:

* Standardizing spelling, punctuation, and usage.
* Correcting sentence structure and verb tense.
* Ensuring uniform instructions.
* Deciding whether to use brand names or generic names of ingredients.
* Standardizing terminology—for example, deciding to use "beat" instead of "whip."
* Generally ensuring clarity.

Once the copy editor has gone over the manuscript, it will be returned to you. You will usually have three to four weeks to go over it and accept (or reject) the changes. Then it will be set in type and proofs made, and you will see those for the final proofing.

*Proofing galleys* is a purely technical process that is ob-jective and requires no decision making. It is done to eliminate any errors in the finished product and is con-cerned with spelling, punctuation, the proper order of things, and making sure that everything has been picked up accurately by the typesetter and that nothing has been left out. A publisher will have your book proofread several times (usually once in galleys and once in pages), but even the best proofreader cannot second-guess your in-tentions and may let a mistake go by. Try to come to an understanding with the publisher about when you will see the proofs and make corrections. You will usually have at least two weeks to read proofs. Enlist a careful friend and go over everything meticulously, comparing the proofs with your copy of the manuscript. Be sure the recipes are in the right order, that all ingredients are listed and appear in the order of use, and that nothing has been omitted. Be especially careful about numbers. There is a big difference between ¼ cup and ¾ cup of sugar. Since it is your work, you will catch things a typesetter might not.

# ALTERNATIVES

The big-name publishing companies are not the only route to fame and fortune, so if your book is turned down by Knopf or New American Library, don't despair. There are many smaller publishing companies that may be a more appropriate home for your book. There are small publishing companies all across the country that may be looking for authors or subjects with a regional flavor. A smaller company may allow you, the author, more say in the final design of the book. A smaller company may be more innovative than a large one in matters of design. There are more small publishers today than ever before and lots of them publish cookbooks very successfully. A few of them publish *only* cookbooks.

Of course, there is always the good news and the bad news. A smaller publisher may have almost no budget for promotion and may lack the channels for marketing that a big firm has. Also, they are harder to find. Once again, look for listings in *LMP* and *The International Directory of Little Magazines and Small Presses*. Another source is *Small Press: The Magazine of Independent Book Publishing* by the R. R. Bowker Company, also available in your library. See our appendix, too. When you find a possibility, ask for a list of their publications. Contact some of their authors and ask a thousand questions about anything that you don't fully understand before you sign anything. Ask did you work with one person or with several people? Were they pleasant and cooperative? Were many changes made? Did you have control over the changes? Did they keep to their schedule? And most important: would you publish with them again? You want to know what to expect, and there is no better way to find out than by talking to other writers.

There are two more possibilities for getting your book in print that come under the category of self-publishing, but marginally—and one is hard to define.

The type of press that is "hard to define" and exists in "never-never land" in the publishing industry is what is known as the *vanity press*. Vanity presses advertise or report themselves to be publishers but in reality are companies that charge you for the privilege of having them publish your book. Although they list as publishers, they charge you, the author, for everything—book production, storage, promotions, etc., and you receive payment after everything else is paid for. Generally they make no effort to market the book since all their money is made by the fees they charge you. Vanity presses are under investigation because of their practices. We think *this is the worst option of all*.

The next chapter deals thoroughly with self-publishing, and we'll tell you from start to finish how to self-publish a Classic. For those people with a small budget and with no desire to reach the national market, there is another viable, very reliable alternative: *formula* or *standard publishing*.

There are several companies in the United States that specialize in producing small runs of 1,000 or less economically. You supply the recipes and they offer you a set or choices of covers, paper, dividers, and so on. They can even produce a "specialized" book for you. The company will send you a packet of samples; you choose Cover A, Dividers B, Color C, and so on. Your book may look like someone else's three states away, but if you are aiming at a limited local market, that doesn't really matter. If you don't have an idea about a theme or a source for artwork, these companies can help you. Your book will not be a Classic and it won't sell 500,000 copies on the national market, but for a small group or an individual with a $2,000 budget and the desire for a limited number of books, this is a good option. These companies advertise in the medium-priced cooking and craft magazines.

Some of these companies don't typeset. The printed reproduction comes straight from the typewritten manuscript you originally produced, but some are fairly sophisticated and there are several very good ones. Some offer "state-of-the-art" typesetting and printing at very low costs. Again, contact some of their customers to ask questions about their service, and ask to see samples of their work.

# CHAPTER 3

# Self-Publishing

THERE ARE SEVERAL reasons why you may decide to self-publish your cookbook. First, as a self-publisher you have total control. *You* are the final authority on how the book looks, how much it costs, how and where it is sold, how it is advertised—the whole works. Second, as a first-time author having trouble finding a publisher, doing it yourself may be the best way to get your book on the market. Third, you will get all the profits without sharing them with a publisher or an agent. Fourth, a successfully published book might be more appealing to a publishing company than an unpublished, untested manuscript. Fifth, your control may ensure the longevity of your book. When sales slack off, a publisher may decide not to put any more money into advertising and let the book go out of print, so that the only available copies appear on the remainder table. When you self-publish, you can decide when more promotion is necessary and can keep the book going for years. A famous publisher once said that a self-published book had a greater chance for success because it was in the hands of someone who cared and believed in it totally.

To give you courage, some of the authors who have self-published are James Joyce, Virginia Woolf, Washington Irving, and Mark Twain.

Self-publishing is the usual procedure for nonprofit organizations that publish cookbooks, and there are many benefits over and above the money raised for the cause. A cookbook becomes an ongoing fund-raising project. It provides a variety of volunteer training opportunities. It fosters friendships and improves morale within the organization. We'll talk more about committee structure and volunteer job descriptions in a later chapter.

When you decide to self-publish, there are several steps you need to follow. This chapter is a guide to finding a printer, arranging financing, signing printing contracts, and pricing your book. What you are really doing in becoming a self-publisher is setting up a small mail-order business. The Small Business Administration says that to run a successful mail-order business, you need a product that is "appealing, unusual, mailable, and nonseasonal." Did you ever hear a more perfect description of your cookbook?

# FINDING A PRINTER

Let's assume you have gone through all the stages of creation we discussed in Chapter 1, and you now have a completed, typed manuscript, an idea of the format and design of your book, and artwork already in hand. How do you find a printer? And how do you decide which printer is going to do the best job for you?

Our "golden rules," which we cannot repeat often enough, are: *ask a Thousand Questions* (we'll give you several for starters) and *get at least three bids!*

There are basically three types of printers:

1. *A full-service printer*—one who can do most of the work on your book in-house and has the staff and machinery to print large quantities of books at reasonable prices. He probably doesn't want to be bothered with the smaller items, for which you need the two other types of printers.
2. *A specialty printer*—one who will print your brochures, flyers, promotional material, letterheads, and invoices.

3. *A quick-print shop*—which offers the lowest prices of all and is used to print forms, letters, some promotional material, press releases, etc.

You may have dealings with all three at different times. Be sure to apply our golden rules to whichever ones you use.

No matter which kind of printer you are looking for, you want to check the same things:

*Reputation*—First and foremost, check with others. Ask for a list of past and present customers and don't hesitate to call them. Ask what he currently prints and see how many of these are reprints. This is a tip-off to satisfactory service.

*Quality*—Ask to see samples of his work, particularly work that is similar to what you have in mind. Ask to see samples of color work if you plan to use color.

*Time*—From the time the printer receives your manuscript, how long will the printing take, start to finish? Average time to print a cookbook, with some exceptions, is three to four months. Be aware that this may vary according to the season. The summer is usually a busy time and this may cause delays. The availability of materials can also cause problems and needs to be checked.

*Service*—When checking with present and former customers, be sure to ask if the printer lived up to all his contractual agreements. Did he deliver when he said he would? Was he cooperative, even helpful? Did he drag his feet on service because he was too busy hustling new customers? How did he deal with problems that arose? Is he easy to communicate with or impossible to get hold of?

*Price*—This will come with the bid. One warning: never tell one printer what another printer bid. This is not fair to you or to the printers.

*Extra services*—Beyond actual printing, many printers offer extra services. Be careful. It may sound good but often it can actually hurt your product. Some of the possible extra services include:

"A great deal" on paper
Indexing
Computer services
Photographs or artwork on hand
Design services
Marketing
"Free brochures"
Wholesale orders shipped (fulfillment)
Storage
Testing ..... and so on

Be sure you understand exactly what is offered and how this affects the cost—and your book.

Remain as independent of your printer as possible. It is our feeling that the more the printer is involved, the more the money interferes with accurate judgment. Also, the success of cookbooks is directly related to their uniqueness and individuality. Too much printer involvement causes sameness. You may find that all the books printed by one company have the same format, the same layout, the same index. That makes it easier and cheaper for the printer, but is it what you want?

Finding a printer is one of the biggest steps in self-publishing a cookbook because of the money involved. Cookbook authors are frequently what printers refer to as "noncommercial customers," which means not as experienced as some of their customers who do regular volume printing. It is true that as a first-timer you may need more help. You may be awed by all the details and tend to get carried away by what the printer tells you. You may think, "Help! The printer is the pro and he knows what he is talking about and I don't." *Stop here!* Remember that you are giving big business to the printer. You deserve service and cooperation.

Somewhere along the way there are going to be problems. There always are. (Sometimes we think that there is something in the ink that must create snafus.) Machines break down, books get lost, mistakes occur. The important thing is *how* the printer deals with it. This is what other customers can tell you. By asking a thousand questions and understanding the answers before you go any further, you can forestall most of the difficulties.

Where are you going to look for a printer? When the word gets out that you've got something to print, they will be looking for you. You can look in the yellow pages of your phone directory; there may be local printers who have the capability to print what you want but they may lack experience with cookbooks. Look under "Book Manufacturers" in *LMP*. Look in the front of other cookbooks to get the names of printers to contact. There are national firms that specialize in cookbooks and will send a sales representative to meet with you.

Then, of course, there's the problem of your neighbor's brother-in-law in the printing business who will give you such a deal. Whoever you deal with, remember our golden rules: ask a thousand questions and get at least three bids.

# GETTING A BID

If you are talking about a reprint of an already existing book, you can take a copy to a printer and simply say, "How much to reprint so many copies of this book?" But if you are talking about a new book, you may feel that you are in a "chicken or the egg" situation. You don't know how much your book will cost and you don't want to go further until you have some idea if your brainchild is within the realm of possibility or too expensive to even consider. You need to find a book that is roughly the size and type of book you have in mind and ask for a "dummy bid." This means an estimate of what the book would cost. If you have your manuscript and your concept fairly well defined, you ask for a bid on that. In any case, you need some sort of a "spec sheet," specifying what you are asking the printer to bid on. It should include:

Description/title
Approximate number of pages
Page and/or book trim size

Cover stock
Content paper
Dividers and artwork stock (paper) if any
Ink: cover (how many colors)
   text
   dividers and/or extras
Preparation (typesetting, color separations, etc.)
Artwork/photographs (how many and description)
Type style
Binding
Boxing specifications
Quantity

Don't panic. You don't know all these specifications right now. There are several ways to get help. First, find those books you like and use samples. Second, get help from your designer, who should have most of the answers. Third, find a printer who can't or won't print your book; for example, a local middle-sized printer. He will be knowledgeable and can give you an unbiased answer since he won't be in competition for the contract.

When you draw up your spec sheet, have several copies made and send one with a cover letter to several different printers to get their bids. A sample appears on the facing page.

One of the most confusing aspects of printing is paper. To quote *Small Press Magazine*: "It's sold by the carton, talked about in sheets, charged by the hundredweight, but discussed by the pound. Make your printer help you through this confusion—he should understand it all." He will also have lots of samples. Show him examples of paper that you like in other books. Suppose you fall in love with an expensive parchment-quality paper. A printer may be able to help you find a cheaper equivalent. Also check on the availability of what you select. We know someone who had her heart set on a particular unusual color. The paper was only made once a year, and waiting for it would cause a long delay. Once you find something you like, the printer should be able to confirm its availability with a phone call.

# SAMPLE LETTER AND SPEC SHEET

Dear Sir:

My organization is preparing for its first printing of our cookbook, *The Classic Cookbook*, and we are very interested in receiving a bid from your company.

The printing specifications are as follows:

*Title*: The Classic Cookbook
*Total number of pages*: 320 (including 14 dividers)
*Trim size*:
    Cover—5½ × 8½
    Pages—5½ × 8½
*Paper stock*:
    Cover—23 point stacon
    Content—60 lb. white offset
    Dividers—80 lb. prime yellow vellum
*Binding*:
    Plastic white comb with title silk-screened in yellow
*Presswork*:
    Printer to type-set entire text
    Full-color photography for cover, printer to do color separations
*Ink/colors*:
    Cover—above
    Content—black ink, both sides, entire text
    Dividers—black ink, one side, line drawing to be furnished, camera-ready
*Packing*:
    To be boxed in three quantities—⅓ in boxes of 6, ⅓ in boxes of 12, and ⅓ in large quantities, boxes to be printed.
*Quantity*:
    10,000 and 20,000 (please quote both)

I would also like to have a list of your company's policies and services, and would need the costs of shipping, storage, possible delivery date, and your payment terms. Please also enclose a list of your customers.

We plan to be ready for press June 1. If you have any questions or need any further information, please feel free to contact me.

Sincerely,

Now is the time to be flexible—about paper, color, artwork, bindings, everything. You may have a million-dollar idea and a thousand-dollar budget. A good printer can help you find satisfactory alternatives. If a printer suggests an alternative, get a separate quote on that.

One of the most important things the printer needs to know to figure your bid is quantity. You can ask for a quote on different quantities: say 1,000, 5,000, and 10,000. As the number of copies goes up, the price per copy goes down, but the total price of the contract is higher. When you are deciding on the number of books to print, consider these points:

1. A first printing is usually smaller because of the large costs involved in preparation. Also, if there are errors or oversights in the first edition, you don't want to get stuck with too many incorrect books.
2. Printing a large quantity may be a hedge against inflation, for example: rising paper costs, increased labor costs. However, you have to consider the storage. Storing a large number of books for a long time can be costly, and you need to realize that books stored for too long are subject to damage.
3. Your office and promotion costs may rise, too, and you may want to increase the price of the book. You don't want 5,000 copies marked $5.95 when you've decided to raise the price to $6.95.
4. The cost of subsequent reprintings will be less than the original so your profit margin will be greater.

For the first printing, print the number of books you think you can sell in one year. When you sell out, you have a terrific advertising gimmick and a big psychological boost. After that you don't want to have to negotiate a new contract every six months, so reprint what you think you can sell in two years.

How do you know? At first you are making a guess, but after you are in business, good inventory controls and sales records will help you. If you have been selling 50 books a month, you know it's time to reprint when you are down to 300 or so books.

5. Remember that you won't *sell* every book. You will give away some complimentary copies to book reviewers, potential large wholesale accounts, etc., and these are recorded in the budget as marketing/promotional expense—at the cost of the book, not the retail price.

6. Only you can make the decision about how much effort you are willing to put into promoting the book and only you know what you want from the sales. If you are part of a large organization that needs megabucks for a new project and has the resources, contacts, and manpower for promotion, you will make one decision. If you are a person whose chief pleasure has been in the creative stage, perhaps you don't want to bother with a big sales effort and only want to sell enough to cover your costs and then give the rest away to friends. You have to make a judgment about what you want and what you can expect from yourself (or your organization). There are Classics in both categories, books that crack the national markets and books that enjoy only a limited local sale.

After the printer has all the information, you will receive a bid in writing. (See sample bid on pages 102–103.) Some printers will send you a written bid, then if you accept it, will send you a separate contract. Sometimes the bid becomes the contract: by signing it you accept it. Either way is perfectly all right. Before you sign *anything*, make sure you understand *everything*.

Remember what we said about always getting at least three bids? Make sure the bids are equivalent. You have to compare apples to apples, not apples to oranges. You have sent the printers the same spec sheet, but the bids they submit may vary widely. One company may include storage in the price, while another's bid may be lower but specify that "Storage will be billed at so much per thousand each six months." Another may give you a bid that says, "Freight included," while another may not mention it.

```
                        ABC PRINTING CO.
                      2345 International Road
                        Memphis, TN  38000


Date:  March 15, 1985


Book title:  The Classic Cookbook


Number of pages:  126 pages, flat board cover


Trim sizes:  Cover - 6½" x 9½"
             Text - 6" x 9"


Stock:  Cover - Kevtone acrylic coated
        Text -  70 lb. Hammermill (beige)


Colors/ink:  Cover -  Two colors, one side only
             Text -  One color, two sides


Dividers:  none


Printer preparation:  Typesetting from provided mauscript


Art:  Customer to provide, camera ready


Binding:  GBC punch, silkscreened (1 color)


Boxing:  Boxed in 5 & 10 count (half & half), boxes to be printed


Quantity:  5,000


Shipping:  Charges to be included in total bid price


Extra:  Storage - to be provided by printing compamy for 1 year at
                   no charge
        Inventory - printing company to provide customer with
                    quarterly inventory report, in writing
```

Be sure that everything is clear and specific and that
you understand the terms. For example, one bid may say,
"Cover will be plasti-coated," which is a term describing
a specific waterproof coating that is a good product. An-

Delivery date:  120 days from date completed manuscript and art are
delivered to printer.

Payment terms:  1/3 payment with signed contract, 1/3 payment upon
book delivery, 1/3 payment in 30 days.

Price:   $10,500.00    ($2.10 per book)

Signed:  _____

        ABC Printing representative          date

Signed:  _____

        Customer                      date

Please note that when this bid sheet is signed, it then becomes the
contract.

### ABC PRINTING COMPANY POLICIES

1. ABC guarantees delivery of all books in condition that is
   acceptable to customer.
2. Please note that the price(s) quoted are good only for 30 days
   from date printed on this bid.
3. Paper prices are subject to change at any time.
4. Customer agrees to a maximum 10% over-run/underrun quantity.
5. Ownership of original materials and printing negatives is
   retained by the customer.

other bid simply says, "Cover will be coated"—this can
mean the cheapest kind of varnish which can cause the
covers to stick together or yellow. When you go back to
the printer and say, "This is not what I meant," the printer

may say, "Well, that's all the contract said. We can do it for you, but it's going to cost you a little more."

We've included a glossary of printer's terms (see page 269), but please don't try to use them just to impress the printer. You're sure to get caught if you don't understand exactly what you mean. Ask for full explanations in plain English.

Also, look at the bids for the expiration date. A printer's costs are constantly fluctuating: paper prices go up, labor contracts have to be negotiated, and so on. The bid will usually say, "This price good through October 15—or thirty days." This can create a special problem for volunteer groups that have to present the bid to the finance committee, then the board, and then the membership before it can be approved. Time can run out. You can either ask the printer for an extension until a certain date or ask for a new price. Just pay attention, so that if you take a year to make up your mind, you won't be surprised by a higher price.

If everything is not specified to your satisfaction, write an addendum for the printer to agree to and sign.

Don't ever let a printer tell you that *you* can't do something. That usually means *he* can't do it, and he is not about to give you the name of the man down the street who can do what you want. Shop around, and ask a thousand questions before you sign. If you are the type of person who hates to ask questions, you should not be in this business.

# THE CONTRACT

After you have received at least three bids and compared them, you are ready to sign the contract. If you've paid attention to the previous section, you've made sure that the bids are based on the same specifications. Printing contracts can take many forms. Fortunately, contracts are more likely to be written in plain English today than a few years ago when the legalese was overwhelming. You will probably want a lawyer to check everything before you sign. However, be careful. Lawyers can sometimes tend to overcomplicate printing contracts. There are many permutations and combinations you or the printer may want included. You want everything spelled out in writing—no oral understandings—because this is a legally binding document that is your last recourse in case of difficulty. Now let's go over some of the factors that should be included in your contract, besides those already specified in the bid.

1. *Quantity*—The number of books you decide to print.
2. *Price*—Price isn't everything, but it certainly is important. You figure how much money you can spend, and how you are financing the project. We'll talk more about this later. Don't forget all your other costs: setting up an office, the costs of food preparation, artwork, typing, attorney fees. You also need a promotion budget. If you can't promote, you can't sell. Ask for a total contract price and a breakdown of cost per book.
3. *Boxing*—The boxes should be printed with the name of the cookbook and the business address, and the cost of the boxing should be figured in the "price per book." You will need several different boxing quantities. For retail sales you want the books packed in large quantities, because these are the books that you will keep in your office and mail out one or two at a time. For wholesale we recommend that you have at least two different quantities—for example, boxes of six books and boxes of twelve books. These will be shipped, in the boxes, directly to the wholesale accounts, and having two different quantities available makes you more flexible in filling orders. Don't skimp or try to cut costs on boxing. You will have more trouble than you need. You wouldn't believe the horror stories we hear about books arriving damaged, with combs broken, the bottom of the box fallen out—because people thought

they could save some money. The box weight or sturdiness should be adequate for the weight of the books.

Some books, particularly hardcovers, require heavier boxes or Styrofoam padding. Some books require "slipsheeting"—a sheet of paper slipped in between each copy to protect the cover. The cost of doing this is minimal compared to the damage that can be done without it.

4. *Binding*—The type of binding and any printing on it should be specified.

5. *Shipping charges*—Is this included in the price per book, or is it an additional charge? Charges for this should be enumerated. If you are having large quantities shipped to you, they will probably come by truck. You may want to specify "Inside Delivery." Imagine that you have just had 5,000 copies, boxed in large boxes of 40 each, and the boxes banded together, dumped in your driveway at 5:00 P.M. on a rainy day when your children are crying and the supper is boiling over. It is worth the small extra cost to have the books brought inside where you want them. Since freight rate is usually dock to dock, "Inside Delivery" must be specified.

6. *Time restrictions/delivery date*—The contract should specify a delivery date. There can always be delays, but you want a firm date specified on which you will receive the finished product. Set the delivery date a little earlier than necessary as insurance against an unforeseen delay. Have the printer check on paper delivery before signing the contract since that can cause a delay. You may also want the deadlines on reading proof in writing.

7. *Inventory*—Are you going to store all the books you have printed? If you print a large number, this can be a problem. Will the printer store them? If so, for how long? Is there a charge? What are the conditions? Will they be insured in storage?

If the printer stores, the storage area needs to be satisfactory. We don't mean that the warehouse has to be heated and air-conditioned like your home, but it has to have some temperature control to insure against extremes. We know one story about a printer who had stored books satisfactorily for several years, then moved the books to an outside metal warehouse with no controls, just as a heatwave made the temperature shoot up enough to melt the varnish and ruin the covers.

If the printer stores for you, insist on a regular inventory statement from him. You should keep your own records and receive a statement from him of how many books are left. You'll probably always be a *few* books off—but you want to avoid a problem like finding out you're hundreds of books short as the Christmas orders pile up. If the printer comes up short on the number of books you've paid for, he either has to print more or pay you for them.

8. *Extra services*—Be sure you understand what is offered. Some printers will offer local delivery on large orders, with or without charge. Some will offer to print brochures for you. Some will offer *fulfillment*, which means they will drop-ship large orders directly from the warehouse to the customer. Be sure you know if there are any charges for promotions—you want to know exactly what he is sending out with your name on it. Are there any charges for consulting or for an extra like having extra promotional covers printed? If so, all of this needs to be spelled out, in writing, in the contract.

9. *Proof considerations*—Know the schedule for proofing and the costs for making changes as the process proceeds. A printer's error is the printer's cost, but your error, or alteration, is your cost, and it can cost plenty if you wait too late to change it. When changes are made, you will want to see proofs of the corrections.

10. *Book errors and damage*—Any mistake that occurs at the printer's—broken combs, covers stuck together, pages missing, books incorrectly bound—is his problem and cost, but once the books are in your

possession, the problem can be yours. The contract should say that the printer guarantees delivery of the books in acceptable condition. You don't have to unpack every box that you send out from your office to check. If you send out a shipment and get one complaint, it is probably an isolated incident. You then apologize profusely, send more books, and ask for the damaged books back—you pay the shipping. (You need to know for certain that the books *were* damaged, and you can use them for promotional purposes later.)

However, if you get calls from five different stores saying that the bindings are all damaged, you know you've got problems—and it's probably the printer's fault. Notify the printer immediately, in writing. Check everything you've got on hand, and ask him to check his stock. Determine where the damage occurred and whose liability it is. The contract should specify that the printer will correct anything that does not conform to the specifications of the contract.

11. *Overrun/underrun agreements*—This is standard in printing contracts. You contract for 10,000 books. When the printer cranks up those huge machines there is no way they are going to print exactly 10,000 copies. In the contract you agree to accept a 10 percent overrun or underrun—and that is all. If they print 9,901 books, that is within the 10 percent. You accept that number and only pay for that number. If they print 10,020 books, you pay for that number at the same contract price per book.

Ten percent is standard in the printing industry. Don't agree to 20 percent. An overrun is probably more common because the printer doesn't want to come up short and lose money. Since you own the copyright, the printer can't do anything with your books except use them for samples of his work. We did hear about one printer who sold extra copies of a book from his back door. If that happens, sue! Remember to figure the possibility of a 10 percent overrun in your budget because it is not uncommon.

12. *Payment schedule and terms*—The contract states how much you owe. It will also specify when you owe it. A usual method of payment is one third upon signing the contract, one third upon delivery, and one third thirty or sixty days later. This can vary from printer to printer. Four payments or two payments are not uncommon. In any case, be prepared to write a check for part of the contract price when you sign the contract. A printer's costs are immediate; he has to order the paper, the bindings, and so on, and he needs some money right away. By the time of the second or third payment he will know if there is an adjustment for overrun or underrun and will bill accordingly.

13. *Ownership*—Standard printing contracts have a form printed on the back that says (in hard-to-read small print) something like, "The printer retains all rights to negatives, plates, artwork, etc." You, the author, own the copyright to the contents, but the printer owns the actual materials used in printing. This becomes a problem only if you decide to change printers. Then you might have to buy the negatives or start all over again. The printer cannot use your material since you own the copyright; all he can do if you decide to change printers is to destroy the plates.

Specify in the contract that *you* own the negatives, original art, and so on. Nonprofit groups have been doing this for years, and it is a good idea for any self-publisher to state that ownership is theirs. The big printing companies that specialize in cookbooks are aware of this and give ownership rights to the author on request. We hope your relations with your printer are smooth and that you never have reason to think about changing, but we have heard too many stories from people who do decide to change printers for one reason or another. You ought to be aware of this potential problem.

If you must make changes in your book after you are well into the printing process, keep track of the costs. The timing and the type of change can be crucial. Are you talking about one change on a page or are you talking about a change that realigns the whole book? The longer you wait to make changes the more costly it will be. Ask how much a change will cost and get it in writing. Keeping track of changes will save you some nasty surprises.

Keep your budget to yourself. If you say you have $20,000 to spend, do you really expect to get a quote for $19,900?

If your book is in bits and pieces, the art not in camera-ready form, the text full of additions or deletions, you can expect to pay more for the work the printer has to do to get it in shape.

If you want to see your cover before you end up with 10,000 copies of something and decide you don't like it, you can ask for a "press proof." It can cost you several hundred dollars, but it may be worth it.

If you are dealing with an out-of-town printer (and the majority of cookbook writers do), remember that the big companies have a travel budget and can send a representative to see you. It helps to work things out face to face.

When you change printers for a reprinting, you will go through the same thing all over again, but *this time* it will be easier because you know what you want and you have a copy of the book to work with.

You may think you can save money by having the typesetting done yourself. Some printers won't touch this because it's hard to establish where the mistakes were made. However, the computer revolution is reaching the cookbook printing industry. It may be possible to put your manuscript on a word processor at home that will go right into a printer's process. It's worth looking into if you have computer capability.

Once again, let us repeat our golden rules: *ask a thousand questions*, and *get at least three bids.*

# FINE-TUNING
# AND FINAL STEPS

We covered design considerations in Chapter 1, "Creating a Cookbook," and we have already said that we recommend that you stay as independent of the printer as possible. We have one further warning. Make sure that the printer can do what you want done, and that you and the printer have a clear understanding about the design. Find out in what form he wants the artwork delivered. Some printers will want camera-ready art and others will do some of the technical preparation for you. For example, if you use color photography, the actual printing will be done from color separations. You can supply the color separations yourself, or the printer may do it for you. Be sure you understand who is responsible for what, and what it will cost you.

The contract will state when the books will be delivered, and when you will deliver the completed manuscript. There are other deadlines, or time frames, that you should be aware of. There may be a separate deadline for the artwork. You will receive the proofs for corrections at different stages and will have a certain period of time to go over them and return them with any corrections you've made. Be sure you understand the time allotted. Delays can be costly.

We have already mentioned the difference between editing and proofing, and the role of the editor and copy editor in a publishing house. Self-publishers need to pay attention to this, too. You can be your own editor and copy editor, but sometimes being so close to the work causes you to overlook things. You probably need some help. Whoever goes over your book should have some knowledge of writing, spelling, punctuation, grammar, and cooking. You might consider asking a home economist, a cooking teacher, or the local newspaper's food writer to edit your book. The goal is to have all the material "read" the same way. As we outlined before in Chapter 2, editing includes:

1. Making sure the copy flows in the same style and manner.
2. Standardizing spelling, punctuation, and usage.
3. Correcting sentence structure and verb tense.
4. Ensuring uniform and clear instructions.
5. Deciding whether to use brand names or generic names of ingredients.
6. Standardizing terminology—for example, deciding to use "beat" instead of "whip."
7. Deciding how to give credit for recipes or where to add comments.

What you choose to do in such cases is less important than making a decision and sticking to it consistently. Editing should be done while the book is in manuscript form and before it is given to the printer, because making a number of changes after the type is set will be *very* costly.

The proofing stages are all-important. Nothing is more discouraging to sales than a new book with an "errata" slip stuck to the first page. If you are self-publishing, you will proofread your book at least three times in order to have as error-free a product as possible.

This means reading:

1. The typed manuscript in its final form.
2. The typeset proofs sent to you by the printer.
3. The corrected proofs returned by the printer.

Some printers will give you an overlay, some a non-photo blue line copy, some a blue line proof. Don't worry; these are technical terms and the printer will explain the method of correction to use. What is important is that you and the printer understand the corrections and that they are consistent. In the appendices we have included a sample list of proofreaders' symbols and corrections. Your printer may have something similar to give you. Just be sure you and he are using the same system.

Proofing includes:

1. Making sure the pages are in order.
2. Making sure that everything that is supposed to be on a page is actually there.
3. Checking all spelling and punctuation.
4. Making sure that the cooking terms that you have decided on are correct, consistent, and properly used.
5. Checking all numbers and measurements.

Several people should proof several times; one will always spot something another has missed. One method that works well is for one person to read aloud from the manuscript while another checks the proof. Now is the time to enlist your most careful, detail-conscious friends.

Don't make big changes after the book has been typeset. Each time you change your mind it is going to be *very* expensive. The time for that is while the book is in manuscript form. The proofing stage is simply to correct errors. Remember to watch your deadlines and know just how long you have for each proofing stage.

# BOOK REGISTRATION

If you have sold your book to a publisher, the publisher will take care of book registration, but as a self-publisher it is something you must do yourself. There are several important reasons why your book should be properly registered. They include:

> Protection
> Identification
> Location
> Sales and promotion

There are at least three ways you should register your book: with a copyright, an International Standard Book Number (ISBN), and a Library of Congress Catalog Number (LCCN).

## Copyright

A copyright assures you the right to print, reprint, and copy the material you are publishing. It also assures that no one else may do so without your permission. Your copyright must be registered if you ever want or need to enforce it. It can be expensive to defend your copyright legally, but it is your only protection. We know too many stories about people finding that their material has been reprinted and is making money for someone else.

The new copyright law of 1978 insures your work for 50 years after the last surviving author's death. To obtain a copyright, write to the address below and ask for Form TX, an application for copyright registration on a nondramatic literary work.

> Register of Copyrights
> Library of Congress
> Washington, DC 20559

Do this at least four months prior to publishing; you are dealing with the government, remember. Go ahead and have the copyright symbol printed in your manuscript and book before you receive the final registration—this is standard and necessary. As soon as the book is printed, register your claim to copyright by sending the completed Form TX along with two copies of the book and a check ($10 most recently) to the copyright office.

There are three essential elements in the display of the copyright in your book:

1. The symbol © or the word "copyright" or the abbreviation "copr." must appear on the final publication.
2. The name of the owner of the copyright must appear. This will be the name of the individual author or authors or the name of the organization.
3. The notice must appear in the copies of the book "in such a manner and location as to give reasonable

notice of the claim of copyright." This is usually printed on the title page verso (the back of the title page).

If you want more information, send for *A Writer's Guide to Copyright*, listed in the appendix, or ask the Library of of Congress for Circular R99.

## ISBN

The ISBN, or International Standard Book Number, is the way booksellers can identify and find your book. Write to the address below and request an application for an ISBN:

> R. R. Bowker Company
> 205 East Forty-Second Street
> New York, NY 10017

Or, call Bowker at (212) 916–1600. You will receive a form with questions concerning you as a publisher. Fill this out, return, it, and you will be sent a ten-digit number that is permanently assigned to your book. This, too, should be done at least four months prior to publication, as the number needs to be printed in the book. It goes on the title page verso along with the copyright.

Why is this so important? First, it is the universal identification for your book and makes it simple for a bookseller to find it if he is interested. Second, all the bookstore chains and most of the independent booksellers now use computers. The ISBN system was chosen to enter books into the computer system since the number identification was already there. This number records a bookseller's stock, sales, and reorders when needed. If a book does not have an ISBN, it cannot go into the system and will eventually be lost to all intents and purposes.

Once an ISBN has been assigned to a title, it cannot be assigned to any other book. The number is printed in catalogs and international bibliographies. Any distributor must use the ISBN in all promotional materials. This is how the bookseller can find your book and reorder it, and you certainly want that to happen, don't you?

Once you have an ISBN, write to the same address and request an ABI (Advanced Book Information) form. When this is filled in and returned, your book will automatically be listed in *Books in Print*, an annual publication listing all titles in print and forthcoming—the "Bible" for book sellers.

## LCCN

This is the Library of Congress Catalog Number. It can only be obtained on an unpublished or new book, so it, too, must be applied for in advance. This allows your book to be cataloged in the library system. Right now, few libraries are cataloging cookbooks except for hardbacks, but our philosophy is "be prepared." A few years ago (before computers) no one thought an ISBN would be critical. The LCCN is also printed on the title page verso.

To obtain it, write to:

CIP Office
Library of Congress
Washington, DC 20540

and request a form for a pre-assigned Library of Congress Catalog Card Number. There is no charge, but one copy of the completed book must be sent to the Cataloging Publication Office of the Library of Congress.

## Universal Product Code Symbol

There is one more way that you can register your book, the Universal Product Code Symbol. You know those dark vertical bars and white spaces that an optical scanner reads on packages in the grocery store checkout line? You will notice that most mass-market paperbacks have them printed on the back cover now. According to the Uniform

Product Council, no bookstores are currently requiring them, but it may only be a matter of time. The vertical bars and spaces translate to a 10-digit number that is printed under them, which goes into a computer and relays the information to the cash register. The first five digits of the UPC number are the manufacturer's identification number assigned by the Uniform Product Council, and the last five digits are the product number assigned by the manufacturer. Having these numbers will make it easier to get into retail outlets that use computerized checkout. For more information, write to:

> The Uniform Product Council, Inc.
> 7051 Corporate Way, Suite 201
> Dayton, Ohio, 45459–4294

or call 513–435–3870.

# FINANCING YOUR BOOK

In all the books about self-publishing, the shortest section (and frequently no section at all) has to do with financing your book. It's as if the subject were too painful to discuss. We hope that the sales from your book will pay for reprintings, increased promotion, business expenses, and a tidy profit. However, there is that moment when you have to pay the printer, and it comes before the profits begin to roll in.

That bill can be large or small (we'll talk about comparative budgets in a little while), depending on the scope of your book, but it is going to be there, and you'd better know how you're going to pay it.

The best way, of course, is to pay it from your own savings. If you work on your book over a period of time, you might open a savings account or buy a CD just for this purpose. We know one lady who financed her book with a legacy from a grandmother. Perhaps you have a friend or a family member who has faith in your book and will look upon a loan for its publication as an investment.

Banks tend to regard all self-publishing as a poor risk and are not likely to accept a stack of unsold books as collateral. You can get a loan from a bank or a savings and loan company, but it will probably have to be a personal loan, with your house or your car as collateral. Other places you might look for money are credit unions, retirement plans, or insurance policies.

Perhaps you have a group of friends who might invest in your book as silent partners, or even as partners, sharing some of the responsibilities of promotion and distribution for a share of the profits. Be businesslike. Consult a lawyer and get everything in writing to avoid misunderstandings later. If you choose this route, there are several places you can go for assistance and advice. The Small Business Administration has a series of helpful publications which you can get by calling the number listed in your telephone directory. Perhaps the SBA will refer you to a counsellor from SCORE (Service Corps of Retired Executives), retired businessmen of all sorts who assist small businesses on a voluntary basis. The SBA can also assist with information on minority small businesses (and women are still considered a minority in business). Call your congressman's office for information.

Another alternative is to look for a sponsor, or a co-publisher. Does your book deal with a certain food or a certain appliance? Perhaps a manufacturer or a food association would be interested. Perhaps an appliance store might sponsor you in return for some advertising in your publicity and enough free copies to give one book away with every microwave. Perhaps a local grocery store chain or a gourmet shop would be interested. Even unrelated businesses—a bank, a resort, a corporation—might sponsor you in return for copies to use in promotions. If your book has a regional theme, a chamber of commerce or tourist bureau or a local event may be potential sponsors.

Another possibility along this line is to raise money through pre-sales. Instead of enlisting "X" company as a sponsor, you pre-sell them a thousand copies at a discount to use in their promotions. If you are trying to sell a yet-to-be-published cookbook you have to have the concept thoroughly established and have sample recipes and illustrations; in other words, you need a really good presentation. No one is likely to buy a pig in a poke.

A symphony in New Mexico earned money at a big event, put those profits in a high-yield money market fund for two years while they gathered recipes, and had a nice profit to pay for their book.

A museum in West Virginia rounded up ten investors who put in $1,000 each as a loan. After the book was printed and selling, the investors were paid back, with interest. Then the investors in turn donated the interest paid back to the museum for a tax write-off. Some books have included a listing of corporate and patron sponsors.

You might sell ads to appear in the back of the book, if you don't think this will make it look like a high school annual. We have never seen a Classic yet that did this, and large book chains will not accept them, but it is a last-ditch possibility.

You can be as creative in raising money as you were in writing the book. Just like cooking, funding the book needs advance planning. Before you start looking for money, know how much you need. Be thorough and realistic.

# BUDGETS

There will be four major costs in creating, producing, and marketing a cookbook, and each one requires a budget at the proper time. They are:

1. *Set-up money to create a cookbook*—food, artists, lawyers, accountants, correspondence, recipe collection and evaluation forms, copying, etc. These are one-time costs in creation.

2. *Actual printing and artwork*—the largest single cost of all. This is a cost and budget factor that will always be with you.
3. *Set-up of office*—buying office equipment and supplies (if necessary). The original cost will be larger, but the costs of supplies, postage, paper needs, etc., will be ongoing.
4. *Promotion budget*—if you can't afford to promote, you won't be able to sell. We'll talk more about this later, and there are lots of angles, but you will need a good budget in the beginning. If your book is successful, the promotion budget should grow every year.

Set a budget for each item and stick to it as well as you can. The variables in each budget are enormous, and you can choose to do things any one of a number of ways, but by planning in advance and knowing what to expect, you can save yourself money and some nasty surprises.

The *set-up money* is one of the largest variables. Who is doing the testing? And who pays for the food? You've obviously spent money in developing the recipes. Now you're asking other people to test them. Are you going to pay for the ingredients or will the testers absorb the costs? Perhaps you will offer to pay only for certain expensive items like crabmeat or crown roast.

You will need money for duplicating recipes and for printing evaluation forms. It may not be much, but don't forget it.

You will need a lawyer to look over your contract and an accountant to set up the books. Do you have a friend who will do this for free, or do you need to budget for the professional fees?

Typing a manuscript can be expensive unless you are a good enough typist to make a perfect copy. There may be costs for correspondence—soliciting recipes, getting bids on printing, and so on.

The cost of the art and design can come under this section or under the printing section, but it must go somewhere. Artwork and design can cost lots of money—or very little, but it is an expense that must be budgeted.

We have covered the *printing costs* pretty thoroughly. However, in your budget you must estimate costs for 1,000 copies of a 50-page book or 10,000 copies of a 400-page book, or whatever it is you plan to print.

*Office costs* are next. Do you already have an adding machine and a typewriter? You're going to need them. You will also need to budget for postage, invoices, letterhead, and supplies. We'll go over a complete list when we talk about office systems.

You can spend a fortune *promoting* your book and you can also get an amazing amount of publicity for very little. You need to plan ahead in order to have some way to get the word out so the books don't end up on your bedroom floor. Are you trying to sell them locally through your own contacts or are you planning to hit the national market?

There are no absolutely right or absolutely wrong answers to any of these questions. The decisions are up to you, and depend on the kind of book you have written. You want to be in the position to *make* the decision, rather than have the wrong decision forced on you as a result of lack of planning. Only by thinking ahead can you really be in charge.

A lady from a small town in Mississippi phoned Helen and wanted to know how much it would cost to print a cookbook. Helen went on at some length about different types of books, numbers printed, and on and on. The lady was insistent; she had to have an answer. Her organization had to know how much it would cost before they could vote on whether or not to do it. Helen asked how big a book they had in mind and how many copies they thought they could sell. Well, the caller really didn't know any of that, but she had to have an answer. So, ever helpful, Helen pulled a figure out of the air. "You could print a cookbook for around $35,000."

Horrors! Gasps from the other end of the line. "But we only have $15,000!" Well, of course, you can print a cookbook for that amount, too.

To illustrate the many variables you have to deal with in planning a budget, we want to propose two different cookbooks. The first, Cookbook A, is to be published by a woman's organization with many members and a fat bank balance. The second, Cookbook B, is to be published by Mrs. B who had saved a little money to get it off the ground and plans to sell it to her church group and some friends. Both will have to consider the same things.

Food testing: Group A decides to pay for everything; they expect to test 500 recipes, so they budget $1,000 for testing. For Cookbook B, Mrs. B and her sister-in-law are testing everything, and they decide to count on $150 to cover the ingredients. Group A hires an artist—$1,500. Mrs. B's daughter draws, so that item is zero. Group A wants a lawyer to look over the printing contract and an accountant to set up the books, so they plan on $300 each for these two fees. Mr. B is a lawyer and his brother has a little accounting background, so zero again.

Group A figures that recipe and evaluation forms plus copying 500 recipes will cost about $250, and a typist will charge $175. Mrs. B plans to be very systematic, but she intends to type and copy everything herself; she puts $50 in the budget and thinks this figure is a little padded.

Printing, of course, is the biggest cost for both. Group A decides on a first run of 10,000 copies and budgets $40,000 for printing. Mrs. B wants about 2,500 copies and her book is small, so she thinks she can get it done for under $5,000.

Group A already has an office with adequate equipment, but they decide they will need a new typewriter, two new adding machines, a desk, plus, of course, invoices, letterhead, and mailing labels with their new logo— total $3,000 for the office. Mrs. B has a typewriter and an adding machine of her own, she sets aside a corner in the guest room, moves her son's old desk in, and orders office supplies to the tune of $500.

Group A wants to market their book nationwide, and plans a first-year promotion budget of $18,000. Mrs. B and her daughter draw up a nice-looking flyer, decide to run one ad in the weekly paper, and think that word of mouth among the church members is the best tool. She sets aside $1,000 for promotion.

The two books come on the market at the same time with budgets that look like this:

|  | Group A | Mrs. B |
|---|---|---|
| Testing | 1,000 | 150 |
| Artist | 1,500 | 0 |
| Lawyer | 300 | 0 |
| Accountant | 300 | 0 |
| Copying | 250 | 50 |
| Typist | 175 | 0 |
| Printing | 40,000 | 5,000 |
| Office | 3,000 | 500 |
| Promotion | 18,000 | 1,000 |
| TOTAL | $64,525 | $6,700 |

Both books are classics of their kind, and both books fulfill their publisher's dreams. Book A goes into a second printing after nine months and has been mentioned in a national magazine. Mrs. B sold 1,200 copies through her church and club friends; her sister in another town sold 300 copies. After a year she has paid back all her investment, and whenever the next 900 copies sell it will be pure profit. She has the satisfaction of being the most famous cook in the Methodist Church and having something to show to her grandchildren.

Two success stories. Two different budgets.

Record-keeping on all these items is most important from the very beginning. Have your books set up early on, and keep careful records on everything you spend. Some of this may be tax deductible. Also, all of these costs should be added into your calculations when you decide on pricing your book.

We'll get into promotion in great detail later, but for a guideline in budgeting, let's think about what costs you might plan on originally. In promotion the word is *creative*. You can get lots of free help if you are creative about it. Here is a sample budget for a small cookbook aimed at a regional and national market.

## PROMOTION BUDGET FOR A NEW BOOK

| | |
|---|---:|
| Feature article in newspaper | $    0. |
| Press release to 400 newspapers | 161.00 |
| Party given by local gourmet shop | 0. |
| Party to kick off book, tickets sold | 0. |
| Special brochure for wholesale accounts | 300.00 |
| Flyer printed for retail buyers | 200.00 |
| Mailing and rental list, new customers | 2,500.00 |
| Local TV show appearances | 0. |
| Total | $3,161.00 |

One more piece of advice: pad your budget a little. It is so much better to overestimate and be pleasantly surprised than to underestimate and be appalled. Be realistic, but be aware that unexpected items will crop up, costs will rise. Be prepared.

The promotion budget will be lower the first year because you can get more "freebies" as a new book. After that the budget should increase. Good books usually spend at least 10 percent of gross profit on promotion.

# PRICING YOUR BOOK

How are you going to make a profit? Well, people are going to buy your book for more than it cost you to print it. If you have paid attention to the preceding pages, you have set budgets for all the additional costs, not just the printer's bill.

Your book is unique—or should be. While a customer won't pay more than he thinks it is worth, if your book is a good one, he is going to want it and will pay what you ask. Underpricing a book just because you think that a low price will increase sales is often a big mistake. In fact, it may undermine the credibility of the book. Price also has a reverse impact when a book is purchased as a gift. Don't underprice it, but don't go overboard in the opposite direction. Know the market. Look at lots of books so that you are familiar with the going rates that people are paying. Our experience as book distributors taught us that none of the books that fall far outside the reasonable margins does very well. Cookbook buyers are not dumb. They know what books are worth from comparison shopping. You should, too.

To figure the price of your book, you start with the contract price, basically the cost to print per book. You've found a printer who will print 10,000 books for $20,000, so you have a price per book of $2. However, this does not include the cost of selling the book. You must also include: overhead, postage, packaging, supplies, promotional materials, advertising, etc. The total of these costs must be prorated over the 10,000 copies and adjusted to a per-book cost. The first time you do this it is hard to estimate the costs of all these additional items, and you will be making an educated guess (with your budget as your basis). Every time you reprint thereafter your estimates will be more accurate (because of the good records you kept). Plan ahead; postage may go up, inflation is always with us, etc. Give yourself a slight pad for error or adjustment.

Here is one way to estimate:

|  |  |  |
|---|---|---|
| Cost per book | $2.00 | |
| Overhead | .05 | |
| Packaging | .08 | |
| Supplies | .03 | |
| Promotion | .10 | |
| | $2.26 | cost to you |
| Remember to add some pad: | .14 | (roughly 5 to 7 per cent) |
| | $2.40 | cost per book |

Now you know what each book costs you. Figure your price this way:

| | |
|---|---|
| <u>Price ceiling</u>: $10.95 | this is an educated guess as to what the market will bear. Let's say that you look at other books that compare with yours and see that they are all $10.95. This then is your "ceiling price." |

Your price

| | |
|---|---|
| <u>Price floor</u>: $ 2.40 | this is firm. If you sell below this figure, you will lose money. |

Most people try to figure the selling price at three to four times the cost of the book. Most, today, are around three times the cost. If the margin is much below this, you will have to depend on large volume sales to make any profit. It will also make it unrealistic to offer much discount, which will hurt your wholesale market.

A few years ago the average price of a community cookbook was $5.95 and there was an imaginary price barrier at $10. If you've been looking at any kind of cookbooks lately, you know that the prices have gone way up. The average price today is $9.95, and there are some very strong sellers at much higher prices.

For our book, a price of two to five times the basic cost of $2.40 would be between $4.80 and $12. After looking at comparable books, let's decide on a price of four times the cost, or $9.60, which we'll round up to $9.95. This is the *base retail price*, from whch you figure everything else. However, it is not the only price you need to figure.

| Retail price (base) | Cost if bought in a store. | $9.95 |
|---|---|---|

| Retail mail order | Mrs. Jones orders your book. You charge for the book, the mailing bag, and the postage. | 9.95<br>1.50<br>―――<br>$11.45 |

|  | If the sale is within your state, you add sales tax. | 11.45<br>.56 |
|---|---|---|
|  |  | $12.01 |

| Wholesale price | What you sell to stores for them to resell it— minus the standard 40 percent discount. | 9.95<br>−3.98 |
|---|---|---|
|  |  | $ 5.97 |

| Distributor's price | If you deal with a distributor, the standard discount is 50 percent. | 9.95<br>−4.97 |
|---|---|---|
|  |  | $ 4.98 |

Now you have the basic price levels you will need if you plan to go into the wholesale/retail book business. The prices will look like this:

| Retail | $ 9.95 |
|---|---|
| Retail mail order | $11.45 |
| In-state retail mail order | $12.01 |
| Wholesale discount | $ 5.97 |
| Distribution | $ 4.98 |

Notice that all of these prices are *based* on your $2.40 per book cost and your basic retail price of $9.95. Now you can also see why you must have at least a three- or four-time mark-up on your price. Without this profit margin, discounts of any type would be impossible.

However, depending on the type of sales you intend

to try, other prices are also possible. *Volume discount* means a new price, below the standard wholesale 40 percent, given only for a large order. For example, if someone wants to order 1,000 books, you can set a special rate, say 45 to 50 percent off the retail price.

Some books that have been on the market for a long time and have sophisticated systems offer "sliding scale" discounts. An example:

| | |
|---|---|
| 1–50 books | 40 percent discount |
| 51–100 books | 42 percent discount |
| 101–250 books | 44 percent discount |
| 251–500 books | 46 percent discount |
| over 500 books | 48 percent discount |

You can even set a "sale price" for a one-time offer, i.e., special seasonal offer, premiums, convention sales, etc.

Obviously, all of this can become a bookkeeping nightmare, but some people use all these prices. The only prices you *need* in the beginning are the retail price, the retail mail order price, and the wholesale price. These will put you in business. Then, as you grow and learn more about the book business, you may want to try some of the other prices or discounts available.

Remember, if your profit margin is too low, say two times cost, you don't have any room for discounting. You've limited your options; after 40 percent, you're dead, and you aren't making much of a profit at 40 percent. So set your price high enough to allow yourself some flexibility in offering specials and getting into new markets. Also, remember that offering a special will require some money spent on promoting it. If you can't promote, you can't sell, so figure those costs before you get carried away and offer a big Mother's Day "Special" and lose your shirt.

Every time you reprint your book, you will have to refigure all the costs. Despite the fact that sometimes the cost per book will drop on a reprinting, inflation is always with us. Paper and printing costs go up every time. When you figure your first printing contract, you may want to ask the printer to quote you a reprint cost. You may want to use the two figures in pricing the book.

Don't change the price of your book until you reprint it. Nothing looks more unprofessional than books with the first price marked out and a new one written in in magic marker. Stores hate it because their customers think that they've marked it up, and most distributors won't even take them. If you want to raise the price, consider having a big sale and getting rid of all the old copies at $6.95, then start with a whole new printing and a whole new price structure based on $7.95.

# CHAPTER 4

# Starting the Business

"CREATING A BOOK is just the beginning," says self-publisher Ellen Abbay, owner of Kudzu and Company in Walls, Mississippi. "The future is in being able to set up a business and run it professionally. If you can't tell a purchase order from an invoice, your book will stay on your dining room table forever."

Because you will be dealing with professionals, you must be professional, too. You will save yourself much time and trouble by setting up systems correctly in the beginning, and thinking of your efforts as a business from the very start.

## CHOOSING A COMPANY NAME AND LOCATION

You will want a name for your business for several reasons. First of all, it makes you look more businesslike and serious about what you are doing. If you were the owner of a bookstore or a gourmet shop, who would you be more likely to do business with, Mrs. Mary Lou Jones or MLJ Publications? Second, it makes record-keeping easier when you keep all the records and accounts separate from your personal checking account. The name of the business/company should be printed on all your letterhead, invoices, boxes of books, and advertising. You need to register the name of the company with your county government and with your bank, no matter what type of company you decide to form.

The name you choose should be unique; you don't want to be confused with somebody selling widgets or publishing porno magazines. To begin to check, look in the local yellow pages, and also in *Literary Market Place* and the *International Directory of Small Presses*. You can also have an attorney check to see if the name you have chosen is registered in your state. Think, too, of the future. If you choose the name of your cookbook as the name of your company, as many people do, you might be limiting your future. When your first book is a huge success, you may want to publish another. Or your company might go into other sidelines, like selling recipe cards or aprons, so try to select a general name.

Your company headquarters may be a table in the corner of your bedroom or in a major office complex, but your customers don't need to know that. Consider, in the beginning, getting a post office box for your address. This has several advantages: it saves trouble if you ever move; it discourages drop-in customers who might come to your house to buy a book, and it keeps book orders entirely separate from your personal correspondence, like bills and invitations to the PTA Open House. You'll be going to the post office anyway to mail books, and the cost of box rental is minimal. Also, remember what we said about the cookbook business—it is a wholesale/retail *mail*-order book business, and you don't need expensive overhead in a large commercial building to be successful.

About your headquarters: if you establish your office in a spare room or even a boarded-off section of the garage, a space that is set aside for business purposes only, it may be deductible. However, be certain that when you talk to your lawyer and accountant you go over this matter carefully. The IRS has *very* strict rules and regulations covering deductions for home-based businesses, and some of them are conflicting. Be sure to get expert advice.

Get all of your plans in line. Be sure you understand everything you are doing before you do it. Consult a lawyer and an accountant, in the beginning, and discuss every aspect of your proposed business with them. Keep good records from the start. You'll save yourself worry, time, trouble, and money.

# COMPANY PRODUCT

Obviously the reason for establishing this business is your product—your cookbook. You must have your product and its sales future defined clearly at this time. Is there an obvious by-product of the book that could become a product in itself? Some cookbooks have such beautiful color dividers that they are printed and packaged as a separate sales item "suitable for framing." Or you may want to have specially designed recipe cards to sell as a package with the book and also as an entirely separate product.

The majority of the people who go into this business start with their cookbook as the single product. You may want to do this, too, but always keep your eyes open for obvious sidelines or future products.

# CONSULTING A LAWYER

One of the first and most important persons to contact in setting up a business is a good attorney, preferably one who has had experience in starting new companies. You must be able to explain to him what your business and product will be, and he should then be able to advise you as to what form your business should take.

There are three major ways to set up a business: sole proprietorship, partnership, or corporation. There are advantages and disadvantages to each type.

The simplest form is the *sole proprietorship*. One person owns the business and supplies all the assets. The proprietor hires other people and has responsibility for all legal requirements. The income is reported as personal income. The advantage is great flexibility, total control, and the greatest freedom from regulation. However, the proprietor also bears all the liabilities.

A *partnership* can be either *general* or *limited*. Either one should begin with a written agreement setting out the responsibilities of each partner. A general partnership has fewer legal requirements and the liabilities are shared equally. A limited partnership protects the limited partners from liability beyond the amount of their investment but requires more complicated legal steps. A limited partner is by definition an inactive participant in the partnership; if the limited partner assumes an active role, the liability changes.

If you have written the cookbook with someone else, you are obviously partners. You may take in a partner solely to raise capital or to share in the work. You might contribute the creative work (the book) and take a partner to handle sales and distribution. Both partners need to fully understand the terms of the partnership, and it should be spelled out in writing. It's a little like a marriage in that care must be taken in choosing a partner or partners.

A *corporation* (and there are various types) is more complicated but has the advantage of limited liability. A corporation becomes a separate legal entity in the eyes of the state and lasts beyond the death or retirement of any individual. A corporation can be formed by an individual or by stockholders. Ownership can be transferred. A corporation pays salaries to its employees and dividends to its stockholders, both of which are taxed as personal income. A corporation is taxed on its profits, except for a "Sub-Chapter S" corporation, which is suitable for many small businesses and passes the profits through to the stockholders with no federal income tax on the corporation itself. Obviously you will need a lawyer to explain to you the ramifications of incorporation.

How do you know which legal structure is best for your business? There are many factors that will play a part in your decision: your own finances, the need for additional capital, your tax bracket, the availability of stockholders or partners, your plans for the business and its future potential. Legal advice is important. Before you make any decision, be sure you understand the advantages and disadvantages to your personal situation. Many accountants have very definite opinions on this subject, also, and they should be consulted before you make a final decision. The Small Business Administration and your public library have many publications that can help you. If you decide to open your business, whether it is in your home or in a building, a lawyer can advise you on other subjects, too. He will know what permits and licenses are needed and, for a fee, can even obtain them for you. Laws regulating new businesses vary state to state and city to city, and these laws must be followed. You may need a permit to operate; many localities have registration requirements for new businesses. There may be zoning regulations governing home businesses. The name of the business needs to be registered. You will definitely need a resale license that enables you to buy merchandise (since you buy books from the printer) and resell it to the public. Some of these permits or licenses may require a fee.

It may be startling for you to think of your beloved brainchild as merchandise, but it is if you plan to do more than just give it away.

# CONSULTING AN ACCOUNTANT

Next on your list to contact is a good accountant. He will be invaluable in helping you set up the financial end of your business, and will also have helpful thoughts on some of the subjects you have discussed with your attorney. Your financial status has a lot to do with the type of company you want to create, and your accountant is your "financial" person.

Money should be the main topic. After you've explained your company and its product, plus your financial status, an accountant can draw up a "prospectus" of your business—show you on paper what your costs, profits, and investment will be for a certain period of time (six months, a year, two years). This is a must for budgeting and future planning. With this professional direction you will have a better picture of how to finance, how much it will be, what to expect in costs, and what kind of profit can be possible.

An accountant will also advise you on how to set up your *bookkeeping system*, and a professional bookkeeping system is a *must*. There are many ways to keep books, and you need advice on a system that suits you best. You will definitely need a *general ledger* and a posting book for *accounts receivable*. You may want others. If you have a computer, here is a perfect place to put it to work.

Just remember that although your ledgers and posting books may not be the most interesting part of the operation to you, they are of extreme interest to Uncle Sam. You need to keep basic records of:

1. Sales (what you sell)
2. Purchases (what you buy)
3. Costs (the cost to do both)

Bookkeeping is the visual and factual record of all factors that affect the financial condition of a business. A business magazine reported that 87 percent of small business failures occur because of lack of proper records or the inability to understand them.

The Small Business Administration said a good record-keeping system must be:

1. Simple to use
2. Easy to understand
3. Reliable
4. Accurate
5. Consistent
6. Designed to provide information on a timely basis

There are also regulations on what records must be kept and for how long, and you need to know these answers.

Two other topics to review with your accountant are taxes and insurance. Most states require a sales tax, and this necessitates excellent record-keeping. The sales tax is collected only once, at the retail level, or point of final sale, when the book is sold within the state. If a book is shipped out of state, no sales tax is charged. A book can be sold several times (printer to publisher, publisher to distributor, distributor to bookstore) before the final sale is made and tax must be collected. Therefore, you, the publisher, are not responsible for the sales tax on books you sell wholesale to bookstores or distributors; the final seller, the store, collects the sales tax.

You *are* responsible, however, for sales tax on those books that you sell retail, or directly to the final customer, when those books are sold within the state. For this you have to have a certificate of registration and a sales tax number.

It sounds more complicated than it is. The point is that you need to know all this in the beginning and keep good records. Otherwise you might find out that you owe the government a big chunk of what you thought were your profits, and that could certainly take the fun out of it.

There are other taxes that you may be required to pay

either as your business grows or depending on the type of company you decide to form. You may decide to hire outside help, and this involves taxes, too. Even if you only use a neighborhood teenager part-time to help with mailing, you may be required to report how much you pay. Your lawyer and accountant will explain local and federal tax laws to you, and your accountant will set up your books so that you can keep track of all the necessary information.

One last item is *insurance*. You will need to investigate this factor if you store an inventory of your books and/or if you are leasing space for your operations.

A lawyer and accountant are critical if you intend to set up a business properly and operate it in compliance with business and government regulations. Once again, *ask a thousand questions* and then make your final decisions.

Now you have your product (or products), have decided on a company name, and have spent a great deal of in-depth time with an attorney and an accountant. With all of this information you are ready to establish your new company and sell thousands of books. We have discussed budget items and financing, and now you know how to make an intelligent decision in these matters. You open up a bank account and begin.

# THE BIRTH OF A BOOK BUSINESS: A TRUE STORY

Before we go into the details of an office system and sales, let us tell you a story to show that it really is possible to start a business—and succeed.

In 1977 Ellen Rolfes was fresh from an invaluable learning experience as chairman of the Memphis Junior League Publications Committee, which marketed and distributed two cookbooks nationally. Her mother-in-law, Peggy Rolfes, was a TV personality. One of the most popular features on Peggy's noon news show was a segment on household hints sent in by viewers. The two women combined their talents and experiences to self-publish *Why Didn't I Think of That?*, a collection of tips for homemakers.

The television station gave Peggy encouragement as well as written permission to develop the book. They hired a graphic artist to design it from a concept in Ellen's head: color-coded cards (each category—sewing, cooking, gardening—printed on a different color) held together by a metal ring.

They began by borrowing $5,000 from Mr. Rolfes, Senior, and setting up a Sub-Chapter S corporation, PER, Inc., with the two couples as stockholders. The $5,000 had to cover the artist's fees, printing, and a meager amount for office supplies and promotions.

There was no promotion budget at first. A local bookstore gave a party for the TV personality's book, and Ellen picked up 200 advance copies from the printer. To everyone's surprise, a huge crowd came and those 200 copies sold in forty-five minutes! Ellen went down to the printer's the next day to help put together some more books in a hurry.

The worst moment came later that week when a red pickup truck delivered 4,800 copies to Ellen's house. "I couldn't sleep a wink all night wondering how I was going to get rid of all those books in the attic. And wondering what I had done with my father-in-law's money and my mother-in-law's reputation," Ellen says.

That good old volunteer training stood her in good stead. She had budgeted enough money to buy some office supplies.She created an office in the utility room with a desk, a filing cabinet, and a storage cabinet. The next day she loaded up some books in her station wagon and went around to local bookstores and gift shops to sell them, opening wholesale accounts locally first.

Ellen's husband, Barney, a CPA, set up the books and invented a ledger sheet. Ellen had gotten a post office box because she didn't want people coming by the house or calling and waking the new baby. PER, Inc. was in business—in the utility room.

"I'd go to the post office box every day, hoping something would be there. Some days there was, some days there wasn't. But gradually the orders began to come in— retail orders from the coupon in the back of the book and from Peggy's television viewers, wholesale orders from a flyer we sent out. I learned to stuff a reorder form in every box I shipped wholesale. I'd put the baby down for a nap, and while I washed a load of diapers, I'd process the orders."

She learned that it was easier to process the wholesale orders first and let the retail orders stack up for a few days, then do a whole batch at once. Whenever she had a few minutes she'd sit down and call a key account, asking if they were ready to reorder and thanking them for their business.

Gradually PER, Inc. started marketing nationally, sending a promotional flyer, an order blank, and a copy of the book to stores across the country. Ellen began to offer volume discounts. The book took off, and she was ordering reprints of 5,000 copies often. A college student was hired to come in two or three days a week to handle the orders, leaving Ellen to deal with unusual correspondence and promotions. In 1980 Peggy and Ellen published *Why Didn't I Think of That? II*. In seven years the books have sold in every state in the union and several foreign countries, a total of over 80,000 copies! And the children got raised and the laundry done, besides.

# OFFICE SYSTEMS AND SUPPLIES

Now you are ready to establish your office systems. We've said it before and we will say it again; it is important to present yourself to the world in the most professional manner possible. There are two reasons for this, one external and one internal.

First, *externally*: you will be dealing with professionals. You will be negotiating contracts in the thousands of dollars, you will be servicing the accounts of large-volume book buyers, in some cases you will be trying to collect overdue payments. Businesses, particularly big ones, aren't going to bother with books whose offices don't keep accurate records and operate in accordance with certain accepted business procedures.

One of our friends is the head buyer for the book department of a major department store chain. Their stores sell thousands of cookbooks every year and she knows that cookbooks are big business. She prefers to do business through distributors rather than with individuals or charitable organizations because she says, "I haven't got time to teach someone how to fill out an invoice."

If you are going to deal with professionals, you must be professional, too.

There are *internal* reasons for professional office systems, too. You want your system to stress accuracy, efficiency, and expediency. You want your system to be as error-free as possible. To save yourself time, trouble, worry, and money, you want a system that works efficiently and minimizes errors. Most of the horror stories we hear about collection problems and mixed-up orders could have been prevented with careful planning in the beginning.

Now that we've stated our case for a businesslike business, let's define what we are talking about. What you are doing in selling cookbooks is establishing a *wholesale/retail mail order business*. Let's be very clear about the terms.

## The Wholesale Business

This covers those books sold to qualified, licensed dealers for the purpose of resale. You sell books at a wholesale price (discount) to a dealer who has a license to do business and who sells your books to individuals at retail price. The dealer/retailer collects the sales tax. Ninety-five percent of wholesale business is charged on a 30-day net account—you ship a quantity of books to the retailer; you charge the wholesale price per book plus shipping costs; you have an account due (receivable) on understood terms that is payable 30 days from the day the retailer receives the books. You *cannot* add "handling" charges on whole-sale orders.

## The Retail Business

This covers those books sold to the actual user (person) of the book. There is no middleman; you sell directly, at retail price to an individual. In most states, the last person to buy the book pays sales tax, so you add that to the retail price if the book is sold within your state. Most of your retail business is cash, check, money order, or credit card. A charge account for individuals is not recom-mended because it is more trouble than it is worth. In the retail business, if you are mailing the book, you charge the retail price, plus sales tax (if sold within state), and most businesses add a fee for "shipping and handling," which includes the actual cost plus some extra for time, effort, and mailing materials.

We speak from experience about office systems both on the basis of our volunteer training and our professional careers. What we are about to outline may sound com-plicated, but it will save time and trouble in the long run and will ensure accurate records of all the business you transact.

First of all, you will need certain supplies and equip-ment. Remember that we said you'd need to set a budget for this? Well, now's the time to spend the money. Here is a *suggested* list of office equipment and supplies. Notice that we say "suggested." You will develop your own needs and lists, too. Also, if some of the list is unfamiliar to you, don't panic. It will all be explained, with examples, as we go through the office system.

## SUGGESTED LIST OF EQUIPMENT AND SUPPLIES

1. Financial
   Checking account
   Savings account
   Ledger/bookkeeping
      system
   Statement/billing system
      and forms
   Monthly report forms
   Year-end audit
      requirements
   Sales permit
   Tax numbers
   Inventory report form

2. Promotional
   Brochures (wholesale
      and retail)
   Reorder cards
   Press kit
   Testimonials
   Reviews
   Bulk mailing supplies
      (stickers, mail bags,
      permits, etc.)

3. Office Supplies
   Space (office)
   Desks and chairs
   Typewriter
   Adding machine
   Scales (for weighing
      books)
   Filing cabinets and
      filing folders
   Storage space
   Postage
   Filing baskets
   Company address
      rubber stamp and pad

4. Shipping Information
   Zip code directory
   Postal regulations
      and supplies
   UPS information
      and supplies
   Trucking information

5. Paper and Correspon-
   dence Needs
   Stationery and
      envelopes
   Postcards
   Statements/billing
      and envelopes
   Invoices and envelopes
   Wholesale order blanks
   Retail order blanks

6. Shipping Needs
   Address labels
   Packing slips
   Invoice-enclosed
      envelopes
   Jiffy bags or boxes
   Strapping tape
   Heavy-duty stapler
   Weight/price charts
   Magic markers
   Package ripper/knife
   Postage (book shipping)
   Gift wrapping supplies[?]

7. Systems
   Operations notebook
   Job descriptions
   System procedures
   Filing system
   Policies

This is only a basic supply list and may include more or less than your needs demand. It also does not include obvious small items such as paper clips, Scotch tape, scissors, etc. Adjust to your system's demand.

There are also other items that may be added as needed, or as your business grows, such as postage machines, delivery services, etc. However, it is recommended that these items, which are costly and considered "extras," be added only when your sales and profits require and warrant them.

# GETTING THE ORDERS OUT

Now let's see what you do with all this. Let's go through the system of getting orders out, after addressing a few basics.

At this point you should have obtained a post office box, had letterhead stationery and envelopes printed, opened your bank accounts, and set up a work area. You will have contacted potential customers, both retail and wholesale, and orders will now start coming in. You will have three basic steps:

1. Receiving an order
2. Invoicing the order
3. Shipping the order out

Let's begin with the wholesale system and work through that process first. It is the more difficult of the two systems, and the one that must be handled with the most efficiency and care.

## The Wholesale System

In order to open up the wholesale business and begin getting customers you will be contacting stores and asking them to become an account. In the beginning, all wholesale accounts will be *new* accounts, and certain information must be obtained. When the ABC Bookstore sends in an order for your books, you should immediately send a credit information application that asks for two major items—credit information and the store's "resale" number. You want all of the information possible since with wholesale accounts you ship the books and invoice for payment. This credit information will allow you to check on a store's financial stability and payment record. It also lessens the chances of getting stung with a no-pay account. (See sample form on facing page.)

As soon as the credit information is returned, *check* on the information. If it all clears, you can ship the books and you have now opened an active wholesale account. A store is aware of these procedures and understands this information request. If the store is not willing to send it, you can bet a dozen books it wasn't a good account to begin with. As your business grows, you will constantly be opening new wholesale accounts, and this process should be followed *every time*.

There is one other suggestion that has worked well for others. Set a limit on the first order—say six or twelve books—and don't ship a second order until the first is paid. Ellen remembers a horror story. "One store sold out so fast they called and ordered a second box of books within a week. I was thrilled! I sent more, and they called again, they just couldn't keep them in stock. I sent even more! That was really dumb. I had shipped three orders to a new account within one thirty-day period before they sent any payment. And I never did receive payment," she remembers. RED FLAG: a sale is not a sale until the money is in hand. Watch out for repeated orders without payment. Don't let them fool you, too! Once a store has ordered and paid promptly several times, they have established their reliability.

Wholesale orders will come in different ways:

1. The order form in your brochure
2. A store's purchase order
3. A letter (preferably on business stationery)
4. By telephone

# GOODLETT PRESS, INC.

P.O. BOX 11465     MEMPHIS, TN 38111

Name of Account: _____

Mailing  Address: _____

City & State: _____ Zip _____

*(If the above address is a P.O. Box, please give a physical location or address below.)*

_____

_____

Store  Resale  Number: _____

Phone Number: (area code) _____

Owner's Name: _____

Home  Address: _____

City & State: _____ Zip _____

Phone Number: (area code) _____

Bank: _____

Branch: _____

Address: _____

City & State: _____ Zip _____

Account Name _____ Number: _____

Banker's Name: (contact) _____

**Please list 3 other credit references with complete addresses: (Please do not use publishers.)**

1. _____

_____

2. _____

_____

3. _____

_____

I agree to the payment terms of GOODLETT PRESS, INC.; and state that the above information supplied is correct.

Date: _____     Signature: _____

Title: _____

Orders can and do come in all shapes and forms. However, they should all contain the same information:

Name of the company ordering
Address of the company
Number of books ordered
Purchase order number (not usually in letters)
Shipping address
Name of the person placing the order (nice,
    but not always supplied by store)

The order may also have shipping information—how and where it is to be shipped, and specific billing information—method or specific address. All of the large stores and chains and many of the small stores have their own printed purchase order forms. These can sometimes be very complicated. Read all purchase orders carefully and follow the instructions completely. *Warning*: if you do not follow the instructions completely, you may delay your payment for months—and large stores deduct a penalty charge from their payment for not doing it their way.

Now the first step is completed—the wholesale orders are coming in. You have the purchase order (in whatever form) in front of you. You have now arrived at the second step, that of invoicing the order. Your invoices should be printed with the name and address of your company. These invoices are three- or four-part forms that you can buy at any office supply company; they can be imprinted with your information and numbering system. They come with all four parts in a different color, and you need either the kind with carbon paper between or self-carboned (which are easier and much cleaner). You can also buy invoices with a mailing label attached, which saves typing the address twice.

You type—repeat *type*—all necessary information on the invoice. This will include sold-to and ship-to addresses, price per book, and extended price for total, shipping costs, and the total due. Never hand-write a wholesale invoice; nothing looks so unprofessional. In a pinch you can hand-write a retail order, but *always* type the invoices going to businesses (see example, page 147).

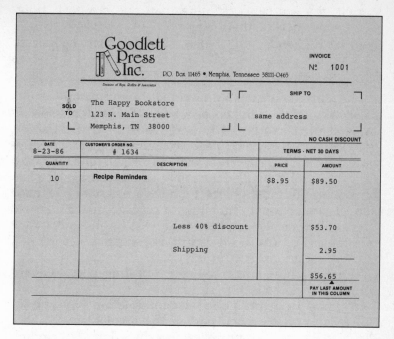

The next step is shipping the order to the customer. For shipping you need:

1. Address label of good quality, printed with your company name and return address.
2. "Invoice-enclosed" envelopes—printed plastic envelopes for your invoice with a gummed side to attach to the box of books.
3. Your invoice number written on the box itself—if the address label comes off, and the books are returned to you, you can track the order back.
4. Postage or UPS number and weight.
5. Your shipping boxes should be printed with your book and company name and address and the number of books contained.

Other items to consider are:

1. Some stores will request that you write on the box their purchase order number and sometimes other information as well.

2. If you are sending more than one box to a store, mark each of them clearly "1 of 3 boxes," "2 of 3 boxes," and "3 of 3 boxes." This lets them keep track of the order, and lets them know if one of the boxes did not arrive.

The store pays the shipping costs, and of course wants the books shipped the cheapest way. Some stores specify method of delivery—UPS, post office, or truck line (on very large orders). You need to know the rates for shipping the different size and weight boxes. Getting the boxes to the post office with the proper amount of postage can be a chore, but it's a perfect job for a neighbor's teenage son. If your budget will allow, a postage meter that will prepay the postage can be rented. UPS has the advantage of billing you. You will need to investigate what method is cheapest and/or easiest for you.

There are now two more steps: posting your sales information and collecting the money.

You begin posting your sales information with the invoices you typed. Each part of the invoice should be a different color, and a duplicate of the original, including the number. The invoice is your record of the transaction. You can disperse the invoice this way:

*Original* (usually white)—retained and filed numerically in a file or on a spindle

*1 copy* (perhaps pink)—sent with books in the invoice-enclosed packing envelope

*1 copy* (perhaps yellow)—goes to the bookkeeper (you or someone else) and is filed in the customer's file after it is posted

*1 copy* (perhaps blue)—can be kept and mailed if the store requires another copy. Some people use it as a "statement" and mail it separately the day the order is shipped to expedite payment

The copy that is sent to bookkeeping is used to "post" your accounts receivable book. This is a book with a separate page for each wholesale account, which records all amounts due and paid (see example, page 149).

| | | DATE | ITEMS | FOLIO | | DEBITS | CREDITS | BALANCE |
|---|---|---|---|---|---|---|---|---|
| | | 5-13 86 | 10 RR | | | 56 65 | | 56 65 |
| | | 6-1 86 | 10 RR | | | 56 65 | | 113 30 |
| | | 6-3 86 | payment (ck #1422) | | | | 56 65 | 56 65 |

SHEET NO. 1
RATING good
CREDIT LIMIT $500.00
TERMS net 30 days

ACCOUNT NO. 322
NAME The Happy Bookstore
ADDRESS 123 N. Main Street
Memphis, TN 38000

FORM N1-D

An efficient business should keep a filing system on all wholesale customers. For every wholesale account you should have a file folder that contains the original credit information sheet with resale number, your credit check information, and all correspondence and sales information. You would now take the bookkeeping copy of the invoice, attach it to the customer's original purchase order, and file it in the folder. This ensures an accurate record of all correspondence and transactions between you and your account.

If your printer is "fulfilling" or "drop-shipping" your wholesale orders for you, you need to send the copy of the invoice that goes with the books and the address label to him for shipping.

Then there is one final and most important step: collecting your money. We hope that the stores will pay promptly, but here again there are certain steps you must follow.

Small stores sometimes consider the invoice sent with the books the bill, and will pay from that. However, the majority of your accounts will not, and you will need to bill them by sending them a statement. Once a month, on a determined day, you or someone else must send statements. These too can be bought at an office supply house and imprinted with your company name and address. You choose a day of the month and, using your accounts receivable book, you bill every wholesale account that has not paid. You include all of the information that was on your original invoice (see below).

| | | Statement | | | | |
|---|---|---|---|---|---|---|
| From | Goodlett Press, Inc. | | | | | |
| | P.O. Box 11465   Memphis, TN 38111 | | | | | |
| | | Sept. 15 | | | 19 86 | |
| To | The Happy Bookstore | | | | | |
| Address | 123 N. Main Street | | | | | |
| City Memphis | | State TN | | Zip 38000 | | |
| Terms | Net 30 days | | | | | |
| 8-23-86 | 10 Recipe Reminders | 56 | 65 | 56 | 65 |
| | | | | | |
| | | | | | |
| | | | | | |
| | | | | | |
| | | | | | |
| | | | | | |
| | | | | | |
| | | | | | |
| | | | | | |
| | | | | | |
| | | | | | |
| | | | | 56 | 65 |

Wilson Jones
GRAYLINE FORM S1600 © 1977 • Printed in U.S.A.

Some people use the last copy of the invoice as a statement, but it is more professional to have separate statements for this. One accounting firm recommended billing on the 20th to the 24th of each month in order to be in the stack of bills on your customer's desk to be paid the "first" of each month.

If payment has not been made 30 days after the books were received, and a statement/bill has been sent, you need to take prompt action. A letter on your company letterhead should be sent, informing the customer that his payment is overdue. It can be a form letter like this:

Goodlett Press Inc.

P.O. Box 11465 • Memphis, Tennessee 38111-0465

Division of Hays, Dollar & Associates

March 6, 1986

The Happy Bookstore
123 N. Main Street
Memphis, TN   38000

Gentlemen:

We must have your help in clearing the past due amount shown on the attached invoice copies.

We must require that full payment be mailed to us within the next 10 days since books have been received by your store without payment.

Your prompt attention to this bill will be appreciated.  Please forward payment so that we may clear your credit record.

Very truly yours,

Helen S. Hays
President

Enclosures:  Invoice copies

A date on which payment is due should be specified. If payment has not been received by that date, your next recourse is a phone call. This is frequently the most effective way to get your money. If you still aren't paid, send in your lawyer. Don't delay too long in trying to collect. The longer you wait, the harder it is to get the money.

Ellen remembers getting stung more than once in the early days of PER, Inc. She says, "I assumed that because it was a lovely store, a store where all my friends shopped, where I even had a charge account, that, of course, they would pay their bills. Wrong! My father-in-law finally had to go in and ask for the money. But I don't recommend that as a collection method."

## The Retail System

The retail business and system are much more fun than the wholesale business. First, since you are selling directly to the customer with no middleman, you are making more money per book. Second, instead of dull old purchase orders, you will find that your retail orders will come with personal letters telling you how much they love your book or where they first had one particular recipe. Keep a folder with some of the most enthusiastic orders—they make a great promotional tool.

Remember, since this sale is final, a state sales tax must be added if it is sold within the state. Also, retail orders should come with full payment, eliminating a bookkeeping step. It is money in the bank, literally.

Retail orders come in different forms, too:

1. Reorder coupon printed in the back of your book (This is one of the most effective marketing tools.)
2. Brochure response
3. Unsolicited letters
4. Verbal or telephone orders (Ask them to send a check.)

Whatever way the orders come in, you will need a system for shipping and recording. You will also have invoices. They should be three-part, self-carboned or with carbon, and prenumbered (use a different set of numbers from those on the wholesale invoices). They should be slightly different from the wholesale invoice and should contain the following information:

Sold to/shipped to address
Name
Date
Form of payment (check, cash, credit card, etc.)
Quantity ordered
Unit price and extended price
Shipping/handling charges

GOODLETT PRESS, INC.
P.O. Box 11465
Memphis, TN 38111


RETAIL SALE


Name: _Miss Jane Doe_____

Address: _123 N. Maple Street_____

City: _Austin___ State: _TX_ Zip: _37442_


Date: _____8 - 6 - 86_____

Form of payment: __ck # 437_____


_2_ copy(ies) Recipe Reminder
　　　　　　　　$8.95 each　　　　$ 17.90

　　　　　　　　1.50 p&h each　　　3.00

(TN residents) .69 tax each　　N/a


　　　　Total Payment　　　$ 20.90

When the order comes in, you type the invoice. Write the invoice number on the original order.

After the order is invoiced, you put the book in a box or Jiffy bag, type a label, put on the postage, and mail it. You can enclose the last copy of the invoice if you want the customer to have a receipt. Retail is that simple.

For your office records, the parts of the invoice should be dispersed as follows:

*Original* (white)—filed alphabetically (by customer's last name) in a file.

*1 copy* (yellow)—goes to bookkeeping with the payment. After it is posted, it is filed numerically.

*1 copy* (pink)—can be mailed to customer. (Since a statement is really not needed, all these copies can be kept as the basis for your future retail mailing list and promotions.)

Take the original orders (letters, coupons, etc.) and file them by *month* (just rubber-banded together is fine). This is convenient as another cross-check. The beauty of this system is the cross-checking it allows. You end up with excellent records: one color filed alphabetically by the month, and at the end of the year all placed in a "1985" file. If an irate customer calls up to complain that the book she ordered for her sister's birthday never arrived, you can quickly check to see if you actually received the order and when it was sent.

Since cookbooks sell by word of mouth, you definitely want to print coupons and reorder information in the book so that when someone's guests rave about the meal and want the recipes, she can point them directly to the source.

## More Office Suggestions

Since some of your retail and wholesale orders can come by phone, we have a helpful suggestion—and a necessary one for records. A phone order can present special problems. Local stores, which will frequently be your best customers, will often call up and say, "I need a dozen more books." Most of us would have a tendency to jot down the order on the back of an envelope or on a grocery sack and say, "I'll tend to it later." This can *never* be permitted.

We suggest a system we all *WOB/ROB*—which stands for Wholesale Order Blank and Retail Order Blank. Type these up and have a quick printer produce printed forms in two different colors.

---

### WHOLESALE ORDER BLANK

Date _____

Store: _____

Address: _____

_____

Person Ordering: _____

Purchase Order Number: _____

<u>Number of books ordered:</u>  6    12    18    24

                           30    36    42    48

Special Instructions: _____

_____

_____

---

One like this can be designed for retail, also. Keep these by every telephone, and fill one out for every verbal order. These forms should contain all of the information found on a regular invoice or order form. Never accept a verbal order without filling out the appropriate form. This is your only record of the transaction. If someone besides yourself is taking orders, be sure they initial the order form.

*Postage* and *shipping charts* are other useful office tools. (Samples appear on page 156.) They can be placed on the office/shipping area wall.

It is easy to find out all rates, both wholesale and retail, and create these forms. Then, when an order is received, you can simply look up and find the costs without having to check or figure them out every time. Having these charts on hand also has the wonderful quality of eliminating money errors, which tend to irritate customers.

## WHOLESALE POSTAGE CHART

| Quantity | Price | Postage | Total |
|---|---|---|---|
| 6 | $ 36.00 | $ 3.00 | $ 39.00 |
| 12 | 72.00 | 6.00 | 78.00 |
| 18 | 108.00 | 9.00 | 117.00 |
| 24 | 144.00 | 12.00 | 156.00 |
| 30 | 180.00 | 15.00 | 195.00 |

## RETAIL POSTAGE CHART

| Quantity | Picked up | Mailed out-of-state | Mailed in-state |
|---|---|---|---|
| 1 | $10.60 | $11.50 | $12.10 |
| 2 | 21.20 | 23.00 | 24.20 |
| 3 | 31.80 | 34.50 | 36.30 |
| 4 | 42.40 | 46.00 | 48.40 |
| 5 | 53.00 | 57.50 | 60.50 |

# FILING SYSTEMS

We've already suggested ways of handling the filing of invoices for both wholesale and retail systems. You also need to keep up with many other things: correspondence, bills, tax forms, customer lists, promotional ideas, etc. Filing systems are very personal. Your filing system must

## SUGGESTED FILING SYSTEM

A. Purchase orders (filed by the month/12 folders)
B. Correspondence
    1. General correspondence
    2. Correspondence with other cookbook authors
    3. Correspondence—potential wholesale accounts
    4. Correspondence—retail customers
       requesting information
    5. Account problem correspondence
    6. Delinquent account correspondence
    7. Delinquent account notices
C. Office administration
    1. Company's paid bills
    2. Credit memos
    3. Form letters
    4. Insurance forms and contracts
    5. Inventory tally sheets
    6. Inventory memos
    7. Job descriptions
    8. Monthly reports
    9. Opinions and policies
    10. Permit mailings, records, and forms
    11. Sales tax forms
    12. Wholesale customer account list
D. Promotion
    1. Testimonial letters
    2. Advertisements: camera-ready artwork
    3. Cookbook promotions/publicity
    4. Other cookbook promotions/publicity
    5. Future promotional plans
E. Printing
    1. Copies of contracts (original in lock box)
    2. Printing bids
    3. Future cookbook revisions/corrections
F. Year-end
    1. Auditor's financial report
    2. Your year-end report
    3. Year-end net profit record

work for you. It doesn't do any good to put something neatly away, if you are then not able to get your hands on it.

You may prefer a strictly alphabetical system, or you might want to file things by subject. A list of possible categories for such a subject index system appears on page 157.

# INVENTORY CONTROLS

At the end or beginning of each month, someone needs to count the books on hand. This is the easiest thing *not* to do, but it does need to be done.

We know a group in Oregon who were selling books so fast they forgot to stop and count. When they ran out of books and back orders were piling up (a nightmare!), they went back for a reprint, but the delay in filling those orders was several months. They should have negotiated a new contract well before they ran out. This is one major reason for taking inventory.

There are other reasons. Counting the books regularly tells you how many you've sold and serves as an independent check on your bookkeeping system. A physical count keeps books from walking out the door with friends or visitors. You need to know how many you have on hand, and, if your printer is storing books for you, his *written* inventory of how many he has left should match your records. Your printer should give you written confirmation of his inventory of your books periodically, at least several times a year.

You also need to keep a record of books that are not on your shelves; for example, a dozen books sent as complimentary copies to food editors, or two dozen books on display at a convention, or several sample copies sent for printers' quotes. Just because there was "no sale" doesn't mean the books didn't leave your inventory. You need to create some sort of inventory memo.

```
                    GOODLETT PRESS, INC.

                      Inventory Memo

Title: _____

Number of copies: _____

Purpose: _____

_____

_____

_____

_____


Date: _____         Signed: _____
```

Another use for an Inventory Memo occurs when a customer tells you that a book never arrived. In this case you have to trust the customer and send another book. You've made one sale but two books have left your inventory. Fill out an Inventory Memo "One copy lost in mail."

Damaged books are another example. If a customer reports that a damaged copy arrived, ask for the damaged book back first, then mail another copy to the customer, making an Inventory Memo. (You need the damaged copy back to see how the damage occurred—printer error or shipping damage. We'll talk about uses for damaged books in Chapter 5.)

Inventory Memos can keep you on your toes and make you aware of where slippage is occurring. You might discover that you are losing money by sending too many complimentary copies.

To keep up with your monthly count, we suggest an Inventory Tally Sheet. Each month you count what you have on hand—those books you have accounted for by Inventory Memos, books sold, books stored at the printer's—and total it. This way you have a good idea of what is selling and what is on hand.

| INVENTORY TALLY SHEET | |
|---|---|
| Book Count | Description |
| | _____ Boxes of 6 count |
| | _____ Boxes of 12 count |
| | _____ Boxes of 30 count |
| | Retail ("loose" copies) |
| | Damaged books |
| | Inventory memos/miscellaneous |
| | HOUSE TOTAL |
| | Printer's inventory |
| | Book inventory TOTAL |

Month _____
Date _____

# POLICIES

As your cookbook gains fame and your business booms, thousands of questions will come up. You need to deal with them consistently and efficiently. We suggest you have *written policies* to help you. Deciding in advance how to handle a certain problem, writing down the decision and keeping it on file will keep you from having to reinvent the wheel over and over. Of course, unique situations will always come up and require instant policy-making, but a file of written policies can save you hours of worry. Policies are a necessity: to maintain continuity and build long-range plans, to avoid potential errors, to make your operations more businesslike.

Written policies are particularly important for volunteer organizations where the leadership of the cookbook committee changes each year. Each new chairman needs to know what was done and why. This does not mean that once a policy is made it can't be changed. Events and circumstances change.

Hays, Rolfes sets policies on everything we do, and we can't change them without a "corporate meeting." For example: both of us must make all major decisions. Other policies we set are that we never endorse or recommend commercial companies and that all information taken in confidence from any cookbook publisher is kept classified. These and many other policies have helped immeasurably over the years.

You will want to make your own decisions to suit your personality and situation. Your first decision may be who is involved in the policy-making process. There are two types of policies: those that are strictly business policies and those that we think of as philosophical policies. To get you started thinking about policies, we offer the following list of situations that you will probably face. The decisions are up to you.

## General Business Policies

1. *Prices*—We've discussed this in detail, but your pricing schedule, and the exceptions you make to it, come under policy and should be written down and filed or posted.
2. *Bad checks*—We hope this won't happen, but if it does, you need to be prepared. There are several things you can do.

   • You can keep the original, sending a copy with a letter asking for payment to the store or person who issued it.

- You can ask for payment by cashier's check or money order on the second try.
- You can, and should, charge a "bounced check fee" in addition to the original amount since you will have to pay for it.
- If the bad check comes from a wholesale account, flag the account. Ask for prepayment on future orders.

3. *Consignment sales*—You will probably be asked to offer books for sale on consignment at some time. Before you decide whether to do it or not, weigh the pros and cons. It can help you in getting accounts for a new book, and many use this as a way to get started. It can be useful in placing your books at certain events, like meetings or charity fairs. Many nonprofit groups do this reciprocally for seasonal sales.

   However, allowing consignment sales can wreak havoc with your inventory control; you don't know whether the books are actually sold or on their way back to you. It is hard to ship books several times and display them for sale without some damage, and you may find that you get back books in poor condition. Payments may be delayed for even longer than 30 days.

   If you do decide to allow consignment sales, we suggest you have the customer sign a consignment agreement that sets time limits and specifies the condition of the returned books (preferably in unopened boxes).

4. *Returns*—Publishing companies and many distributors allow booksellers to return unsold books after a certain length of time. Charitable organizations have traditionally *not* allowed this practice. An individual self-publisher may lose some accounts if he or she tries to enforce a no-return policy. We don't recommend accepting returns, but if you do decide to, print on the invoice, "Authorized returns only within six months" (or some specified time).

The bookseller understands this to mean that he must call or write before shipping books back to you. Never print anything about returns in your wholesale promotional material—it implies the books might not sell, and that's a real downer.

5. *Damaged/lost books*—There will always be some of this, but fortunately the problem doesn't occur too frequently. If a book is lost in the mail to a customer, you must replace it (filling out an inventory memo to account for it).

   If books are damaged in shipment to a dealer, you must replace them, too. Always ask for the damaged books back (offering to pay the shipping costs) so that you can determine where the fault lies. Damage in shipment is your loss, but damage in manufacturing is the printer's cost. If the fault is yours, write it off at cost.

   You can sell damaged books at a discount or use the pages as promotional material. Never use a damaged copy as a review copy; this leaves the impression all the books are faulty or easily subject to damage.

6. *Charge customers (retail)*—This is definitely up to you. Usually retail orders should be prepaid. Wholesale accounts are allowed 30 days with some exceptions.

   You may decide to let retail customers use charge cards, but this is not "credit." Consult your bank for the proper forms and procedures. It is a lot of trouble but can increase retail mail order sales.

   Some groups allow "members only" to charge. Traditionally these are the slowest-paid accounts, and it requires setting up a new billing system in the office.

7. *Delinquent accounts*—Set up a system in advance and follow it. You might decide on first billing, sending a letter with the second bill, sending in the lawyer on the third, or some variation of that procedure. Don't forget that the telephone is a good reminder. Decide when to use a lawyer or a collection agency (for large amounts).

- ◆ You can state that you will hold future orders until current payment is made, or ask for pre-payment of future orders from delinquent accounts.
- ◆ You can offer percentages: a discount for early payment, a penalty for late payment.
- ◆ If you bill by the 24th instead of the 30th of each month, you're more likely to get into a store's first-of-the-month payment cycle.
- ◆ *Exception*: the large chains and department stores and most distributors never pay net in 30 days; you need to flag these accounts for your own information, but don't handle them as you would a small account that habitually pays late.

8. *Book inventory control*—We've discussed this in detail, but it needs to be written down under policies. You must take a monthly count and keep records, and if the printer is storing, he needs to give periodic reports in writing to you.

9. *Promotional books*—Again, this is your decision. You will definitely want to give some promotional books away, but the trick is to decide how many. Set a limit for each time period (a year, six months). This keeps you from giving away too many or too few. Decide who is to get them: book review editors, food editors, well-known individuals who might give endorsements, buyers at large stores or chains, courtesy copies for friends or visitors.

   Figure the actual cost of books given away into the promotional budget.

10. *Free delivery*—This can be good local public relations, but be careful; as your customer list grows, it can get to be time-consuming and troublesome. You can decide to do it locally or out of town as a special marketing tool or as a one-time offer for a new account.

11. *Advertising/promotions*—We are going to devote a whole chapter to this, but some policies need to be included in your policy file.

- ◆ Keep testimonial letters in a special file for future use.
- ◆ Never advertise or promote without coding the return so you can evaluate the results.
- ◆ Research every new approach and budget carefully.

12. *Gift wrap (retail)*—If you use this as a promotional tool, do you gift wrap upon request, do you charge for it, do you supply cards for enclosure, how do you advertise it, and do you do it seasonally or all year round?

13. *Overpayment/underpayment*—This will happen eventually on both wholesale and retail, particularly as the book goes into additional printings with price increases.

   *Retail:* If your book continues to sell for years, cards will come in from the back of old books with out-of-date prices. Most cookbook buyers are nice people and will understand. Devise or design what we call the OOPS Card! It is usually designed as a postcard so it may be mailed alone (when order is held) or enclosed with book (when book is sent).

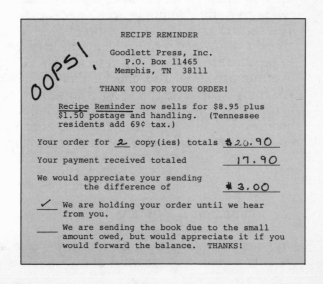

RECIPE REMINDER

OOPS!

Goodlett Press, Inc.
P.O. Box 11465
Memphis, TN  38111

THANK YOU FOR YOUR ORDER!

Recipe Reminder now sells for $8.95 plus $1.50 postage and handling.  (Tennessee residents add 69¢ tax.)

Your order for  2  copy(ies) totals  $20.90

Your payment received totaled              17.90

We would appreciate your sending
       the difference of              $ 3.00

  ✓  We are holding your order until we hear from you.

____  We are sending the book due to the small amount owed, but would appreciate it if you would forward the balance.  THANKS!

If the amount owed is large, hold the check and don't invoice the book until the full payment is received—and then send the book. Hold the order in a basket until the balance is sent. For overpayment, nonprofits usually keep the money as a donation; an individual can send it back by check or stamps, or send a letter issuing credit toward another book.

*Wholesale:* This can cause real bookkeeping headaches. Underpayment can be deposited and credited and a new bill sent with a letter asking for the balance. Overpayment can be deposited and credited, but it is probably easier to write a check and return the difference, simplifying your bookkeeping.

14. *Correspondence*—Keep a copy of everything: letters, complaints, etc. Put a copy of any correspondence with a wholesale customer in their file for reference.

Always be polite—even when it hurts.

15. *Form letters*—Decide when to use form letters and when not to. There are two types of form letters.

- Frequently used letters or notices which can be mass-produced—for example, the OOPS card, answers to routine inquiries, promotional material.
- The second type is not mass-produced but is an already composed letter which you keep on file to personalize and mail as needed—for example: overdue accounts, bad checks, damaged books. We think a mimeographed letter in some cases is inappropriate, as it gives an impression that your business handles lots of bad accounts or damaged books. However, having the text written in advance saves time and ensures consistency.

## Philosophical Business Policies

1. *Future sales*—Think long-range. No major company plans only a year or six months at a time. (This can

be a large problem in an organization where the
chairman has a tendency to think only "My Year.")

2. *Classified information*—Remember, you are now a
   company. You will always have some information
   that goes under this heading, such as printing bids,
   confidential records, or problems or special circumstances that should be preserved for future reference.

3. *Business image*—A *must*! Everything that goes out
   should look good. Procedures must be businesslike,
   clear, consistent, and efficient.

4. *Customer relations*—The customer is the lifeblood of
   business. "It costs five times as much to acquire a
   new customer as it does to maintain an old one."
   So remember, the customer is always right and deserves: courtesy, reliability, and promptness in service, delivery, and handling problems, etc.

You will develop policies of your own as times goes
on, but these will give you some idea of the issues that
may come up. By having policies written down and easily
accessible you will be able to carry on your business in a
much more consistent, worry-free manner.

# CHAPTER 5

# Marketing a Cookbook

WE'VE SAID IT BEFORE and we'll say it again: even the best cookbook won't sell unless it is marketed properly. Barbara Metcalf, who has had experience as cookbook buyer for Marshall Field and as the owner of a retail cookbook mail order business, says, "I have studied ads this past year for cookbooks from bagels to hot sauce, from traditional to nouvelle cuisine, from $2.95 to $50. That's the beauty of the cookbook product—cookbooks can reflect the diversity in the population; there is so much to choose from that there is a cookbook just perfect for everyone!"

You can write an absolute gem of a book and it will stay on the shelves unless someone makes an effort to sell it. In this chapter we are going to talk about finding those buyers who are perfect for your cookbook and selling it to them. Marketing can be as creative and exciting as writing the book. First, let's discuss what happens to your book once it is published and what you can do to help it become a best-seller.

## WITH A PUBLISHER

A large publishing company will have a big publicity department and an active staff of sales representatives who travel regionally selling their company's books to stores. Let's say a book is to be published in March. It appears on the publisher's spring list of new titles. Early in January, bookstores and distributors will receive that catalog, then a visit from the sales rep, whose job it is to sell the books to the retailers. A major company will have numerous representatives throughout the country who regularly call on accounts in their territory. Because a smaller publisher can't afford a big sales staff, it may use commission salesmen who represent books from several companies, may sell its books only through a wholesaler, or may rely strictly on direct mail sales.

The store's buyer looks at all the lists of new titles and places orders, or the sales rep and the buyer sit down and go over the new list. An experienced salesman knows the market and can tell which stores will be good outlets for particular books. The big chain bookdealers have buyers who specialize in different fields, including a cookbook buyer. The buyer (in independent stores, frequently the owner) knows what his customers want and will place orders accordingly. Perhaps your book doesn't catch the buyer's eye right away. It needs some publicity to push it. Or perhaps the sales rep can offer extra inducements to the buyer by offering to supply posters or a counter display (like the one below); or they may say something like, "This author will be featured in the May issue of *Family Circle*."

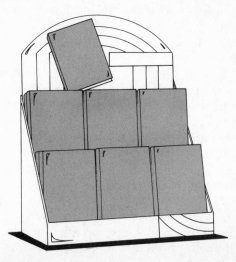

What kind of promotion your book gets from the publisher depends upon several things: the size of the first printing, your reputation, the company's expectations for sales, where your book fits into their list. (Is it the first of its kind? Does it complete a series?) A publisher will figure a budget for promotion of each new book, which may include an author's tour, posters, flyers, review copies, ads, and so on. A new novel by a famous writer whose last book sold a million copies is obviously going to get the whole works. A first book by an unknown is not. The budget will not send you on a nationwide tour, book you on Johnny Carson, run ads in *The New York Times* and *Gourmet*, and pay for stunning floor displays for 5,000 bookstores. More likely it will cover inclusion in the publisher's catalog, press releases and review copies, and a couple of ads in book trade journals. Then, as the book begins to sell well and goes into a second printing, more publicity will be called for. A small publishing company may rely solely on the inclusion of your book in its general publicity mailings.

What can you do to help? Well, making yourself famous—even locally—will help. When you've got a published work, you can get on local radio and TV talk shows or interest a local store or two in giving an autograph party. A feature story in the local paper not only sells books, it provides quotes to be used in the next press release: "Outstanding chef shares succulent secrets in her new book."

If you have an agent, the agent may be able to bargain for additional publicity for your book. You can even hire a special public relations person to get your picture printed in all sorts of places, but this can be really expensive, and it is something you can do yourself.

Being available and eager to help your publisher's publicity efforts is important. You can suggest specialized markets for your book: food associations, trade fairs, conventions of appliance dealers, or nutrition magazines. You know your book best and you know who is going to be interested in buying it. Draw up a list of specialized publications that will be likely to print a review of the book or do a feature story on you (the newspaper in the town where you grew up, for instance). You can suggest ideas for premium sales (to a trade association, for example). You can get quotations from all sorts of people to use in publicity.

Supply interesting facts about yourself and your book to your editor to share with the rest of the company. When the sales rep goes out to sell the book, he needs to know what distinguishes your book from all the others. Establish your credentials—as a teacher, a personality, or the heir to a long tradition of ethnic cooking. It's your job to get your publisher excited about you and the possibilities for your book.

When you can show your publisher how much interest you've aroused in one market, even if it is your hometown, you can become a hot property for other markets, too. Make a name for yourself by public appearances regionally. Get a speaking engagement at a food convention. Get yourself photographed serving your famous cheesecake to a visiting celebrity. When you travel, call on food editors, book in hand.

Publicity generates more publicity. Everything that you can do to sell your book will help to show the publisher that you are worth his investment. If your book sells well in one city, it will sell in another, with the same effort.

If your book does well, and your publishing company attends the book trade shows, you will have the exciting prospect of seeing your book promoted during one, or all, of these shows. The biggest book show is the American Booksellers Convention, which is held in a different major city every year. The large New York publishing houses plus many of the small publishers attend this event and show attending booksellers what books they have available for the year. The convention is held over the Memorial Day weekend, and literally thousands of booksellers attend. Seeing your book displayed there is an exciting and educational experience.

# MARKETING A SELF-PUBLISHED COOKBOOK

As we mentioned before, an editor once said that a self-published book stands a greater chance of success because it is in the hands of someone who cares. When you self-publish, the whole thing is in your hands, and you can be just as creative in marketing the book as you were in writing it.

Let's define our terms. *Marketing* covers the whole field and includes planning, the product itself, its production, sales, distribution, and advertising. *Advertising*, or *promotion* (we use the two words interchangeably), is just one part of the total effort. When we say "advertising," people usually think of the news media—radio, TV, magazines, and newspapers. We think that advertising—or promotion—includes anything that presents your book to the public:

| | | |
|---|---|---|
| newspapers | TV | brochures |
| magazines | billboards | press kits |
| radio | direct mail | handbills |
| catalogs | posters | banners |
| displays | logo design | stationery |
| postcards | aprons, mitts | bookmarks |

We also want to make a distinction between publicity and advertising. *Advertising* you pay for. It is a controllable expense that requires planning and budgeting. You control how much you spend and when you spend it. *Publicity* is free and adds credibility to your book. A feature story in a newspaper, an endorsement from a celebrity, a quotation from a satisfied reader—you don't pay for these things but you do capitalize on them.

There is also an important difference in promoting your book for the wholesale and retail markets. In *retail* promotion, you are aiming at the individual who will buy your book either to use or to give as a gift. Therefore you appeal to that buyer's emotions:

"You can be the best hostess in town with these recipes."

"This book will make you healthier."

"Giving this book marks you as a person with good
taste."

Retail buyers like to know what they are buying; they like
to see sample recipes and see what the book is like if they
can't see the actual book before they buy, so ads should
be specific.

*Wholesale* promotion aims at the stores that will sell the
book. Remember that the sellers don't have to be bookstores; wholesale outlets can include food specialty stores,
hotel and airport gift shops, distributors, cooking schools,
even strange places like trout farms. Any retail outlet that
will carry your book is a potential account. What the
owners of these outlets want to know is that the book
will sell and make a profit for them (and you). They don't
care if you have the recipe for the all-time greatest crabmeat soufflé. They want to know that the book will sell,
and to whom, so you approach wholesalers accordingly:

"A must for health food fans."

"10,000 copies sold in three months."

"Now in third printing."

Wholesalers want to know the facts that will help them
sell the book.

Retail sales can lead to wholesale sales. When a potential buyer hears about a book from a friend, she will go
to her bookstore and ask for the book. Retails sales are
very important (and fun, because you get more of the
profit), but on a book that is marketed nationally or regionally, 75 percent of the net profit will come from wholesale accounts because of the volume.

Of course, there is a big difference in marketing a brand-
new book and one that has been around for several years.
In fact, there are three stages to marketing a book:

The *pioneer* stage—a brand-new book that has to be
introduced to the public, where every wholesale account is a new account.

The *competitive* stage—a book that has established a track record and can quote its past successes but has new markets still to develop.

The *retentive* stage—a book that has been around for a while and needs continued attention to established accounts and new incentives to buyers.

As we talk about techniques and methods of promotion, you will see ideas applicable to each stage. Marketing is an ongoing process. You can't stop without seeing your profits decline. In marketing your book, there are four basic decisions you must make, whether you are beginning with a new book or continuing with one already on the market.

First of all, are you aiming at a local, regional, or national market? If you plan to sell all your books to members of your PTA or church group, or to only sell once a year at the Harvest Fair, you will allocate your resources in one way. If you plan to aim at nationwide distribution within two years, you need other kinds of plans.

Second, which methods of marketing are best suited for you? You know how much money, manpower, and time you have. You can't do everything at once and do it well. You will probably try different things at different times. This chapter contains many ideas. You will have to choose.

Third, what is the unique quality of your book? Define your strengths and build everything around them.

Fourth, set a budget (money) and a schedule (time) and a goal (the profit you want or the number of books you want to sell) and stick to them.

As you make these four important decisions, you will want to base them on some information. You need to *define your market*. Establish a customer profile. Who is going to buy your book? What kind of people are they? Where are they going to shop and what is going to be most likely to attract their attention? Do some research. There are dozens of books in the library about marketing. Read whatever you can about the field. Talk to people— book and gift shop owners, cookbook buyers. Find out what sells and why. Keep a file of "bright ideas." Save "junk mail" or advertisements that appeal to you—and not just those dealing with cookbooks. Borrow ideas from any source. Finally, don't forget student power. We know one nonprofit group that got a professor at a local college to use its books as an assignment in his marketing class. The students came up with detailed plans and wonderful ideas. Perhaps a student might be interested in using your book as a project.

When you define your market you will know what makes sense for your book. You wouldn't advertise in *Road & Track* magazine, nor would a manufacturer of cam shafts advertise in *Bon Appetit*.

Finally, always key your advertising so that you will know what is most effective. Remember that we said advertising was a controllable expense, one for which you can plan both timing and budget? It is important to know what works so you will know whether to do the same thing again or try something new. You can test the results by inserting a key into an ad: "Order from Department AB, such and such address." Put a different code on a direct mail flyer, "Department XY." Then you have a way to measure the results of each.

With this background we're going to talk about many different ways to market your book. Our purpose is not to give you a definitive outline to follow, but to suggest a variety of ways to consider as you make the decisions that are best for you and establish your own marketing plan and budget. For each idea that you try, make a plan and record its success. Even if an idea bombs and you want to tear up the paper and never think about that disaster again, don't do it. Fill out the results honestly. Remember, "Good judgment comes from experience, and experience comes from poor judgment."

Eighty percent of all books sold are sold by word of mouth. One person likes the book and recommends it to another. So let's get busy and start people talking about your book.

## MARKETING PLAN & REPORT

*General Description:* _____

_____

*Needs:* _____

*Manpower:* _____

*Time Schedule:* _____

*Expenses:* _____

Gross Income: _____

Expenses: _____

Net Profit: _____

## *The Kick-Off*

The best time to get lots of free publicity is when a book is brand-new. A new book is *news*; after it has been around for a while it is just another product. You want to take advantage of the newness to get as much publicity as possible.

Back in Chapter 3, we talked about the calendar for producing the book, and we said to allow six to eight weeks' time from the day you expect the book to be delivered to you until the official date of publication. This gives you time to send press kits or review copies, arrange for news stories and interviews, and plan a big splash for the day the book officially goes on sale.

You start locally, for that is where your first big sales will be. If you have contacts in other cities, try to repeat the same procedures as often as you can. Here are some ways you can get publicity for a new book:

Newspaper articles
Radio and TV interviews
Party for press, dignitaries, friends, book people
    to introduce the book
Autograph party at local store or stores
Special appearances by author at club meetings,
    stores, fairs, charitable events
Present a cookbook to mayor or celebrity
Local cooking school uses recipes and sells the book
A food specialty store gives samples and sells the book

We'll talk in detail about press kits for newspaper food editors. For the first story in your local papers, you will probably want to send a review copy to the food editor and make a personal call, after first sending a press release to alert the editor well before the official publication date. Don't forget about neighborhood newspapers; many cities have several small publications as well as the major dailies. Contact the newspapers in any city where you have a connection: where your mother lives, where you once lived. Editors love the "local person makes good" angle.

A phone call to radio and television stations will tell you the name of the person who schedules guests for talk shows. Having the correct name is important. Send that person a press release and follow up with another phone call. All the stations have time to fill and are constantly looking for material.

You can make the contacts yourself, hire an agent, or persuade a friend to act as your agent in this first period. A nonprofit organization will have a committee responsible for a new book's publicity.

When you make a radio or TV appearance, be prepared. Find out if the station will let you do a cooking demonstration or bring some appealing-looking samples. (You may consider your chicken gravy your best dish, but it won't photograph as well as a kiwi tart.) If the format of the show is strictly an interview, have in mind some funny stories about writing the book, a couple of short, easy-to-read recipes, a few cooking hints. The interviewer should be prepared with the written material in the press release you've sent (we'll warn you—sometimes they will have no idea who you are), but you must be ready to put across in a few seconds why your book is different and worth buying. Aim for short answers; don't embark on some long story or recipe. We can't all be Erma Bombeck, but heaven preserve you from sitting there answering yes or no and forgetting your own name. A radio or TV appearance can be a good tool for getting wholesale accounts, too. You can say to a store owner, "I'm going to be on the Happy Homemaker's Hour; may I mention your store as an outlet for my book?"

An autograph party at a bookstore or gourmet shop needs to be scheduled well in advance. Stores frequently include invitations in their billing cycle. Some stores love to do this because it brings new customers into the store, and they will want your help in drawing up a big guest list. When you ask a store to give an autograph party, don't act as if you are asking for a huge favor. Tell the store owner that you will be glad to do an autographing session for them. Present it as a matter of mutual benefit; you are helping them to sell more copies. (Of course, you could always offer to bring a tray of your original tidbits, too.) One self-publisher managed to arrange a hookup with a radio talk show from the autographing party.

Organizations frequently give marvelous debut parties that attract lots of attention and lots of buyers.

*Applehood & Motherpie* first appeared at a party at a historic home in Rochester.

The Junior League of Atlanta previewed *Altanta Cooknotes* at a party at Lenox Square Shopping Mall with a well-known band for entertainment. All the cooks were there to autograph their recipes, and 7,000 people attended.

The Beaumont, Texas, Junior League issued clever citations to the whole community to appear at the old jail house for a "booking party."

*Minnesota Heritage Cookbook* was presented by the Minnesota Cancer Society at an early morning breakfast at the Minneapolis Farmers' Market.

For the St. Louis Museum's *Artist in the Kitchen*, Neiman-Marcus gave a huge party in a shopping center with chefs from the city's restaurants doing the cooking.

Mickey Schaffler and Suzanne Henley, authors of *Sauce for the Goose*, gave a huge lawn party to introduce their book to all their friends and acquaintances.

*A Man's Taste* was introduced by two parties: first, a wonderful series of private dinners at members' homes, ending with a dance and skit held for the Memphis Junior League's membership; second, a public function, at a gift store with autographing and food samples.

If your organization has the manpower, you can make the kick-off a fund-raiser, too, by selling tickets. Some groups have used tasting teas both to make money and to build up interest in the book. Other groups have auctioned off the artwork at the kick-off.

If you plan a big public kick-off event, plan your guest list carefully. Invite all the media people who might mention the book, store owners who will carry the book, anyone you can think of who will buy a copy, and any dignitaries you can think of—the mayor, city officials, civic club presidents, local personalities. Unless you sell tickets and make the party self-supporting, you will have to budget it in your promotion expenses. However, it doesn't have to be expensive, particularly if you can hold it in a public place. Creativity and originality are more important than a big budget.

If you can arrange public appearances anywhere, do! Most club program chairmen need all the help they can get. If you can plan a cooking demonstration at a store, a fair, or a meeting, you will sell books. Two words of warning. First, remember that the ingredients for a demonstration will cost and have to be included in your budget. Second, if possible, take a friend along to help with the sales. It is very difficult to talk charmingly, answer questions, autograph books, and make change at one and the same time.

First make a sample budget, a guideline, for the kick-off of your book. The example on page 180 will give you some ideas.

```
┌─────────────────────────────────────────────────────┐
│                    BUDGET                            │
│                                                      │
│  Party at bookstore         Free                     │
│  Review copies to two                                │
│      food editors               2.40 × 2 (cost to you) │
│  TV appearances             Free                     │
│  Cooking demo in store         25.00 (ingredients)   │
│  Press releases                25.00                 │
│  Party for press & friends    100.00                 │
│                               ───────                │
│                   Total       $154.80                │
│                                                      │
└─────────────────────────────────────────────────────┘
```

For under $200 we hope you have gotten lots of attention and generated lots of sales.

## Press Kits

Book reviews sell books. It's the most effective and least expensive avenue into retail sales because consumers trust what they see in print. When a cookbook is featured in a newspaper or magazine, the consumer thinks, "Aha, that sounds like something I should have." An endorsement in print adds credibility to the book. Press coverage can also lead to wholesale accounts because booksellers will stock a book that they know their customers will be asking for. If you know ahead of time that an article is forthcoming, write to the stores in the vicinity announcing the coverage.

One self-publisher estimated that each newspaper story on his book sold from 50 to 200 books. Another received 1,500 mail orders from one story in *The New York Times*. When the *Ladies' Home Journal* did a story on *Party Potpourri*, the Memphis Junior League received 6,000 orders, and resales from the coupons in the back of those books are still coming in years later.

So how do you go about getting coverage for your book? Plot a campaign with the use of a press kit. Whether you aim only at local sales or are trying to expand your market nationwide, a press kit will be a useful tool. The purpose of the press kit is to attract the food editor's attention. Sometimes a story will appear right away and sometimes she will file the press kit away until she has a slow week. The more professionally your material is presented, the better your chances.

Let's go over what goes in a press kit.

COOKBOOK PRESS KIT

1. Cover letter—personalized and typed
2. Book cover—facsimile or dust jacket
3. Press release
4. Selected recipes
5. Promotional fact sheet
6. Testimonial—copies of significant review coverage
7. Author's biography or information about the organization
8. 5″ × 7″ black and white glossy print photograph
9. Reply card with stamp offering complimentary copy if reviewed
10. Request for two copies of article
11. Ordering information—address and postpaid price (include tax for in-state)
12. Name, address, and telephone number of contact person (author or chairman)

Obviously, putting this together is going to cost some money. Now is when you need the Quick-Print for copies of the press release and other items. Figure in your budget how many you can afford to send at one time, coordinating with your efforts to get new accounts in that city or region. You might start with one region and gradually expand your market.

The cover letter should be personalized and typed. We'll go into some detail about how you know who to send it to in a minute. In the letter, ask for two copies of the article when it appears.

Don't send a copy of the book. Instead send a tantalizing sample of its contents and a stamped reply card, asking for a complimentary (not free) copy. If someone takes the time to do this, you can be pretty sure a story will appear. When you choose the sample recipes to include, select those that are really unique, that illustrate your theme, or that are featured in a photograph. If you take recipes to the Quick-Print rather than sending sample pages, consider having them printed on colored paper for variety.

Send the cover of the book or a facsimile so that the reviewer knows what it is like. You can either use the overrun pages or ask the printer to run a few extra covers for you, or use the covers (and sample pages) from damaged or incomplete books. The Junior League of Wichita Falls, Texas, turned a disaster into a selling tool for their book *Home Cookin'*. They had quantities of damaged books after a hurricane, and rather than tossing the lot, they reassembled small booklets from undamaged covers and pages, tied them with a ribbon, and included them in the press kits.

The press release should be short and organized into the journalistic formula: who, what, when, where, and how. It should stress a human interest angle and tell what makes the book unique. For a new cookbook you can write about how the book was written, give humorous anecdotes about the testing, tell why you wanted to write this book, how you learned to cook couscous in Morocco, why the organization decided to do a fund-raiser. A new book has certain built-in news angles, but there are many stories about older books, too. For example, selling a million copies was a natural story for *River Road Recipes* (so is going into another printing). You can write a story on a season, an event, or a holiday; for example: Christmas dinner ideas, after-theater suppers, tailgate picnics in football season. You can write about your theme, or about what's happened to you since you became a famous cook. You can write about anything that you want people to know about your book.

The press release should be typed and double-spaced on 8½" × 11" paper, using one-inch margins. In the upper right-hand corner give release instructions: "For immediate release," or "For release April 23, 1984" (the official publication day). You can make a press release out of almost anything: announcing the members of the new cookbook committee, a tie-in with a news event, the celebration of an anniversary, a special event, an appearance on TV, cooking classes, winning a contest, meeting a celebrity, reemphasizing a theme.

The promotional fact sheet is different from the press release, although they may cover some of the same ground. It should be printed with bullets so that the writer of the story can pick out a few facts. For example:

* Sold in 48 states
* First printing sold out
* Author featured on TV
* Contains 250 recipes
* Proceeds support the symphony
* All recipes triple-tested

For the photograph you'll need to spend a little money for a professional look, but you can create a scene out of your own imagination. The photograph can feature the author holding the book, or it can feature the book in a scene that illustrates the theme. Look at photographs in catalogs and magazines for ideas. You might use a tablecloth or an old quilt as background. In your kitchen you can find lots of things to use: a tureen, a copper pot, a picnic basket, a plant, a colander, or a bowl. You could use some prepared food that looks particularly appetizing, or apples, artichokes, or fresh vegetables. You can have fun designing the picture. *Winning Seasons* capitalized on the Alabama Crimson Tide and Coach Bear Bryant by having eight photographs of Bryant enjoying food at pre-game parties. Be sure that the book is the most prominent thing. Attach a caption to the bottom of the photograph and be sure to mail it between two pieces of cardboard.

If your book has already gotten significant review coverage, include that. You can either quote from the review or take a copy to the Quick-Print and ask to have it shrunk. One author made a collage of the reviews and had it reduced to letter size. If you have a testimonial from a famous person, be sure to use that. If you use the actual names of people, you should get permission, but you can always use initials.

"The desserts are a big hit with my family . . ."
    Mrs. A. B., Houston

"The Quick Quiche is a lifesaver . . ."
    L. M., Dallas

Be sure to include biographical information about the author, or the history and purpose of the organization, and most important of all, ordering information, including price, postage, and tax, if required.

The whole point of this is to attract attention, so it stands to reason that it should be attractive, eye-catching, and as professional-looking as possible. A sheaf of plain typed pages can be boring. Be creative in the packaging; use a bright folder tied with a ribbon, use colored paper, use gimmicks that illustrate the theme.

The Junior League of Tampa's *The Gasparilla Cookbook* used a story about pirates and enclosed a fake gold coin.

*Tea Time at the Masters* sent the information on a golf scorer's clipboard.

*Lone Star Legacy* sent the packet tied in a Texas croker sack with a packet of bluebonnet seeds.

The Pine Bluff, Arkansas, Junior League enclosed pine cones with the information about *Southern Accent*.

*Gulf Gourmet* sent Spanish moss in their press kit.

*La Piñata* sent a piñata.

You can be really creative here. You might even design two press kits and keep a record of which one gets the best results.

How do you know where to send this after you have assembled it? There are over 60,000 magazines in the United States, hundreds of major daily papers, and over 9,200 secondary community newspapers. You will have to be selective about which ones you want to approach. When you have selected the cities or the newspapers, you need the name of the particular person to address the letter to—the food, home, or woman's page editor. Once again, the library is your source. *Literary Market Place* has a complete listing of newspapers and book review editors. Book review editors are likely to pass a cookbook along to the food editor or wait until they have several to do one story on many books. A better resource is the five-volume series *Working Press of the Nation*. One volume covers newspapers, another magazines, another feature writers. Here you will find the listing of food, home, or women's page editors. It's worth the effort to make a few phone calls to the newspaper switchboard to verify that Mary Jane Doe is still the food editor.

Other resources include *Editor & Publisher Books, International Yearbook*, which includes separate listings of departmental editors, syndicates, and feature services, and *The Family Page Directory*, which lists family-page editors of the 500 largest daily newspapers in the U.S.

Publicity generates more publicity. Once you get reviews, use them! Put them in your next press kits and brochures. You can have a pressure sticker made that says, "Featured in *Family Circle*" and apply that to the books. Or use a cigar band that quotes a particularly good review. Or make a poster of good reviews and testimonials to send to wholesale accounts. When the *Ladies' Home Journal* featured *Standing Ovations* from Davenport, Iowa, the cookbook committee got the maximum mileage from it in a four-city area: one person did a story on the editor who came to town, another wrote about how the cooks prepared the food for the photographs, a TV station featured a demonstration of the recipes used in the story, a radio station interviewed the chairman about what it was like, and a cable TV station got the whole photographic session on video tape. Magazines like the *Journal, Redbook,* and *Good Housekeeping* will supply tearsheets of the article prior to publication, which can be sent to bookstores.

It pays to be persistent. You can say in your cover letter, "I will telephone you next week to answer any questions," or you can write a follow-up letter.

Capitalize on all your successes. *River Road Recipes*, the guru of community cookbooks, recently sold its one millionth copy. *The New York Times* noted this, which led to a picture story in *People* magazine. We don't know of any other cookbooks that have had this kind of success, but it proves that anything is possible.

## Brochures

One of the first marketing tools that you will want as you expand your market is a brochure. Remember the difference between wholesale and retail sales. You will need to pitch your message differently for each market. To get your book carried in local stores, all you have to do is load up some boxes of books and a batch of invoices in the car and call on the booksellers. You can persuade them to carry your book because of your personal charm and salesmanship, because of the local interest, and because you can show them a copy of the book. However, when you are ready to expand your market to a wider region or even nationally, you need a brochure that will sell the book in places where you cannot go.

There are two parts to a brochure, and both need to be effective: the copy and the layout or design.

### 1. THE COPY.

The words that tell your story. Its purpose is to sell the product. A brochure aimed at the *wholesale* market needs to present facts: the reasons the book will sell and make money for the store.

Copy should follow a basic outline:

Headline or opening
Amplification and details
Proof and reassurances
Closing

Here are a couple of good examples.

**The Stuffed Griffin**
*The Utility Club of Griffin, Georgia*
"What is *The Stuffed Griffin?* It's not just another cookbook. It is the cookbook you want on your shelf—a

guaranteed, proven seller. We've been handled, thumbed, and purchased in stores from Connecticut to Colorado and 75 percent of our bookstore customers reorder!"

### Home Cookin'
*Junior League of Wichita Falls, Texas*
"A unique blend of Southern hospitality, Spanish heritage and Texas taste. A great success story—*Home Cookin'* has expanded its wholesale outlets *1000 percent* in one year!"

The headline or opening must catch the reader's attention immediately—engage the reader before he tosses it in the wastebasket. There are several approaches you can take.

- The direct promise—"This book will be a holiday bonanza for your store."
- News—"Five million Americans bought bok choy last year."
- Curiosity—"Why did the first five printings sell out in three months?"
- Selective—"Dieters will want this book." (special market)
- Marketing help—"1000 copies sold in nine weeks by placing them in a basket near the checkout counter."

The opening statement can use any of these approaches; remember that its purpose is to engage the reader's attention quickly. The opening statement is usually, but not always, set off in a headline.

Next, you should provide concrete information about the product: size, physical description, type and number of recipes, index, illustrations, what makes the book unique. A good example follows:

### Quail Country
*The Junior League of Albany, Georgia*
"Because *Quail Country* offers features every cook wants and expects in a cookbook and more, it is destined to become a bestselling classic:

- 750 triple-tested recipes
- Extensively cross-referenced index
- Hardbound and Smythe-sewn to lie flat
- Ribbon marker
- Menus
- Measurement chart
- Plantation recipes
- Men's recipes
- Wild game recipes
- Special hints and tips throughout
- Original drawings by Georgia artist Rena Divine"

The next section—proof and reassurances—is the place for testimonials or endorsements. Here, too, is the place for bragging about past performance—proven sales record and so on. For a brand-new book, define the potential audience.

In closing, give specific instructions on ordering. This is the climax: you've gotten attention, presented the facts, reinforced them, now you tell the reader what you want him to do: buy the book.

### Southern Accent
*Junior League of Pine Bluff, Arkansas*
"Thousands of happy cooks have told us we couldn't improve our recipes. So we decided to improve our offer, just in time for Holiday giving, close on the heels of national recognition in *Good Housekeeping*. So, take advantage of this free offer and return the attached card today. We will ship your books immediately via UPS."

For a *retail* brochure (one you can use in a direct mail campaign to individual buyers), you use the same format. The difference is in the approach. A bookseller wants to know that a book will make money for him, so you present the facts. For a retail customer, you can appeal to the emotions.

"This book will make your next party a success."
"These recipes will help you become healthier."
"A discriminating person gives this book as a gift."

The individual buyer likes to know what she is getting. In a store, she will thumb through the book. In a retail brochure, give a sample recipe or two, a sample menu, a list of sections or titles, even a bit of the index. The appeal should be direct, emotional; you want the reader to say, "This looks so good I'll have to buy one."

### Dinner on the Diner
*Junior League of Chattanooga, Tennessee*
"Crisp white linens, fresh flowers, flickering candles, the music of the train zooming across America, and, of course, an elegant dinner. The romance of gourmet dining during the era of the great passenger trains has been recaptured in the Junior League of Chattanooga's *Dinner on the Diner.*"

Copy should be clear, concise, vivid, and specific. Short, uninvolved sentences are more effective. Try to use the vocabulary of the person the copy is aimed at. A bookseller wants to know about profits. A cook, a cookbook collector, or a gift giver wants to know why she will like this book. Never feel that there is nothing new to say; just look for a new approach. Always keep in mind the goal: getting a specific audience to buy the book.

### Plain & Fancy
*Junior League of Richardson, Texas*
"*Plain and Fancy* is a regional cookbook that truly breaks the mold! In concept and content, it's unlike any community cookbook you've ever seen or read and may well become a classic in its own right. Written for today's cooks, *Plain and Fancy* offers shortcuts to quality yet highlights the creative side of cooking. The results: hundreds of recipes that range from 'divinely simple to simply divine!' "

There are many ways to gain attention with the *layout* or *design* of the brochure: size, striking design, use of color, extra white space, emphasis on one element, distinctive style, artwork. You want the brochure to be so attractive that it will influence the recipient in your favor and not end up in the trash. Think about these criteria:

Is it arresting?
Is it distinctive?
Is it clear?
Does it quickly communicate the idea to the reader?
Does it encourage reading the whole thing?
Is the most important idea given the most attention?
Does it give the desired impression about the product?
Does it reflect the theme of the book?

For wholesale brochures, posters or stand-up cards are good ideas—something that the bookseller can display that will help him sell the book. Be careful with the design: if you get too elaborate or gimmicky, you may obscure your message. Make it easy, not hard, for the reader to know what you want him to do.

Believe it or not, sometimes the simplest things get overlooked. We hear horror stories about beautifully designed brochures that forget to list the price or the address to order. Also, do a little research at the post office. Will it mail and for how much? We once printed a wonderful brochure in a large size. If it had been a fraction of an inch smaller, it would have mailed at a cheaper rate.

How do you create this marvelous brochure? The same suggestions we made about designing a cookbook hold true here. Start collecting things that appeal to you—ads, flyers, things that come in the mail or that you pick up in stores. If you can't design it yourself, a graphic artist or an art student can help you. So can the printer, but not necessarily the one who printed the book. Go to different printers, get estimates, and, as always, ask a thousand questions.

The brochure should be attractive and professional-looking, but it doesn't have to cost a fortune. There are many ways to save money, as you discovered in creating your cookbook. There are tricks with color, type, size, and design that create a great effect and can be done to fit your budget. Many beautiful books have sold poorly through direct mail because of poorly executed brochures. The brochure is the "face" of the book and must sell it.

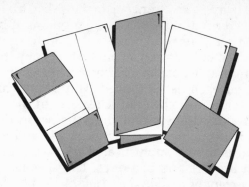

## Wholesale Direct Mail

Now that you have this dynamic wholesale brochure, what are you going to do with it? You're going to mount a direct mail campaign toward your target audience. The *Wall Street Journal* reported that more books are sold today by direct mail than are sold through the stores. Done correctly, direct mail is the most important tool of the independent publisher.

Let's define the purpose once again: to sell your book to stores that will sell it to individual customers. You mail a brochure that persuades a bookseller to order a quantity of the book. The book sells, the bookseller reorders again and again. You have a good wholesale account. If you are marketing the book locally, it is not hard to identify the likely prospects, but as you expand the market, it becomes more difficult.

You knew we were going to say it: the library is your best resource. Of course, you could go to the telephone directory section, look in the yellow pages of various cities, and make a list of stores. However, you can also turn to *The American Book Trade Directory*, which has almost 20,000 listings of bookstores in the United States and Canada, with the address, phone number, and name of the manager/owner/buyer. Twenty thousand addresses is a little frightening and would take lots of time and effort to sift through, but is a great resource if you want the name of an outlet in a specific city.

A quicker way is to "rent" a mailing list from a list broker. You "rent" the list rather than buying it because what you get for your money is a set of addressed labels that you can use only once. Get all those sneaky thoughts about copying the list out of your head. In the first place, it is illegal and each list is seeded with decoy names so that the company can check on cheaters. In the second, it is cheaper and easier to rent the list a second time. A good list of 1,000 names costs between $35 and $100.

Direct mail is a very sophisticated business, and there are good list brokers and bad ones. *LMP* has listings. So does the *Directory of Mailing List Houses*, which has over 3,500 names of mailing list houses, brokers, and specialists. Rather than picking a name out of the blue, we suggest you talk to someone locally who has had experience with direct mail. An advertising agency executive or a department store marketing person will be able to recommend a dependable broker. A good list broker will supply a list that is up to date and accurate.

If you are interested in assembling your own list, you can ask retail customers to give you the names of possible outlets in their area. You could include a mail-back card in each book sold or in retail brochures. An organization can ask its membership for names and addresses; each person who supplies the names of five stores that become accounts can win one free cookbook.

A direct mail house will do the whole thing for you for a fee: design the brochure, write the copy, select the target, mail the brochure, and analyze the results. If you have more money than manpower, this can be the way to go, but if you want to handle it yourself, rent a list from a broker. You can get almost any kind of list: bookstores by state or region, gourmet shops, specialty food stores, large stores, small stores—even lists tailored to your specifications combining other lists. To choose a list you should make a long-range plan. Don't just mail to the first 500 names you can get. Target one area, then move on, after analyzing your success rate.

When you rent a list, you get a set of addressed labels. Labels come in two types: pressure sensitive, which you peel off a roll and apply to the brochure or envelope, and Cheshire labels, which require a special machine to apply and are used by list houses and companies that do great quantities of direct mailings. Be sure to specify which type of label you want. All lists come in zip code order.

There is a formula to successful direct mail advertising. First, you have to have a good list. Second, you have to have a good promotional piece that is eye-catching and informative. The third factor is timing. You can have the list of the century and a gorgeous brochure and mail it out on January first, and you just wasted money. January is "dead time" for the wholesale business; store owners are taking inventory and cleaning house. For the spring wholesale market, do mailings in February and March. For the Christmas market, mail in August and September. The biggest shopping day of the year is the one right after Thanksgiving. If store owners are to be ready for their customers they need adequate time to have their shipments processed and delivered by the wholesaler.

The fourth factor in the wholesale direct mail formula is frequency. Experts say that 2 percent is a good return for a mailing. That may not sound like much, but when the same mailing is repeated three to four weeks later, the return may jump as much as 12 percent. It's the old "Where did I hear of this before?" angle. The first time the bookseller may pay no attention to the mailing, but the second time it looks familiar. He wonders where he heard of this book. Was a customer asking for it? Better order a few copies.

Of course, you must also consider your budget. The good part about direct mail advertising is that it is a totally controllable expense and one on which you can figure your return nearly exactly: printing the brochure cost $200, the list rental was $50, the postage was $75. Within a short period of time you will have the results and know how many orders you received from that mailing. This kind of accountability lets you know quickly what works. Did more gourmet shops than bookstores place orders?

Did more orders come from small cities than from large ones? You can expand on these strengths in the next mailing. Some people have even sent two different types of brochures to test which has the greater drawing appeal. Testing is an excellent idea in direct mail.

To sum up, remember the formula for successful direct mail: a good list, an effective brochure, correct timing, planned frequency, and budgeting. Of course you will remember what we have said before: always use a coded coupon so you can analyze the effectiveness of your effort.

When you plan the budget, plan the time, too. If you want to do a wholesale mailing for the Christmas market, work backward from the projected mailing date (say August 15), and estimate how long it will take you to find a good list, get the brochures printed, and handle the actual mailing. You must be prepared to handle the orders as they come in, too, with enough books on hand and enough manpower to process the orders.

Some nonprofit groups get mailing lists by swapping with other groups, and this is a money saver. Frankly, we've heard both good and bad reports. One group had what looked like an excellent list that turned out to be a disaster. The list had not been cleaned in several years, and over half the pieces came back labeled: "Address unknown," or "No longer in business."

Several thoughts on some ideas that have been given to either increase your return or analyze results in direct mail. It has been proven that a "postage paid" return card will directly increase your response. It costs a little, but always remember that you will be paying the postage only for concrete orders—a small price to pay. Also, many people add their own name or the name of a friend to the mailing in order to see when the piece was actually delivered.

The best list you will ever find is your own. You can't use a rented list more than once, but every store that makes an order becomes your customer. Over the years you will develop your own list, which becomes invaluable. If you don't have access to a computer or automatic addressing equipment, you can type a "master list" of all your accounts and have the list run off on labels when you need it.

Those cookbook publishers who have had the most success with direct mail have established a long-range plan and a budget. Say you start with a February mailing to 500 book and gourmet stores in Florida, Georgia, and the Carolinas, and repeat the same mailing one month later. After you've saturated that market, you move on, with an August mailing to 500 stores in Virginia, Maryland, Delaware, and the District of Columbia, followed by the September follow-up. This way you can build a basis of accounts and broaden your market.

Target your market and establish timetables and budgets for a direct mail effort.

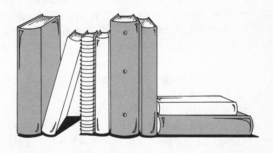

## Retail Direct Mail

The approach here, as we've said, is to tell the individual buyers what the book can do for them:

Make you a better hostess or cook
Save you money
Save you time and effort
Teach you something you don't know
Make a wonderful gift for hostess, teacher, friend
Make you feel better, lose weight, be healthy
Should be on every collector's shelf

Lists for retail mailing are harder to come by and are likely to be much more expensive than wholesale lists.

To date, we haven't heard anything good about those lists of individuals available through brokers, but we understand that some of the cooking magazines are beginning to rent lists of people they say are cookbook buyers. These lists may be worth a try.

Again, the best list is your own, and that takes some time to assemble. The first source of names is the pink invoices you filed from books already sold. Why, if they've already bought one, should you bother to send them a mailing? They are the very people most likely to give the book as a gift.

You can make up lists from church directories, club memberships, school directories, lists of symphony sponsors, advertisers in a charity program. Organizations frequently swap lists of this kind successfully. Analyze the potential of any list you get for your book. Members of a jogging club might be a good market for a nutrition-related cookbook but not for one on chocolate desserts.

Retail mailings should be made on a different time schedule than wholesale. The biggest shopping day of the year is the day after Thanksgiving. A retail mailing should go out in late October or early November, reaching buyers as they make their Christmas lists. A spring mailing might go out in March or April for a special sale. A retail mailing might be tied to a particular promotional idea: "Great ideas for summer picnics," "Christmas gift ideas by the dozens"; or tied to an event: "Featured in *Good Housekeeping*," or "New printing."

Of course you'll code this mailing, too, but it may be harder to tally the results. The flyer may cause someone to go into a store and buy the book and you won't know the cause of the sale. You will receive a response from the retail mailing within one week, and within two weeks, 50 to 70 percent of the results will be in. Convenience is the main reason that people buy through direct mail, and they will order pretty quickly.

One retail sale leads to another through the coupons in the back of the book, so the spin-offs from a retail mailing may keep on coming in. There are three keys to success in a retail direct mail effort:

*First*, the quality of the list. Is it pure? Is it current? Is it the correct audience?

*Second*, the correct timing of the mailing.

*Third*, the quality of the mailing piece.

A 2 percent response is considered good for retail direct mail, but don't forget the long-term spin-offs. By 1985, direct mail was expected to sell over $150 billion worth of goods and services. It is growing by 92 percent each year.

As with wholesale direct mail, offering ease of incentives will always increase results. One of the most effective means is to offer Master Card/Visa/charge card convenience. It is trouble but will increase the response. Some people have offered other incentives:

1. Post-paid reply envelope
2. Prepublication discount
3. Discount offered for orders received within a certain time frame
4. Discount to "first 500 who order"
5. Free trial examination for a fixed time
6. Refund offered if customer is not satisfied
7. Premiums (recipe cards, potholder, etc.)
8. Charge on major credit card allowed

If you decide to go into direct mail marketing, you should investigate a bulk mail permit. There are many varieties at different costs. Talk to your local postmaster.

Since the post office changes its rules frequently, check with your postmaster about savings, and also check the weight, size, and handling of your material.

Use the following checklist for direct mail marketing.

---

1. Decide general purpose and list
2. Decide printing process and cost
3. Select paper, design, and copy
4. Get printing estimates, choose printer
5. Get proofs
6. Receive finished brochure
7. Arrange for addressing and mailing
8. Judge returns

---

## Wholesale Marketing

Those independent publishers who have had the greatest success in wholesale marketing will tell you that they have tried many different methods to achieve their success. There is no one sure-fire key to big profits. You will learn what methods work for you and which are not worth the time and effort, but remember that marketing is an ongoing effort. Frequency and continuity are important. When you slack off in your promotion efforts, your sales will slack off.

Try different approaches, keeping records so you can analyze the results, but whatever you try, make it easy for your customer to buy your book. Always include a coded order card with all the pertinent information.

Although the biggest markets for cookbooks are bookstores and gift stores, almost anything can be a good market, as the following list indicates:

| | |
|---|---|
| Airports | Cooking schools |
| Gourmet shops | College bookstores |
| Specialty food stores | Military bases |
| Grocery stores | Conventions |
| Distributors | Special fund-raising events |
| Catalogs | General stores |
| Real estate companies | Unexpected places— |
| Florists | trout farms, |
| Hotels and resorts | filling stations, etc. |
| Restaurants | |

Any retail outlet that can and will sell cookbooks is a potential account. One warning: the gift industry is different from the book industry. Gift stores are used to a higher discount than the standard 40 percent on books, and you may run into a buyer who says that he would like to carry your book, but he *always* gets a 50 percent or more discount. Don't do it. It's not fair to the bookstores. If you establish a pricing schedule (including volume discounts), stick to it. This happens less often now that gift stores are aware of the popularity of cookbooks. You *must* charge the same basic price for everyone.

Your approach to all wholesale accounts must be professional. They are used to dealing with big businesses, so all your correspondence, brochures, order forms, and invoices must be professional. There are three ways to meet your market: a personal visit, publicity and advertising, and direct mail. Whatever you do must be done in a businesslike and efficient fashion.

*Distributors*: Some self-publishers don't want to handle the distribution themselves and prefer to use *distributors* or *wholesalers*. Some large stores and chains that do big volume business don't want to deal with 500 purchase orders for 500 independent publishers and prefer to deal only with distributors. Distributors are middlemen and work on a small margin. They buy from you at 50 percent (sometimes more) off retail price and sell to bookstores at 40 percent. You have to figure your profit margin exactly to know if you can afford this. There are all sorts of distributors—regional and national ones, specialized ones, and good and bad ones. Some of the big nationwide distributors have other requirements, too: you pay the shipping, you pay a sizable fee to be included on their microfiche lists, and you are required to pay for co-op advertising.

If you decide to use a distributor, don't look to them for all the promotion. They will include you in their catalog, but you still need to promote your book yourself. A good distributor will tell you that you must continue your own promotion.

Most book publishers don't go with distributors originally because they want more profits at first. Be warned that if you already have a lot of accounts, you may lose some when you go to a distributor. Stores will buy from a distributor instead of an independent publisher because it is easier for them and they get the same discount. You may lose some accounts that you had at 40 percent when they go with a distributor that buys from you at 50 percent plus prepaid freight. However, there's always the good news and the bad news. The good news: you may pick up a hundred new accounts.

You need to know your own profit margin, and you need to investigate the distributors. Ask for a list of their clients (suppliers) and ask a thousand questions. You can use several distributors simultaneously—regional and national ones. However, the secret of a distributor is volume sales, and you can spread yourself too thin. Never give a distributor exclusive rights. Talk to bookstore owners to find out which ones they use and which ones are dependable. Contact several distributors and ask for their rates and their catalogs. Talk to their customers and be careful. There are some very real horror stories about distributors placing big orders and not paying their bills. However, there are also many good distributors. The advantage to using one is the saving in manpower and space for storing books. The secret to success in this field is *big* volume. You have to analyze what you need and can expect.

*Agents or reps*: Once again, there are reps and there are reps. A representative or agent sells books in a particular territory, just like the sales reps for the big publishing companies. They sell the books to the dealers and open accounts for you, but you still handle the actual shipping. Some reps may not want to handle just one title, preferring to work for large or small publishers with longer lists. Their percentages usually work out to about 50 percent, too. If a rep has opened an account for you, it is his account forever; every time the store orders from you, even if he hasn't called on the store again, you have to pay the rep his percentage. You usually pay his percentage once a month or once a quarter.

If you want to use a rep, ask the bookstore owner which ones he recommends. If you use a rep in one territory and it works out well for you, and you want to expand this market, ask him to recommend someone in another territory. Book reps are also listed in *LMP*. If you chose to use one, ask for a list of his customers and call them with your questions.

*The telephone*: People tend to forget one of the simplest

marketing tools: the telephone. Now that the cost of long distance service is competitive, the telephone becomes even more attractive. Nonprofit organizations can frequently persuade a local company with a WATS line to give them the use of it in available hours.

It's very effective to send press kits to editors, then call them, or to do a direct mailing, then follow up with phone calls. The telephone is a good way to keep up with regular accounts; call every two or three months and say, "Don't you need to reorder?" It is also a most effective way to collect delinquent accounts.

If you can't be there in person to call on an account, the telephone is the next best thing.

*Catalogs*: Mail order shopping has become such a major force in the American marketplace that getting a good catalog account can mean big money and can sell your book coast to coast. There are many kinds and types of catalogs, put out by book and gift stores, mail order houses, book clubs, and stamp companies (to name just a few).

Getting into one of the big ones usually takes either incredible luck or "knowing someone," but some self-publishers have gotten in through sheer persistence. A catalog company will ask a percentage higher than the standard 40 percent and call it by different terms, but this is standard, and once you get in, it takes very little effort; just ship them large orders periodically.

List of catalogs can be obtained from list brokers and there is a directory of catalogs that can be found in the library. Be sure you know what you're getting into; you don't want your book to end up next to a porn magazine. Ask to *see* a copy of the catalog if you're not familiar with it, and talk to others who have been included to see if the company orders regularly and pays its bills.

To get into a catalog, tie your book into their theme; for example, make a collage of game recipes as a sales tool for a hunting catalog. To sell your book to catalogs, stress its uniqueness. You might offer them an exclusive for one season.

*Advertising*: Here, too, there's the good news and the bad news. Nonprofit organizations should certainly take advantage of the availability of public service time on radio and TV, and billboards, too. Ads in newspapers and magazines can be terribly expensive, and most self-publishers have found the results disappointing. (Of course, if you do it, you will remember to put a key in the ad so you can check results.) Ads are really aimed at retail buyers, and the results may be hard to track because people will see an ad, then buy from a bookstore. It's one more way of getting your book's name before the public.

Advertising in book trade journals is a way to reach wholesale accounts. The main ones are *Publishers Weekly*, *American Bookseller*, *Gift & Decorative Accessories*, and *Entrée*.

If your book is aimed at a specialized audience, like health food addicts, or Armenians, or hikers, or lovers of artichokes, an ad in a trade association journal or club magazine will make sense.

Another frequently used tool is *co-operative advertising*. A store will run an ad for your book, saying that it is available at their store, and split the cost with you. You could offer co-op advertising as an incentive to get a big new account. Be careful not to offer this to 600 small bookstores; they might all take you up on it at once.

## Incentives for New Accounts

When you are going after new accounts, remember that there are certain points you can emphasize about the salability of the book. The first is the uniqueness of your book—why it is special, what makes it different or better, what special audience will want to buy it. Stress, too, the super sales records of cookbooks; many bookstore owners say that cookbooks pay the rent, that they are the one class of books that almost never ends up on the sale table. Cookbooks are a most versatile product; they appeal to cooks and cookbook collectors and are the perfect gift for weddings, showers, graduations, birthdays, Mother's and Father's Days, Christmas, Hanukkah, get-well, thank you, housewarming, favors, and anything else you can think of. A book is easy to wrap, easy to mail, easy to carry.

Service is another thing that you can sell. Stress quick delivery and attention to orders and correspondence. Independent publishers have the advantage here over most large publishing companies.

There are several other incentives you can offer to get a new account. They include:

Free shipping for a predetermined number (12 or more)
Free shipping with prepaid orders
Free shipping for a new account, first order
S.T.O.P. (S.C.O.P) orders*
Order six books, bill for five (etc.)
Free book display with first order
2 percent discount for early payment

Bookstores operate on a slim margin with lots of overhead and inventory. Postage and shipping have gotten to be dirty words. Postal rates have gone up an unbelievable 350 percent since 1970, while book prices haven't. Today it costs the stores more to sell books because of this jump in rates. Here's a comparison:

|                       | 1970   | 1984   |
|-----------------------|--------|--------|
| Retail price of book  | $6.00  | $7.00  |
| Wholesale price       | 3.60   | 4.20   |
| Postage               | .49    | 1.10   |
|                       |        |        |
| Cost to store         | 4.09   | 5.30   |
| Profit to store       | $1.91  | $1.70  |

You can see why offering to pay postage/shipping for certain orders can be very appealing. To offer this, you have to put pencil to paper and make sure that you can afford to do it. If you can, it's a great incentive.

Offering six books for the price of five, or twelve for the price of eleven is like offering volume dicounts on a small scale, or offsetting the shipping costs. You have to know if you can afford to make the offer, and then offer it only for a limited time, or only to new accounts.

* S.T.O.P. = Single Title Order Plan; S.C.O.P. = Single Copy Order Plan.

A S.T.O.P. order or Single Title Order Plan (sometimes known as S.C.O.P. for Single Copy Order Plan) is now accepted industrywide. It means that a bookseller can buy a single copy of your book at the regular 40 percent wholesale discount. In order to receive the special order, the bookseller prepays, enabling you to process the order at a saving and eliminate billing. There are many advantages to this plan. It allows a bookseller to order one copy when a customer requests the book, and it allows the bookseller to see a copy of the book, which may lead to more wholesale orders. Store owners have said that they almost always order a book after they have seen it and been assured of its quality and sales potential.

This adds one more category to your wholesale bookkeeping, but it is a minor inconvenience. The postage and handling on these orders are the same as for retail orders. If you decide to do this, always include a wholesale order form in the book package. Include the information about S.T.O.P. order availability on wholesale promotional material. Simply add a line that says, "We accept prepaid S.T.O.P. orders. Please add $1.50 [or whatever you charge] for postage."

Another incentive to booksellers is a display, which can be as simple as a poster or as elaborate as a free-standing rack for the books. We've seen inexpensive racks that hold six or twelve copies that allow the dealer to display your book prominently. We also heard one tale about a group who had a member design an elaborate cardboard book rack. It was large and attractive, and the group paid to have thirty of them constructed. They took the displays proudly to their best accounts, only to discover that the thing was unsteady on its feet and too big to fit in most stores' aisles. We don't suggest you do something elaborate, but you can offer a bookseller a banner, a cardboard tent to sit on the counter, a poster that fits on the back of the cash register or in the window—anything that helps him sell your book and attract attention to it.

Nonprofit organizations have used the method of "trip kits" in order to have their members obtain new accounts for them. You can do this yourself, or you might press

SINGLE
TITLE
ORDER
PLAN

DO NOT BACK ORDER

PACKING LIST

DATE _____
LIST PRICE EACH   $ _____
TOTAL LIST PRICE $ _____
DISCOUNT _____ %
NET PRICE        $ _____
POSTAGE          $ _____
**TOTAL**        $ _____

FROM | PUBLISHER

SHIPPING LABEL

ORDER NO._____

SPECIAL FOURTH CLASS RATE - BOOKS

**TO** | BOOKSELLER        SAN # _____

| QTY | ISBN | AUTHOR | TITLE |
|-----|------|--------|-------|
|     |      |        |       |
|     |      |        |       |

INSTRUCTION TO PUBLISHERS:

1. Complete information in upper right hand corner and on check, if necessary. Price information is essential and urgent.

2. Use shipping label above and enclose packing list at top of form.

3. If book cannot be shipped, check reason below. Return this entire form with check to bookseller.

☐ Out of stock until _____  ☐ Price increase to $ _____  ☐ Not our publication

☐ Out of print  ☐ Value of check too low  ☐ Not yet published

Other _____

© Copyright American Booksellers Association, Inc. 1975

your friends into service with this plan. A "trip kit" is exactly that—a traveling sales kit. Prepare a packet in a bright folder or a tote bag for people to take with them on out-of-town trips. In it put a copy of the book, the wholesale brochure, fact sheets, and testimonials (some of the same ingredients that are in the press kit), plus order forms. A group or person might keep two or three trip kits handy and let people or members check them out like library books. Trip kit in hand, you call on stores (resort and hotel gift shops are naturals) as you travel.

Contests and prizes are another way to get new accounts. Offer free cookbooks or gifts to friends or members of your organization for opening new accounts.

## Taking Care of Old Accounts

Whatever happens, don't ignore your old accounts just because they are there; never take them for granted. They are your bread and butter, and if you don't take care of them, there is someone out there with a cookbook who will. It has been said that when a successful salesman makes ten calls, one is to a potential customer and the other nine are to established accounts. A store may order a box of books from you, but when those are sold, you may be forgotten. It's up to you to remind them. Old accounts are responsible for 80 percent of your business, so stay in touch. There are several ways to do this.

Always put a reorder card in every box of books you ship. It's a good idea to mail reorder cards every several months as standard practice.

Let them know of any new decisions or new ideas: a story in a magazine, a new printing, and of course, a price change.

Send a letter at least once a year. If you don't have a reason to write, make one up—or simply thank them for being such a good and valued account. Thanking the store for the business is always a good reason to write and it's superb public relations.

Telephone if you can; it's a most effective way to keep in touch. Certainly you can call all your local accounts regularly.

## Retail Marketing

Retail means that the book sells for the last time to the customer, who will either use it or give it away. Retail sales will account for about 20 to 25 percent of your business. Some people might say, "Why bother? It makes

more sense to spend your efforts on wholesale marketing," but one retail sale leads to another, as satisfied users
talk about the book. Remember that 80 percent of all books
sold are sold by word of mouth, so everything you do is
aimed at getting people talking about your book. Retail
sales frequently lead to wholesale accounts when a customer walks into a store and asks for a book she has
heard about. Also, retail sales mean higher percentages
of the profit for you, as well as greater ease in handling
the orders.

All the things we've been talking about—radio and television appearances, cooking demonstrations, stories in
newspapers and magazines, ads—are directed at the retail
buyer. The most effective retail tool of all is the re-order
forms printed in the back of the book. Every book should
have a page or two of reorder forms in the back. If you
have published two books, the form can advertise both
of them. Whenever one of these is sent in, three or four
more go out, so that retail sales go on and on.

There are three rules that we think should never be
broken in retail marketing.

1. *Target your market.* Use the rifle approach instead of
the shotgun, and aim directly at the customer who will
buy the book. To do that, you must define your market
by building a consumer profile.

Do not assume that you are selling only to women.
Men make about one third of the food purchasing decisions today. Generally, cookbook buyers are between the
ages of 25 and 45, have a high education level and rela-
tively high incomes. They have the money to make im-
pulse purchases, and limited discretionary time. Jerry
DiVecchio, food and wine editor of *Sunset* magazine, says,
"The fascination of the public for books on cookery has
more to do with the vicarious pleasure of reading than
with the use of the books as technical guides. Cookbooks
that reflect the views, tastes, and experiences of the author
are more likely to appeal to these armchair readers."

Cookbooks have an existing market which means that
the awareness level already exists. Unlike some groups

that have to search out and/or create their own markets, cookbook publishers don't have to create an interest in their product—the interest is already there. By conservative estimates there are in this country over 300,000 cookbook collectors who may never go into a kitchen but want to buy every book that is new and different. Both cookbook users and collectors never seem to have too many; one good cookbook deserves another.

To further draw your own consumer profile, talk to booksellers about who buys cookbooks. Talk to your friends about what appeals to them and attracts their attention. Aim your marketing efforts directly at the potential buyer.

2. *Select a combination of strategies* to reach that buyer. No single medium reaches the entire market. Don't sink all the available money into one plan; try a variety of techniques. When you find something that works well, stick with it. If your direct mail brochure is good, use it again and again until it is really outdated. The recognition factor increases your chances of success, particularly when one method of promotion is combined with another.

3. *Determine your product differentiation.* Decide what separated your book from the competition, and keep telling the public about it. Unfortunately, what most self-publishers do is to sell the same way everyone else does. Try to discover the essential difference that sets your book apart and market that.

Think about some of the famous ad campaigns:

"Where's the beef?"—Wendy's
"Melts in your mouth, not in your hand"—M&M's
"The ketchup that loses the race"—Heinz

These companies are touting what makes their product different and therefore memorable. You must do this, too.

Sometimes the differentiation is automatically there if your theme reflects a place, an event, a heritage, a type of cooking. Sometimes the differentiation is within the cookbook in some of the following ways:

+ Triple-tested recipes
+ Microwave conversions

- Outstanding index
- Beautiful artwork
- Elegant and/or interesting menus

What you must do is identify this special characteristic and build on it.

Slightly different from product differentiation is "positioning," which simply means selecting a place in the market, positioning your book there, and constantly reminding the public.

All of Julia Child's books reflect her special position as a cook and television personality.

*River Road Recipes* automatically positioned itself as the leader of community cookbooks by selling the most.

*Tout de Suite* positioned itself as the first cookbook to adapt French cuisine to the microwave.

*Sassafras!* by the Junior League of Springfield, Missouri, positioned itself as "The Ozarks Cookbook."

When you determine the special quality of your book, promotional ideas will follow naturally. Antique shops would be a natural outlet for a book stressing old-time recipes and nostalgia (*Nutbread & Nostalgia*). A cookbook full of game recipes should be promoted in a hunter's magazine (*Quail Country*). A picnic cookbook should be advertised to football fans, to hikers and campers, and seasonally, for summer (*Picnics in the Park*).

There are special "come-ons" for the retail market, too, like:

Free gift wrapping
Free postage with large order
Coupon discounting
Buy one, get the next one at half price
Product offers (aprons, recipe cards, mitts)
Coupon accompanying check will be placed
  in a drawing for a prize
Volume discounting
Christmas gift wrapping and mailing (the customer
  sends addresses and you send books to gift list).

A good appproach to take in retail direct mail is the special sale in the spring or winter. Once a year, offer the book at a discount, using a coupon with an expiration date to measure the response.

The "blow card" is another tool. You know how magazines drive you crazy with all those cards that fall out on the floor? Nonetheless, you do have to pick them up and look at them, if only to throw them away. Blow cards with reorder coupons can be inserted in everything that goes out. If you have written two books, be sure to let one book help sell the other. Insert blow cards and coupons in the back of both books so that you can capitalize on both lists of customers.

One of the smartest uses of television we know of comes from a friend of ours. Whenever she travels, she makes it a point to arrange an appearance on a television talk show. She writes a letter and sends information, then follows up with a phone call to arrange the date for her appearance. Then she smiles sweetly at the camera, gives the ordering address, and says, "Any orders postmarked within forty-eight hours of today get free postage and handling." She makes a point of leaving the address and information at the station's switchboard. At the same time, she reaches the wholesale market by calling or writing to stores in the area, telling of the TV appearance and asking if she can mention the store on the air as a place to buy the book. One hundred percent of the stores contacted respond yes and order books prior to the program.

Your objective is to slowly build your own retail market from all the ideas above. It takes time and it is more expensive to reach the retail customer, but the market will expand itself as the word spreads about your book.

## Special Sales

Special sales are the wave of the future for cookbooks; in fact, some big publishing companies now have whole departments in charge of special sales. This is a hybrid between wholesale and retail. You sell the book for the last time to someone who is going to give it away, but you sell in volume with a discount. For example, a real estate company buys several boxes of books and gives one to each new home buyer or to each person who visits a new development on open-house day. A cookbook is a much more lasting present than a potted plant. An appliance store offers a cookbook to everyone who buys a new freezer during the month of May. A shop gives a cookbook to every bride who registers her china and silver patterns there.

The possibilities are endless. Think of all the premiums that businesses are using now. Banks are constantly giving away things to attract new accounts. If they can give away soup bowls and stuffed animals, why not a cookbook. A bank in Kalamazoo, Michigan, proudly gave *"I've Got a Cook in Kalamazoo!"* with a sticker that said, "You've Got a Bank in Kalamazoo." Department stores offer gifts to customers whose charge accounts have been inactive. Stores offer prizes to the first fifty customers on a special sale day.

Then there is the Christmas market. Think of the number of businesses that send something to their customers once a year. Then think of some of the useless things they send, like paperweights and plastic items, or things that are soon gone and forgotten, like fruitcakes, nuts, or cookies. Who do you know who wouldn't rather have a cookbook than a poinsettia? A company could simply give you their customer list, and you could offer to gift-wrap and mail. All they have to do is write you a nice check and wait for all the thank-you's.

Another fertile field for special sales is the convention market, since some kind of favor is always given there. What better souvenir of your city than a regional cookbook, a wonderful advertisement that goes home in everyone's suitcase.

Hotels that send a basket of fruit to VIP guests could include a cookbook as a permanent reminder of their hospitality.

Visiting executives could be given a cookbook instead of or with a flower arrangement by their hosts.

Salesmen who travel could take cookbooks as gifts to the people they call on.

A cookbook can be personalized so that it is an advertisement for the giver every time it is used. For a nominal charge, a personalized page can be inserted at the binding stage. A pressure-sensitive sticker with a company's logo can be applied to the cover. A cigar-band wrapper with "Compliments of————" can be put on each book.

A phone call to a company will tell you who is in charge of selecting gifts. Make an appointment and do your best selling job. You sell the book at a price between wholesale and retail. The more the company buys, the greater the discount. If a company buys over a period of time rather than all at once, offer to keep a record and allow a cumulative discount on books sold within one year. The local Office of Tourism or the Convention and Visitors Bureau can give you a list of conventions scheduled in the coming year. You need to contact them early, as planning is done well in advance. Look for firms that do meeting management or convention planning; with one contact there you might be able to sell to several conventions.

If there is a natural tie-in between your book and an industry or an event, use it: for example, *Through the Grapevine* from Elmira, New York, and the vineyards of upstate New York; or *Jambalaya*, the "official" cookbook of the New Orleans World's Fair. *A Texas Experience* was designated the official 1984 GOP Convention cookbook and a copy was put in every delegate's bag. A sticker on the front can proudly proclaim the tie-in, and there are opportunities for regular as well as special sales.

Let's look at one more opportunity for special sales: premiums. A premium is using one product to sell another (remember why you used to buy Crackerjacks?). Look in your pantry right now and see how many products are making special offers. Why not cookbooks? Jeno's Pizza offered a choice of Bantam paperbacks to anyone who sent in one dollar and the coupon from a box. (Think of the fabulous advertising Bantam got on 12 million frozen pizza packages! And think of the pizzas it sold.) If Kraft's mayonnaise can offer a kitchen clock for so many labels, and Scott paper towels can offer steak knives with so many wrappers, you can do it, too. It has already worked for the Junior League of Pasadena—so many raisin boxes plus $7.95 brings you a copy of the *California Heritage Cookbook*. *Putting on the Grits* from the Junior League of Columbia, S.C., has a tie-in with a company that manufactures grits. Cookbooks are a natural! Contact the marketing department or the ad agency for a product, and tell them why your book will help boost their sales.

## Product Tie-Ins

If one book sells another, there are other products that can be used to increase sales and attract attention.

*A Man's Taste* sold an apron cut like pants that said, "I wear the pants in this kitchen" and carried the book's logo.

*Quail Country* printed its outstanding artwork on note cards and sold them. They also sold tote bags with the quail design on it.

*Applehood & Motherpie* sold sets of recipe cards with the apple design across the bottom.

Products like these make wonderful advertisements for the book, spreading its fame wherever they go. Additional items can make your book more appealing to stores and create an attractive display in a prominent place in the store. There are many possibilities:

| | |
|---|---|
| Aprons | Metric table |
| Tote bags | Note cards |
| Pot holders | Stationery, postcards |
| Trivets | Cooking kit |
| Recipe files | Wine chart |
| Recipe cards | Herb chart |
| Dish towels | Cheese chart |

You've already got a market for whatever you think of to sell.

The latest development in our technological world is the cookbook on video cassette. You can demonstrate your recipes and techniques for the home viewer with a

VCR and market it, but you'd better look good and be able to talk and cook at the same time. Julia Child makes what she does look effortless, but hours of practice and preparation go into each show. A video cassette would be particularly appropriate for subjects like cake decorating, making sushi, or preparing elaborate hors d'oeuvres. This may be the wave of the future!

And don't forget: another cookbook will fit right into your system and the two books will help sell each other. But why restrict yourself to the kitchen? (Remember when we said to give your company a nonspecific name like ABC Publications so that you are free to expand in various directions?) Any subject that interests you can be the topic of your next book. Volunteer organizations can use their expertise for how-to books: how to put on a charity ball or a decorator show house, how to run a thrift shop or how to motivate volunteers. There are books on historic buildings, tour guides, books for children—books on every subject are being put out by self-publishers every day.

Finally, remember that even the best book will not sell itself without some help. Concentrate on the quality that makes your book special and stress it in everything you do. All of your promotional material needs to feature the uniqueness of your book and needs to be attention-getting and professional-looking. There are a million ways to reach the public. We hope we've started you on the way to some of them.

# CHAPTER 6

# Voluntary Organizations

THE NUMBER of nonprofit organizations that have entered the cookbook market with great success proves there must be something in it: Junior Leagues, cancer societies, symphony guilds, art museum support groups, hospital auxiliaries, church circles, even the U.S. Olympic Ski Team! One reason that these books do so well is that buyers know they are the compilation of many cooks and can be trusted.

All the material in the preceding chapters applies to group efforts as well as individuals, but volunteer groups have special strengths and weaknesses, special opportunities and problems that we want to treat in this chapter. We will discuss committee structures, volunteer training, job descriptions, office systems, and public relations in some detail.

## ADOPTING A COOKBOOK
## AS A PROJECT

When an organization considers publishing a cookbook the reason is usually the need for a fund-raiser, and certainly a good cookbook can supply big bucks for a needed project. There are other reasons that the cookbook can help an organization. Let's go over them again:

1. One of the most important benefits is the *public relations value*. A cookbook advertises your organization and

promotes the cause. Everywhere that book goes, your message goes. A cookbook can make your cause national as well as local.

2. *Career training* is a prime motivator for volunteers these days, and a cookbook business provides invaluable training in marketing and business skills that can be used either in the voluntary sector or to reenter the job market.

3. *Friendships* are made through working together. A well-run business with an exciting product creates esprit de corps.

4. A cookbook business is an *ongoing project*. Once the machinery is set up, it goes on and on, making money predictably. Unlike a charity ball, it is not a "one-time" thing and does not have to be started up again every year.

5. A cookbook is a *proven product*. The market is already there. Through seminars, consultants, and books like this one, a wealth of information is available to help you.

6. Finally, of course, there is the *profit motive*. A good book can be a bonanza for the cause.

An organization has certain avantages over the individual self-publisher. *Manpower* is certainly a big advantage; you have a variety of talents to draw upon, and many hands to do the work. The *reputation of the group* is another. People will support a cause that is worthwile, and the group and the individuals within it have entreé into certain areas that one person will not have. Also, there are many opportunities for *free publicity* that are available to nonprofits, like public service announcements on radio and TV, donated billboard space, large newspaper articles, and so on.

There are also pitfalls that a group must face. An *overworked membership* is one. What other requirements are there for the membership? Is there another big project going on simultaneously that requires membership commitment? These things must be looked at realistically. Another pitfall is volunteer turnover or *lack of continuity*. A new group of volunteers each year can spell trouble, but we think that a good system can circumvent this. Volunteer training is essential and can elimate the potential for problems.

## Presenting the Idea of a Cookbook to the Membership

It is important that the membership support the cookbook from the very beginning. A sure way to program a failure is to have the cookbook rammed through by a small group, so that the total membership has no commitment to the project. If the cookbook committee works in isolation and the membership is not kept informed, resentments can build up.

In presenting the cookbook as a new project to the group, give all the facts—the many good reasons for adopting it, the proposed budget and sources of financing, and the pitfalls, too. Be realistic in the presentation; if the membership can come back six months later and say, "You never told us this," or "We had no idea it would be like that," the cookbook is going to lose support before it gets started.

Make sure that the membership understands its obligations to the new project. One reason that we love cookbooks is that they are not parasites on the organization. The cookbook should be able to stand on its own in the market. In selling a cookbook, you are offering something to the buyer, not just asking for a donation. If the members think that they are going to be required to buy ten books each, they may feel negatively about the proposal. We know of one organization that spent a huge sum on artwork for a proposed book, and then told the members that each would be required to buy six books. The membership voted the project down, leaving the cookbook committee with a big bill and egg on its face.

If your organization decides on membership requirements toward a new book, don't force everyone to buy books. Offer the members options:

- Buying X number of books
- Working X number of hours in the office (wrapping books, mailing, addressing, etc.)

- Supplying names and addresses of X number of retail customers (credit given for sales)
- Supplying names and addresses of X number of wholesale accounts (credit given for actual sales)
- Supplying so many recipes or testing so many

# INTERNAL PUBLIC RELATIONS

We think internal public relations are most important, not only for a new book, but also for one that's been around a while. If you ask the groups that have been the most successful with their cookbooks, "How did you do it?" they are going to tell you, "We tried this and tried that, but mostly, we have the best book you ever saw!" They believe in their book.

There are many methods to get the group involved and excited.

- Skits at meetings
- A panel discussion of pros and cons (be prepared and show how much research you've done)
- A question-and-answer session at a meeting or in a mailing to the membership
- Charts and graphs of projected expenses and profits
- Articles in the news sheet, answering questions before they are asked
- Contests to name the book, supply the most recipes, supply the names of potential customers
- Refreshments at meetings for those who contribute recipes or names
- Parties for testing recipes
- Having the committee appear at each meeting wearing aprons to keep the idea of the cookbook constantly before the membership
- Posters promoting the book prominently displayed
- A regular column about cookbook happenings in the newsletter (Les Passées, a woman's club in Memphis and publishers of *Well Seasoned*, call theirs "Flour Power.")

- Spotlight members who go beyond the call (The Utility Club of Griffin, Georgia, publishers of *The Stuffed Griffin*, declare outstanding volunteers members of "The Order of the Wooden Spoon.")
- An open house to recruit volunteers for next year's committee
- Gift-wrapped books for sale at Christmas meetings

One of the best methods for attracting membership interest and attention is the questionnaire. Polling the membership serves other purposes, too. You have your own random sampling for market research, for in your membership you have a perfect cross-section of cookbook buyers (one group discovered that their members owned an average of twenty-six cookbooks each). Also, a cookbook should reflect the unique character of its publishers. How better to establish this than by a poll of the membership? You can find out what members like and dislike about cookbooks and get a consensus on policy decisions, like the inclusion of contributors' names. A questionnaire can collect positive and negative feedback and can start you on a book that will truly reflect the personality of the organization. Include a self-mailer with a deadline for the answers.

## SAMPLE QUESTIONS FOR THE MEMBERSHIP

1. What are your favorite cookbooks? Why?
2. What don't you like in a cookbook?
3. Suggest a theme or title for the book.
4. What draws you to a cookbook in a store?
5. Are there certain colors you like? Don't like?
6. What have you always wanted in a cookbook that you've never been able to find?
7. What do you consider a "reasonable" price?
8. Do you give cookbooks as gifts? What do you look for?
9. Should the names of contributors be included with the recipes? At the front of the book? Not at all?
10. Can you think of special events to promote the book?

One more thought about internal public relations. Once the cookbook committee decides on a theme and title, keep it a secret as long as possible. If the membership hears about it for too long, they may get bored with the idea. You can build up excitement by planning a special announcement day.

The important thing to remember is that throughout the cookbook's life—whether it is only a fledgling idea or a tried-and-true product—it must have the loyalty of the organization. Internal visibility is important to keep the cookbook alive and well.

# FINANCING

Again, organizations have resources available to them that individuals frequently lack. The reason that nonprofit groups can make a profit on a book priced at 3-to-1 margins is the "no cost" volunteer labor—and that is invaluable.

Most groups finance their books by setting up a special account, borrowing money from the treasury, and paying the loan back as sales begin.

A special one-time fund-raiser like a party could be used to raise the needed money.

One group borrowed money from a group of supporters to print the first edition of the book. The loans were paid back with interest from the sales. Then the "angels" donated the interest to the group and took a tax deduction.

Patrons and underwriters can be solicited. Again, the donation is deductible.

A "special edition" with a different cover was given to the patrons of one book. Such an edition could also be sold at a higher cost to cover expenses.

One group set aside the money raised at a benefit, invested it in a CD for two years while they worked on the book, and used the money and the profit to pay for the book.

Prepublication sales to the membership and patrons have been used to raise money.

Several groups have taken the original art used in the book and sold it at auction to make money.

The same rules for careful budgeting we gave for individuals apply to groups. Treasurer's reports have probably put more members to sleep than any other part of a meeting, but full accounting to the membership must be made if the membership is not to see the cookbook as a drain on the organization.

# COMMITTEE STRUCTURE

We want to suggest three committee structures for a new cookbook, two of which will be on-going. We are going to outline these in detail. Each group will need to make its own adaptations depending on available manpower.

First comes the *steering/policy committee*. This committee is empowered by the board of directors to make all decisions concerning the cookbook. The steering committee is made up of five to seven people: the general chairman and vice-chairman, the chairmen of the subcommittees, and perhaps a liaison from the executive committee of the organization, or one or two others appointed by the president or cookbook chairman, people who are able to make sound, objective decisions without "tunnel vision."

The steering committee begins at the time the cookbook is voted as a project and has the final say about all decisions—title, theme, artist, length, printer, publication date, and so on. After the cookbook is published and selling, this committee operates as a policy committee, making all those decisions which we outlined in Chapter 4.

As the cookbook goes on as a successful project year after year, the members of the steering/policy committee will change, but we recommend that the first general chairman stay in place for as long as it takes to get the book printed and on sale. After that, we are strong believers in the concept of a vice-chairman learning the job for a year before becoming chairman.

Under the steering committee are two other committees. The first committee is charged with creating the cookbook and seeing it through all the stages of publication. Its job is over the day that the cookbook comes off the press. The second committee is charged with selling the cookbook; its responsibilities begin in the last stages of the first committee's operations. This committee handles the marketing and business operations, and it becomes the on-going publications committee of the organization.

*Committee I* has two parts: recipe collecting and design. The recipe collecting subcommittee is in charge of collecting, testing, selecting, then writing, typing, editing, and proofing the recipes. The design subcommittee is in charge of the selection of the artist, design, cover, layout, art, indexing, and any additional text that is required. They oversee the book from the idea stage until it becomes a physical reality. Committee I begins when the cookbook is in the idea stage and dissolves when the book goes to the printer for the last time during the initial printing.

Committee I is made up of creative people: the gourmet genius, the famous hostess, the talented artist, the people who love to be in on something new and different. This committee also needs some people who are organized and meticulous to write, edit, and proof the recipes.

*Committee II* also has two parts: marketing and operations. Their job is to get rid of the product which Committee I has so lovingly assembled. Their work begins when Committee I is in the last stages of its operations, or four to six months before the official publication date. The marketing group begins to lay its plans for the kickoff, plans and orders the promotional material, and gets ready to sell the book. The operations group sets up business systems and is ready to go into action the day of the first sale.

Committee II is made up of supersalesmen, assertive

types who develop schemes to sell the book. It is the place for the business brains and the math whizzes.

As you can see, these committees are made up of different breeds of people, which is one reason a cookbook is such a good opportunity for volunteer placement—there is a place for everyone.

Sometimes, during the stages of publication, tempers grow short and egos grow long. Sometimes the members of Committee I can become like protective mothers: having created and given birth to the book, they cannot bear to see it leave. A major pitfall is that the members of Committee I simply will not let go. Make sure that the committee members understand on the front end that their jobs belong to one of the definite stages of development of the product.

Here are two charts to differentiate the responsibilities. In small organizations, one person will double up on jobs. In a large organization with a lot of manpower, many people can get involved. The point is that each responsibility needs to be defined and assigned.

Board of Directors
|
Steering/Policy Committee
|
Cookbook Chairman
|

| Committee I | | Committee II | |
| --- | --- | --- | --- |
| RECIPES | DESIGN | MARKETING | OPERATIONS |
| Collection | | Kick-off party | Bookkeeper |
| Testing | | Promotional | Wholesale |
| Selection | | material | orders |
| | | Retail sales | Retail orders |
| | | Wholesale sales | |

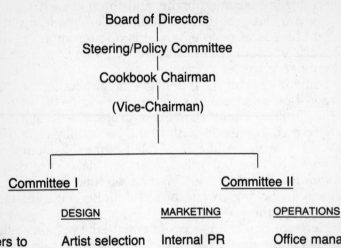

Board of Directors

Steering/Policy Committee

Cookbook Chairman

(Vice-Chairman)

Committee I

| RECIPES | DESIGN |
|---------|--------|
| Volunteers to collect and test recipes | Artist selection |
| Selection of recipes | Author of text |
| Typists | Indexer |

Committee II

| MARKETING | OPERATIONS |
|-----------|------------|
| Internal PR | Office manager |
| Press kits | Bookkeeper |
| Promotional design | Treasurer/banker |
| Direct mail | Credit manager |
| Presentations (TV, radio, etc.) | Wholesale staff |
| VIP solicitations | Retail staff |
| Premiums | Inventory coordinator |
| Local/regional sales | |
| Ads | |
| Pre-publication sales | |
| Kick-off chairman | |

# COOKBOOK PRODUCTION CALENDAR
# FOR SELF-PUBLISHING

1985

| September | October | November |
|---|---|---|
| *Idea!* | *✳Committee I begins✳* | |
| **December** | **January** | **February** |
| | | |
| **March** | **April** | **May** |
| | | |
| **June** | **July** | **August** |
| | | |

1986

1986

| September | October | November |
|---|---|---|
| | *Manuscript finished* | *Bids (self-pub.)* |
| **December** | **January** | **February** |
| *Manuscript to publisher or printer* | *✳Committee II begins✳* | |
| **March** | **April** | **May** |
| | | |
| **June** | **July** | **August** |
| | | |

1987

# VOLUNTEER JOB DESCRIPTIONS

In order to run a more effective organization, please consider the advantages of written job descriptions for each volunteer job, project chairman, and board position. Outline exactly what is expected of each volunteer in her job. Here are some very convincing reasons to go to the trouble of creating a written description for each job:

1. There will be no misunderstanding of responsibilities, and the volunteer will know exactly what to expect.
2. There will be no volunteer "overlap" and confusion.
3. By offering a built-in system of protection for the turnover time in volunteer jobs, a new person, each year, knows what her job is to be.
4. When absenteeism occurs, a new person can "sub" with some background knowledge and direction.
5. It avoids the problems implicit in the total reliance on verbal communication, such as forgotten items or omitted steps.
6. This system gives a measure of accountability for each job.

## Guidelines for Job Descriptions

Each task or job should have a concise formal title.
The job description should include the following categories:

Job title
Job summary
Duties
Skills required (optional)
Skills gained (optional)

The job summary should begin with the phrase "primarily responsible for" and follow with several concise sentences outlining the scope of the job.

The duties should be listed in descending order of importance. It is usually better to list rather than write in paragraph form.

The description should use action verbs to show the action in a job as opposed to a "state of being." Say "Serves on the Board of Directors" instead of "Is on the Board of Directors."

You should make sure that the job description includes any other committees the volunteer may be required to serve on as part of her job. It should also include the length of time the job will be (six months, one year, etc.).

## SAMPLE JOB DESCRIPTION

JOB TITLE: Chairman

JOB SUMMARY: Primarily responsible for coordinating, directing, and supervising the overall concerted work activities of the publication committee.

TYPICAL DUTIES:
1. Serves as voting member of Board of Directors.
2. Initiates and executes committee goals, objectives, and policies.
3. Possesses thorough working knowledge of each committee job and its duties.
4. Devises and implements promotional concepts and marketing techniques.
5. Answers all committee correspondence not covered by form letters.
6. Signs checks, contracts, bonds, etc., in name of organization.
7. Controls committee personnel problems.
8. Assists Vice-Chairman in processing purchase orders.
9. And/or other duties as may be assigned.

Try to use titles that are appealing rather than technical, and make sure that the volunteer knows to whom she is accountable.

In the proposed committee structures, definite duties should be assigned to each person. The *general chairman* oversees the entire operation, from creation to publication and marketing. In the case of a new book, she is frequently given the title of editor, although some books list several editors and/or use outside people. In an already published book, she is the "company president," who oversees the responsibilities of the committee. She should be the long-range planner who formalizes objectives and is the chief policy maker who has charge of final decisions affecting the cookbook and the entire committee.

Ideally, she should sit on the board of directors and the finance committee (if you have one). She represents the board to the cookbook committee, and the cookbook committee to the board. She should be highly visible in the group.

She sets the schedules and timetables, and handles the bidding and contracts with the printer (assisted by the design/format person). She holds general cookbook meetings, handles correspondence, financial needs, general business matters, and personnel matters. All the committee chairmen report regularly to her.

She should be good with people, tactful, organized, and articulate (sounds almost too perfect). She should be a leader, a facilitator and motivator of people. The membership often judges the cookbook on how they feel about the chairman, so ideally she should be someone who commands attention and respect.

She should be slated by the nominating committee or appointed by the president. The vice-chairman serves for a training year before becoming a chairman. We think this is very important. The year as vice-chairman should be spent learning the workings of the entire system, keeping up with all activities, and making plans for the next year.

The *recipe chairman* is responsible for collecting and testing recipes, as well as for selecting the final ones. She is responsible for the final form of the recipes given to the printer; this includes typing, editing, and so on. The final decision about which recipes are selected is up to the committee, which she chairs. She should be organized and a good cook with a "feel" for food and entertaining.

Her committee might consist of *category chairmen*, if enough volunteers are available, each of whom is responsible for one category or chapter, like Beverages, Appetizers, Breads, etc. Each category chairman would be responsible for filling any void or shortage in her section, as well as for the actual testing of the recipes. She calls the contributor of the recipe if there are any questions.

An alternate plan for this committee is organization into *testing captains*. You could set up testing teams that test all categories of recipes. Here the volunteer doesn't get as tired of one recipe type as a category chairman might. The teams could swap recipes for retesting if questions arise.

The category or testing team captains make up the committee responsible for the final decisions. The chairman of the committee is in charge of all mailings, soliciting recipes, making copies of the original to go to testers, and assigning testers. She must be sure that forms are correctly filled out and deadlines are met.

*Design/format chairman* does not personally design the book. Rather, this chairman and her committee acquire the artwork, determine the theme, and make decisions such as type, colors, paper, ink, and format. She works with the professionals who will create the design. She is responsible for the introduction, acknowledgments, extra inclusions, and the all-important index. She is responsible for the final editing, proofing, and preparation of the manuscript.

This chairman should be creative and artistic, with a good feeling for color and design. Her committee should spend a large part of their time researching the cookbook market, finding out what sells and why. The committee can talk to booksellers and retailers, and poll the membership.

The design/format chairman should attend the bidding/contracting sessions with printers, along with the general chairman. Not only are two sets of ears better than one, but the design chairman can also get firsthand information on such specialized areas such as manuscript and artwork preparation.

If the design/format chairman is not a detail person, she should delegate some of her responsibilities to someone who is extremely careful and aware of details.

Let us remind you of one pitfall. Don't put the final decision about design into the hands of too many people. You simply cannot get a large group to agree upon something so subjective.

The *marketing/promotions chairman* is responsible for setting a marketing plan and budget, establishing objectives, seeing that they are carried out, and evaluating the results.

Her committee solicits information from other cookbooks on suggested marketing efforts, contacts professionals in this area, keeps a file of bright ideas, and "brainstorms" for new and innovative approaches.

This chairman is responsible for the image of the cookbook, both within the organization and in the marketplace. The chairman needs to be organized and good at "follow-through." The committee members should be super salesmen who can meet the public well and be articulate and enthusiastic about the book. Party givers can find a place on this committee. The members in charge of the design of the promotional material need to have a feeling for layout, color, and design. Talented writers can be put to work on brochures and press releases. Creativity and originality are important qualifications. Volunteers with backgrounds in graphic arts and photography will be useful. This committee should be responsible for providing the "personal touch" to local accounts.

The committee might decide to seek professional help from a marketing expert, and would be responsible for preparing a budget for this.

The *business chairman* is responsible for the day-to-day

running of the business, for making sure that the systems are in place and working efficiently, and that all volunteers understand their responsibilities and are trained adequately. She should be a supervisor with managerial skills, and will be responsible for volunteers filling and completing jobs such as bookkeeping, banker/treasurer, wholesale staff and retail staff (getting the orders out), inventory, credit operations, and sales.

If you have read the chapter on setting up a business, you will know what is involved in the operation of a mail order wholesale/retail business. These jobs need to be assigned and carried out efficiently by several or many people, depending on your volunteer manpower.

An alternative to traditional cookbook jobs is a *paid* employee. When an organization has an overworked cookbook committee and no more volunteer help available, an office manager or administrative secretary can be the answer. You must, however, look at profits and expenses and judge if you can afford this luxury. Here's a sample ad placed in a newspaper for such a position:

---

### Administrative Secretary

Small mail-order publishing company needs efficient self-starter. Typing, general office work, bookkeeping skills valuable. Hours: 10–2, three days a week. Send résumé to: _____
_____

---

The general chairman and the business operations chairman should interview applicants. A written job description outlining all responsibilities is essential. During the interview discuss the salary and emphasize the distinct nature of working with volunteers. The ability to work with and understand volunteers is the prime requisite for this job.

An essential part of any cookbook structure is the *policy committee*. It is necessary to give the cookbook the strength of group consensus in major policy decisions. It protects the chairman from taking all the blame and protects the cookbook committee from a chairman who cannot make good judgment calls.

The vice-chairman frequently serves as chairman of the policy committee. Members might include: the chairman, the past cookbook chairmen (if you have been in existence long enough), the assistant treasurer of the group, a representative from the board, and some at-large members.

All policies must be written down and kept in a file or a notebook retained by the chairman. Written policies can provide solutions before issues become problems. They enable the work to go on in the absence of the chairman and provide continuity in the turnover of the volunteer system. Written policies lend a professional image instead of the appearance of a bunch of amateurs. Time has a way of making memories fade, which hurts the ability of future chairmen to perform well.

Policy committee meetings tend to be crisis-oriented and should be kept confidential. As much as possible, policies should be determined in advance, with adequate time for discussion, but we warn you, emergencies will occur. We covered policies in Chapter 4. Particular policies for volunteer organizations include:

1. Membership requirements
2. Summer schedules
3. In-house sales
4. Membership charge accounts
5. Who gets to see cookbook information
6. Who takes books on consignment
7. Names of contributors in book
8. Possible discount to members

# VOLUNTEER RECRUITMENT AND TRAINING

The cookbook committee is not the place for everybody. Rather, like the U.S. Marines, we are looking for "A Few Good (Wo)Men." The cookbook business provides unparalleled experiences for volunteers, but you have to let the volunteers know it.

The best recruitment tool is the reputation of a well-run program with meaningful and/or fun jobs. Many volunteers do not want to spend time today in jobs they consider meaningless. It is the chairman's job to define the jobs, determine the skills needed, and actively seek those people that can fill them.

We are firmly convinced, after years of helping to "put out fires" in voluntary organizations, that 90 percent of the fires were caused by faulty communications. A goal for every chairman should be to improve communications with the cookbook committee, with the rest of the organization, and with the cookbook-buying world—your customers.

If you can communicate your enthusiasm for the cookbook to your organization and assure the members that a year spent working for the cookbook will be a worthwhile year, you will get the top volunteers in the organization to work for you.

Written job descriptions are the first requirement. Volunteers want to know exactly what is expected of them, what time and skills the job requires, and what they can expect to gain from it. We believe that the cookbook committee offers something for everyone; there are jobs for creative, artistic types, for the mathematically inclined, for the salesman and the manager. There are also jobs that suit people at different times in their lives: the woman with young children and a job may not have the time and energy to do more than gift-wrap cookbooks one evening a week, while the woman who is looking for new challenges and areas of interest will be ready to accept bigger responsibilities. By placing the right person in the right place you can help her to bloom where she is planted.

To get these top volunteers, do some *recruiting*. Use your organization's newsletter or five minutes at a meeting to tell the membership what's going on and what the opportunities are. Use posters or displays, like the one below.

---

*We're Still Hiring . . .*

*Wanted:* Bookkeeper for small business, must be efficient, meticulous.

*Wanted:* Local sales rep to call on retail stores. Must be charming, intelligent, personable.

*Wanted:* Design coordinator to plan wholesale brochures. Must be creative, talented.

*Wanted:* Promotions person to plan parties, giveaways. Must be terrific hostess.

---

Have an open house (with goodies) at the cookbook office to show prospective volunteers what goes on, and personally invite some members to attend.

Try to make it possible to interview volunteers with an eye to placing them in the right job. When you find someone with special talents (researchers, graphic artists, home economists, copywriters, and public speakers), create a job for that person.

Make sure that your structure has enough flexibility to allow for movement. Flexibility can move "dead weight" from important jobs and move new "stars" into a brighter place. You can't fire a volunteer, but you can move her.

The concerns expressed most frequently by volunteers are:

1. The work is a waste of time.
2. My skills/talents are not utilized.
3. I'm in a job not suited for me.
4. I've never worked in a group before.

*Training* can be the answer to these problems, as well as the solution to the difficulties created by the turnover of volunteers. Training can be as informal as working with your predecessors for a while or as formal as attending a seminar. Some jobs, like computer operator, obviously require a high level of technical training, but no job, even gift wrapper, should be without training. The better the training provided, the happier and more effective the volunteer is going to be.

At the start of the volunteer year, plan a meeting for the whole committee. The purpose of this meeting is to build a sense of teamwork. Some jobs will be done alone, and that volunteer will do it better if she feels that she is a part of the team. Schedule the meeting for optimum attendance (or schedule two meetings) so everyone gets to be present. Give the volunteers the big picture: facts about the cookbook, its history, the goal for the year, the schedule of activities. Present the committee structure by chart so each person knows where she fits in. Introduce all the members. Have some refreshments, have some fun. Above all, communicate your enthusiasm about what you are all going to be doing together.

Training for specific jobs will have to be done individually or in small committees. The written job description is the backbone of this. The person in charge of specific functions is responsible for training her volunteers, but the general chairman must make sure how and when this is done.

Training is an ongoing process. We all learn by doing. Continued formal training opportunities are valuable, too. Plan to schedule an outside speaker on accounting or marketing. Ask your volunteers for suggestions about what they would like in continued training. Schedule a meeting at mid-year for the dual purpose of bringing everybody up to date and getting them together for socializing again.

*Keeping volunteers happy* is important. Each chairman or subcommittee chairman should stay in touch with her volunteers. Knowing that there is constant contact and supervision increases the feeling of accountability. Let the volunteers know at the beginning that there will be evaluations at certain intervals as you strive together to meet the objectives.

Make the work environment pleasant. Be sure the office is a place the volunteers will want to come to. Consider space, light, ventilation, temperature, the availability of soft drinks or coffee. And no children, please! If your volunteers are going to have to bring children sometimes, try to set aside a corner with something for the children to do with some toys, or paper and pencils, then make sure the children *stay* in their corner.

To make the office interesting, we suggest posting:

List of new wholesale accounts
Testimonials
Calendar of cookbook/organization events
Monthly net profit graph (year-to-date)
A map of country or region with active accounts
Library of other cookbooks

# CHAIRMAN'S TRAINING AND NOTEBOOK

We always say, when we give ideas for committee structure, that an organization needs to be flexible, that you can add or eliminate jobs to fit your needs and manpower. However, we believe very strongly that a cookbook committee needs a chairman and a vice-chairman. Ideally, the year as vice-chairman should be spent learning the system and making plans. With no previous experience, it is next to impossible to walk into a cookbook committee as a chairman and run an efficient and effective system.

Obviously, we believe in volunteers, but there are some pitfalls inherent in the volunteer system. By being aware of them and learning to work around them we hope you can avoid problems.

First, *communication*. We've already said that we think most problems arise from faulty communication and that the chairman's job is to communicate with the committee, the organization as a whole, and with the book-buying public. In a sense, a big part of the chairman's job is public relations and communications. Communication needs to be continuous. You started out by welcoming and training your volunteers; don't let it stop there. Stay in touch with your committee throughout the year. Let them know what's going on. Show you're on the way to achieving the objectives, or indicate if any changes are occurring. Plan staff meetings carefully. The committee (and various parts of it) should meet regularly, but no one wants to waste time at lengthy, unorganized meetings. Be accessible—let volunteers know they can come to you with both problems and ideas. And, for goodness sake, let them know you appreciate what they are doing.

Communication with the organization is of major importance. The chairman is the link between the board and the cookbook committee, and it's important to let each know what the other is doing. A new book has high visibility in an organization, but cookbooks go through cycles. After a few years, a cookbook can become a sort of "stepchild." This is discouraging for the cookbook volunteers and devastating for the success of the book. When the membership loses interest in a book the sales will drop, so it's up to the cookbook chairman to keep the membership aware of and proud of the cookbook. Let the organization know how important the cookbook is to them.

Announce or report all special events, and successful sales, funny happenings.

Form an advisory committee that meets several times a year for advice, direction, and information. It could be made up of the president or vice-president, the treasurer, a ways-and-means person, or a PR person.

Offer the membership special prices several times a year to make buying the book extra-attractive. Offer gift wrapping and charge accounts to the members.

Have contests, prizes, refreshments—anything that promotes the positive image of the cookbook.

(We covered communications with the customers and wholesale accounts thoroughly in the market chapter.)

After communications the second major area of concern is *turnover or lack of continuity* among volunteers. Volunteers change from year to year, and each year you will have some dropouts due to pregnancy, illness, transfer, or just plain not showing up for the job. This is a built-in part of the volunteer system. You can avoid some problems by having as much systematized and written down as possible: job descriptions, policies, procedures. Have contingency plans to cover the worst emergencies, and be aware that you're going to have to be flexible enough to cover some gaps.

*Planning* is frequently a weak spot in volunteer organizations. No business can run without planning. Things have a way of catching up with us and we find that we never have the time to sit down and do the planning we intended to do. The vice-chairman should be making plans for her year as chairman early. She may feel that she's stepping on the chairman's toes, but it must be done. The vice-chairman has the time to plan, and also to read and research and to attend seminars.

We want to suggest a tool to help you: a chairman's notebook. It should include all the important information about the business (all of this is in the files; you just gather it together in one place) so that if a Mack truck hits you, your successor can carry on. The notebook contains information about all aspects of the business, things not every committee member knows or needs to know, but that the chairman must keep up with. Having a notebook forces you to plan ahead. It is up to you to formlate this tool, which is very individual; the notebooks from fifty different organizations would differ widely. Yours should contain all the *basic* information to run your business.

# OFFICE SYSTEMS

Because we covered the systems necessary for a wholesale/retail mail order business in Chapter 4, we won't go over the whole thing again. However, a volunteer organization has certain problems. An individual self-publisher handles all the orders herself/himself, or at most has one other person helping. A volunteer organization will have many people in and out of the office, several people performing each function and some people wandering around with no function at all. Obviously, superior organization is called for.

We suggest you establish three separate, clearly defined work areas: one for wholesale, one for retail, and one for bookkeeping.

Label everything clearly. Train volunteers to keep everything in its place.

Color-code eveything so it can easily be identified.

Prominently display posters listing:

Procedures
Pricing information (charts over appropriate desks)
Shipping information (postal and UPS charts)
Schedules for marketing plans
A calendar with the year's schedule

Limit access to the files. Files need to be clearly labeled so volunteers can find what they need, but not every volunteer needs access to every file.


# PROMOTIONAL IDEAS
# FOR NONPROFITS


Because of their tax-exempt status, voluntary organizations have access to a gold mine of publicity. Radio and television stations will give public-service air time, billboard and bus card companies will donate unrented space. Banks, stores, and businesses are glad to help because it is good for their image to help "the cause."

The membership of the organization is another gold mine. Not only can they supply manpower and ideas, but they have all sorts of friends and connections. We can suggest many promotional ideas; your membership will come up with dozens more.

♦ On donated billboards or bus cards, advertise a seasonal tie-in;

> September—tailgate picnics at football games
> October—Halloween cookies
> November—Thanksgiving feasts
> December—Christmas gifts
> February—Valentine's Day
> March—Easter luncheon
> June—Bridal gifts
> July—picnics on the Fourth

♦ Ask the telephone company or a department store to put a cookbook flyer in all their bills.

♦ Put your message on grocery sacks or milk cartons. Many dairies and grocery stores donate this space to charities. Think how many kitchens you can reach!

♦ Tie a press release in to National Volunteer Week in April.

♦ Get a sorority or fraternity to help with sales as their community service project.

♦ Sell through Welcome Wagon or Newcomer's Clubs.

♦ Give a birthday party for the book in a public place.

♦ Have the mayor (or governor) declare "Cookbook Week."

♦ Swap retail lists with other organizations.

♦ Try co-op advertising with another organization—an ad that features two different cookbooks costs each advertiser half as much.

♦ Ask another organization to let you have a booth at their show house, charity fair, or Christmas shop.

♦ Swap ideas—and even books—with another organization. Offer a special to their members in exchange for the same favor.

♦ Have contests for members—win a party given by the cookbook committee for selling the most books, opening the most new accounts, or supplying the most addresses for the retail list. The first prize might be a dinner for twelve, the second prize a luncheon for eight, the third prize a children's party.

* Give prizes to any member who makes an appointment with the food editor of the newspaper in a city where she travels. (Provide a trip kit and brief her carefully.)

* Print a form for members to slip in their suitcases when they travel to bring back with the names and addresses of shops they saw on their trip.

* Make a couple of "trip kits"—encourage members to check it out when they go out of town just as you'd check out a library book. Your own membership can be terrific traveling salesmen.

* Use committee members and recipe contributors in press releases. Send a story and a picture to the member's hometown newspaper.

* Align your book with an organization's anniversary, the city's bicentennial, a major event. Have a sticker made that says, "Special Anniversary Edition," or "Celebrating the Bowl Game."

* Turn a problem into a news release. The Junior League of Tulsa had planned the debut of *Cook's Collage* for a formal party at a new office development. When a strike delayed the completion of the building, the committee quickly shifted gears and threw a "Construction Party" with picnics served on sawhorses and guests wearing jeans and hardhats. The event attracted more attention than the first plan would have.

* Advertise in your retail flyer that buyers can use their charge cards. Check with your bank for the procedure.

* Sell a new book to the membership at a discount; a dollar off each book you buy, or twelve books for the price of eleven.

* Offer special gift-wrapping: Christmas, wedding, birthday.

* If all else fails and you have no ideas for new stories, use the story of the tremendous success of community cookbooks. You can even quote Hays-Rolfes. (Please give credit where credit is due!)

# CHAPTER 7

# What If . . . ?

THERE ARE DOZENS of situations that are going to arise when your book is on the market that will require a decision. In an organization, this is where the policy committee comes into action. An individual self-publisher is her own policy committee, although she may ask for advice. You, as a self-publisher, could form your own policy committee or group of advisors: a lawyer, an accountant, friends, a local bookseller, etc. As consultants, Hays-Rolfes have spent a lot of time putting out fires for self-publishers. We'd like to share some of our experiences with you by playing the "What If" game.

**1.** Catalog sales can be quite lucrative yet hard to obtain. A representative from a catalog company has just approached you, asking for your company's discount scale. He says he is looking for a cookbook to feature in his fall catalog, but you have never heard of the company. He wants a decision in two weeks. What do you do?

POLICY DECISION: Ask for samples of past catalogs. Look at all the items in them. Are they in keeping with the quality of your book? Does each catalog project the image you want to convey? What is the circulation of each catalog? Call some of the other publishers represented in past catalogs. Ask how many books were sold, whether bills were paid on time and all agreements lived up to. Do a credit check through your bank or Dun & Bradstreet. Take your time and get the answers to all your questions before you sign anything. Don't allow an exclusive to one catalog, unless it is for a short period of time—say six months to one year.

**2.** *The Ladies' Home Journal* just featured your cookbook in a terrific story. Orders are pouring in from all over the country and you are working double time to fill all the orders. In the midst of all the excitement and enthusiasm, you begin to get letter after letter from buyers complaining that the book arrived with a shattered comb. The mail brings more complaints every day, from all parts of the country. You just received a new printing of 30,000 copies. What do you do?

POLICY DECISION: First, you cry. This actually happened when Helen was publication chairman for the Memphis Junior League and the *Ladies' Home Journal* article sold over 6,000 copies of *Party Potpourri*.

You must replace the books because the buyers ordered in good faith, but since the complaints were so widespread, it is apparent that the problem was inferior plastic (a printer's error) rather than accidents in the mail. Ask for the damaged copies back, pay the shipping on them, and get hold of the printer as soon as possible. The contract, if well drawn, will state liability for not delivering a product up to the specifications. The printer has to compensate you, and obviously the books must be rebound with new combs as soon as possible. Moreover, you want a guarantee that the next books you ship out will be free from this problem. It would also be correct to ask the printer to repay you for the freight costs of getting damaged books back.

You'll have to flex your muscles with the printer: you'll never reprint with him again and you'll spread the word about his product and service. You're going to lose time, sleep, and money over this one, but remember that the reputation of your book is at stake. Write a letter of apology to every customer and offer to replace their books. And try to make sure the ones you're shipping now are all right.

**3.** Your closest friend or a prominent member of your organization has a brother in the printing business. She has made it absolutely clear to you that she simply cannot attend the family Christmas dinner if he does not receive the contract for printing your book. She is really putting the pressure on you.

POLICY DECISION: Call a meeting of the Policy Committee. This is one time the committee is worth its weight in gold. Announce that it is a long-standing *written* policy that for every contract at least three bids must be taken and that the decision is to be made by the committee, not by you or just one person.

Of course this kind of pressure is unfair, but it does happen. The value of a policy committee is so great in handling decisions of this kind that we think that both an individual self-publisher and organizations need one. An individual can enlist the aid of other people so that she can say, "My advisors recommend . . ."

4. A new wholesaler/distributor has just contacted you in a very professional business letter. He wants to buy your book at 50 percent off and prepaid freight, but wants to buy a large volume. The letter looks good, and he even supplied appropriate credit references. Will you sell to him?

POLICY DECISION: This is another true story, and it turned out to be a disaster for several nonprofit organizations. Several groups agreed to sell to him and shipped quantities of books. Some even checked the credit references he gave, but *no one* bothered to ask for the names of his other customers, and to check his catalog, and no one asked questions of previous clients. No one checked with his accounts to see if he was a reliable supplier.

He received quantities of books, sold them to bookstores, pocketed the money, and never paid the publishers. Participants at one of the Hays-Rolfes seminars discovered that several of them had been taken advantage of by the same wholesaler. They had gotten stung because none had bothered to ask the right questions of the right people. They had been misled because the offer looked businesslike and no one went far enough to check. Beware. There are many honest businessmen out there— and there are also some real rackets going on.

**5.** Sales seem to have leveled off with your twelve-year-old cookbook. Several people, including one bookseller, have commented that the problem might be the cover. Do you change the cover, or change your promotional strategy?

POLICY DECISION: Changing the cover on an established cookbook is a monumental decision. There are many things to consider, and they should be considered by more than one person—the Policy Committee again.

First of all, do a wider market survey, both of individual buyers and booksellers. Getting rid of something that people recognize is frequently a mistake. Also, customers feel gypped if they buy a book for the cover and discover that, although the cover is new, the contents are the same. Consider making subtle changes to update the cover instead of changing the whole thing. Perhaps the type face could be updated or the colors made a little brighter.

If you do decide on a major change, be sure to have a sticker on the front that guarantees "Same Wonderful Contents." (Similarly, changes on the inside should be advertised with a sticker that says "Updated Edition.") An individual self-publisher can make this decision more easily than a group because somewhere in the group there will be people loyal to the old format. It is important for a group to have the decision made by a committee, and to have the agreement and support of the officers and of the people responsible for the original design.

A little change can give an added boost to sales, but be very careful before making a major change. It might be more satisfactory to consider printing an entirely new cookbook. And don't forget that one of the reasons for the sales records might be that promotions have also leveled off, causing this problem.

**6.** A most persistent woman keeps calling and writing you for advice on "just how you did it." Of course, it is flattering when she tells you that your book is such a success, but she is getting to be a pest. How much are you willing to tell her, and how much time can you give?

POLICY DECISION: Remember the things we mentioned as confidential information in the policy chapter. Keep basic information classified. You certainly want to be cordial and answer specific questions—and we do advocate communication between cookbook publishers, but there is a fine line between communication and help, with *hours* on the telephone or the typewriter. Do your best, then advise that plenty of professional help is available. Refer her to a consultant, a seminar . . . or this book.

7. For months the president of your organization has insinuated that she really wasn't "pro cookbook." Suddenly it's come out in the open when she says that all volunteers should be working for the organization's community causes instead of mailing brochures. As cookbook chairman, you are literally red in the face with anger. What are you going to say to her—and to the board?

POLICY DECISION: You, the cookbook chairman, have to accept some of the blame for this situation. You haven't done a good job on the internal PR campaign and the president and probably the rest of the organization have forgotten why you have a cookbook in the first place.

She needs to be reminded that the cookbook provides the "ways and means" that make possible the organization's community involvement. The income from the cookbook makes the group able to support its cause. Go back and read the section on "Internal Public Relations" in Chapter 6. Starting a campaign through the news sheet, meetings, and other tactics is better late than never. And don't forget it again.

Then invite the president (and any other doubters) to a meeting in the cookbook office. Explain not only how the cookbook supports the organization, but also about the wonderful training the volunteers get in a variety of areas, and show how this can benefit the rest of the organization. Invite her to become involved by coming to a meeting of the Policy Committee and/or by participating in the PR campaign.

You can make a believer out of a doubter with a little effort. Practice a little preventive medicine by putting the vice-president on the Policy Committee, so she is already educated about cookbooks and the situation doesn't happen again.

**8.** You had a sixth sense about it all along . . . there was something about her. Now she is on your committee as marketing chairman. Absolutely nothing gets done unless it was her idea. She controls every meeting; no one else can get a word—much less an idea—in. Brainstorming sessions have turned into nightmares. The committee members are all calling you, not her. Are you going to ride out the year and let the situation hurt sales?

POLICY DECISION: This type of personality is the most difficult to handle in the volunteer structure, and it is the job of the chairman to deal with it. Try to direct her into "special assignments," like corporate solicitations or going after premium sales. That way she can be kept busy while working alone. You can also surround her with "chiefs," who are experienced at countering such people. She can be asked to give them updates on the cookbook or write articles for the news sheet. You, as general chairman, can attend her meetings and make a point of asking for others' ideas.

**9.** An internationally recognized company has approached you requesting reprint rights to some of your recipes for a special edition under that company's imprint. It sounds tempting. Are you selling?

POLICY DECISION: Make sure you get the proposal in writing, then get a legal opinion. Ask for copies of some of the other books the company has produced. Ask for a detailed description of their marketing plan (and include this in the final contract). Get references from the company and check them carefully. Find out what other cookbooks have been approached and who has committed so far. Don't let this turn into an exclusive on your mass marketing rights. With care and the proper questions in the beginning, it may turn out to be a wonderful opportunity.

**10.** The first cookbook was fun, so you want to publish another for even more revenue. A company that offers "Full Services" approaches you, offering to do everything from design, recipe collection, printing, and selling, if you sign before you begin. It certainly sounds easy. Should you sign?

POLICY DECISION: If you've read this far, you know that the Hays-Rolfes philosophy emphasizes doing it yourself and keeping the control in your hands. The more you rely on someone else's services, the more your book will become another stereotyped copy of someone else's ideas.

If the company is a publishing company, this will help you make your decision—how badly do you want to be published? If it is a printing company, and you are planning to self-publish, it could be a *huge* mistake.

It is their uniqueness that is so wonderful about successful cookbooks. The true reflection of you or your organization or your area, your taste, your life, your location, is what makes a cookbook a "Classic."

# CHAPTER 8

# Computers and Cookbooks

THE COMPUTER REVOLUTION has already changed our lives in everything, from the way we play games to the way we shop. It can be a potent force in the cookbook industry, too. Software is available for almost everything that a writer or a self-publisher needs to do.

Peter McWilliams, in an article called "Small Publisher Discovers the Small Computer" in the September/October '83 issue of *Small Press*, outlined the many uses of the computer.

*Writing*. Think of being able to file all your recipes on a computer and being able to call them up according to category, ingredients, or the number of people served. There are filing programs that enable you to do this and more. Word processing programs enable you to make changes and revisions with the greatest of ease, with speed and flexibility. Deadlines are easier to meet because of the speed with which you can work. There are programs that check your spelling and insure conformity in the layout of recipes. In the time it took you to read this, dozens of new programs have probably been created.

*Editing*. This process is faster and easier on a computer. Instead of having to make changes by hand in the margins, then retype the whole thing, all editing can be done on the computer itself: the changes are put in and printed out. You can rearrange phrases, sentences, and whole paragraphs. Indexing can be done efficiently. The time saved in this one area alone might pay for the computer.

*Typesetting.* Manual keyboarding, the hardest and most expensive part of typesetting, is already done. Computers offer a variety of typefaces; you can "see" what the type looks like on the page, use a combination of different types and styles (like italics, boldface, and so on). If the printer has the capability, you can send the disk directly to the printer and it can be run through a machine that sets the type in hours, not weeks. The cost-cutting is enormous, and the potential for errors greatly reduced.

*Graphic design.* The range of possibilities grows daily. No longer are you restricted to bar graphs and pie charts. Some computers have amazing graphic potential, and great opportunity for creativity. Also, there are programs available for layout that may eventually replace the drafting board and the X-acto knife. You can size the entries on a page, choose and combine type styles, do spacing and repositioning easily.

*Data management.* There are programs that act as automated file folders and index cards. You can record all your research and have it easily accessible. You can do brainstorming and outlining on the computer. For self-publishers, the business uses include filing past records, current information, and future projections. No more lost files, searches for something you remember seeing, or storage problems for files.

*Sales.* A computer can handle your mailing lists and retrieve them for you according to category. You can track your sales by territory, by account, or by any other variable. A computer can churn out personalized letters in the time it takes you to think about having another standard press release printed. It's easier to keep up with corrections, additions, and eliminations to a mailing list, and the computer can furnish a list of printed labels or envelopes in minutes, not days.

*Correspondence.* Letters can be drafted, revised, personalized, and printed quickly. You can keep the form letters we outlined under "Policies" in the computer, and send them out as needed.

*Accounting*. Invoices, billing, inventory, accounts receivable, tax records, monthly reports, and general ledgers can all fit into the computer system. It may not be any easier, but it certainly is a lot faster.

*Financial projections*. What if the cost per book is increasing by 25 cents in the next printing? What return do you need to make a $1,000 mailing pay for itself? How many copies need to come out of inventory before you start thinking about a reprint? When you enter all the variables of your business into the computer, you can have these answers and many more. All those hours with pencil and paper can be cut down or eliminated.

*Volunteers*. For nonprofit groups the computer opens up a whole new realm. You can keep track of committees and send them a mailing, keep up with hours and tasks and assignments—all those time-consuming jobs are faster on a computer.

Software is already available for all of these chores. If you want something even more individualized, you can write your own program, or have it done for you. As you shop for both the computer system and the software, define your needs carefully. You will be amazed at all the possibilities.

Who knows, maybe your cookbook will even appear on computer disk! You may be able to sell the electronic rights in the same way you sell the foreign rights. With the growing number of home computers, anything is possible. Don't say we didn't warn you!

# Afterword:
# Living with Success

IF YOU'VE STUCK with us this far, we hope that you've got a big success on your hands. Remember that success is relative; it is what you define it as. Success doesn't have to be measured in terms of tens of thousands of copies sold nationwide. It is also your sense of achievement at having done something you always wanted to do.

After all the excitement has died down and after you have achieved your goals, suppose the day comes when you say, "I'm tired of this. I don't want to mail cookbooks out every week for the rest of my life. I want to do something else." There are alternatives to continuing the system you have set up.

The most obvious thing you might want to do is to write another book. With everything you've learned from publishing the first one, you have a good foundation to build on. Maybe you want to write another cookbook and explore new ideas about food. Maybe you want to go into a whole new area: gardening hints, flower arranging, or bookkeeping for small businesses. A new book will fit right into the systems you've already established. You've got an office, a distribution network, a promotion plan. One book helps sell another. Why, you've already got a mailing list of customers who would love to buy another book from you. You could be looking at a future as a small press.

Ellen and her mother-in-law published volume 2 of *Why Didn't I Think of That?* and discovered that the hard work had already been done; the new book dovetailed right into their marketing system and customers were delighted to have something new. When filling orders became too time-consuming, Ellen hired part-time help to take care of invoicing, shipping, and billing. Now she handles only unusual situations and promotions.

Part-time help is a good solution when business becomes routine. Students or retired people can be hired to take over the maintenance functions of the company, while you go back to creating.

Selling your book solely through a distributor is another solution, which leaves only the promotion up to you. An agent can also take over some of the marketing functions. An ad agency would be an expensive but easy way to turn the promotion over; perhaps a marketing student in a local school could be hired part-time.

Several self-publishers have sold the rights to their books to publishing companies. Both Jean Sanderson's *Discover Contest Cooking* and Dede Napoli's *The Starving Students Cookbook* were bought by Warner Books. Pelican Publishing Company has bought the rights to several self-published books, including *Opera on the Half Shell*, compiled by the Junior Committee Women's Guild of the New Orleans Opera Association, and *Herbs: From Cultivation to Cooking*, by the Herb Society of Greater Cincinnati.

A friend of ours decided not to reprint when she sold out her edition of 5,000 books. She had done what she wanted to do and had gotten enormous pleasure out of it. Now her book is a collector's item.

Or perhaps you were lucky enough to have sold your book to a publisher in the beginning. You are now a published celebrity, and the publishing company is asking you to do another book. You can begin again, with the knowledge that a company is behind you from the beginning, or you can say no thank you, and sit back, enjoy your retirement, and cash your royalty checks.

Surely a big part of your success has been the pleasure of creation, the pride of seeing your work in print, and the joy of sharing something you love with others.

# Appendix

## PROOFREADER'S MARKS

| | | | |
|---|---|---|---|
| ℐ delete or take out ~~out~~ | | SET in lowercase ℓetters | ℓc / ℓc |
| ℰ/ delete and close up | | set in capital letters | cap |
| ⊂ close up; no space | | set in small caps | sc |
| # insert space | | set in italics | ital |
| t/ℨ/cn insert leter punctuation word | | set in roman type | rom |
| [ move left | | set in boldface type | bf |
| ] move right | | set in lightface type | ℓf |
| ⌐⌐ move up or down | | insert period | ⊙ |
| ∥ align | | insert comma | |
| align align horizontally | | insert semicolon | |
| ✕ broken type | | insert colon | |
| ¶ ¶ make new paragraph | | insert apostrophe or single quotes | |
| no ¶ no new paragraph | | insert quotation marks | |
| tr transpose | | insert reference | |
| tr words transpose | | insert hyphen | = |
| tr lines | | insert dash | |
| transpose | | do not make correction indicated | stet |
| run on run on | | spell out numeral: ① | sp |
| run over break run over line | | set as numeral: one | fig |
| ℐ turn over | | query, verify: Mosel | ? |

Prentice-Hall, Inc., WORDS INTO TYPE, 3rd Ed., Completely Revised, © 1974, p. 71.
Reprinted by permission of Prentice-Hall, Inc., Englewood Cliffs, N.J.

# A SAMPLING OF
# SELF-PUBLISHED COOKBOOKS

*America Discovers Columbus*, Junior League of Columbus, Inc., 586 East Town Street, Columbus, Ohio 43215

*Applehood & Motherpie*, Junior League of Rochester, Inc., 33 South Washington, Rochester, New York 14608

*The Artist in the Kitchen*, Friends of the St. Louis Art Museum, Forrest Park, St. Louis, Missouri 63110

*Bach's Lunch, Bach for More, Bach for an Encore*, Junior Committee of the Cleveland Orchestra, Severance Hall, Cleveland, Ohio 44106

*Bayou Cuisine*, Saint Stephen's Episcopal Church, Box 1005, Indianola, Mississippi 38751

*The Best Little Cookbook in Texas*, Junior League of Abilene, Inc., 774 Butternut Street, Abilene, Texas 79602

*The Best of South Louisiana Cooking*, Bootsie John Landry, 301 Heymann Blvd., Lafayette, Louisiana 70503

*Beyond Parsley*, Junior League of Kansas City, Inc., 4651 Roanoke Parkway, Kansas City, Missouri 64112

*California Fresh*, Junior League of Oakland-East Bay, Inc., 1980 Mountain Blvd., Oakland, California 94611

*The Captain's Lady Cookbook*, Barbara Dalia Jasmin, 65–69 High Street, Springfield, Massachusetts 01105

*Charleston Receipts*, Junior League of Charleston, Inc., Box 117, Charleston, South Carolina 29402

*Cooking with the Santo Fe Opera*, Santa Fe Opera Guild, Box 2371, Santa Fe, New Mexico 87501

*Dinner on the Diner*, Junior League of Chattanooga, Inc., Box 4384, Chattanooga, Tennessee 37405

*Eet Smakelijk*, Junior Welfare League of Holland, Box 613, Holland, Michigan 49423 *the everyday gourmet*, Junior League of North Westchester, Inc., Box 214, Chappaqua, New York 10514

*Fanny Pierson Crane—Her Receipts 1796*, Montclair Historical Society, Box 322, Montclair, New Jersey 07042

*Feasting Naturally, Feasting Naturally from Your Own Recipes, Feasting Naturally with Our Friends*, Mary Ann Pickard, Box 968, Harrison, Arkansas 72601

*The Fine Art of Delectable Desserts*, Greater Louisville Fund for the Arts, 444 South Third Street, Louisville, Kentucky 40202

*From the Strawberry Patch*, Sharon Kay Alexander, 2521-F North Grand Avenue, Santa Ana, California 92701

*Gallery Buffet Soup Cookbook*, Dallas Museum of Art, 1717 North Harwood, Dallas, Texas 75201

*The Gasparilla Cookbook*, Junior League of Tampa, Inc., Box 10223, Tampa, Florida 33679

*Gracious Goodness*, Junior League of Macon, Inc., 345 Spring Street, Macon, Georgia 31201

*The Gulf Gourmet*, Mothers' Club of Westminster Academy, 5003 Lawson Avenue, Gulfport, Mississippi 39501

*Guten Appetit!*, Sophienburg Memorial Association, Inc., 406 West Coll, New Braunfels, Texas 78130

*The High Museum of Art Recipe Collection*, Members Guild of the High Museum of Art, 1280 Peachtree Street, N.E., Atlanta, Georgia 30309

*Home Cookin'*, Junior League of Wichita Falls, Inc., #2 Eureka Circle, Wichita Falls, Texas 76308

*In the Beginning*, Rockdale Temple Sisterhood, 8501 Ridge Road, Cincinnati, Ohio 45236

*The Jackson Cookbook*, Jackson Symphony League, Box 1967, Jackson, Mississippi 39215

*Jacksonville & Company*, Junior League of Jacksonville, Inc., 2165 Park Street, Jacksonville, Florida 32204

*The James K. Polk Cookbook*, James K. Polk Memorial Auxiliary, Box 869, Columbia, Tennessee 38401

*La Bonne Cuisine*, All Saints Episcopal Church, 100 Rex Drive, River Ridge, Louisiana 70123

*La Piñata*, Junior Service League of McAllen, Box 1656, McAllen, Texas 78501

*The Literary Allusions Cookbook*, Women's National Book Association, c/o Margaret B. Burns, Hillwood High School, 6416 Harding Road, Nashville, Tennessee 37205

*Lone Star Legacy*, Austin Junior Forum, Box 26628, Austin, Texas 78755

*A Man's Taste*, Junior League of Memphis, Inc., 2711 Union Extended, Memphis, Tennessee 38112

*Minnesota Heritage Cookbook*, American Cancer Society, 3316 West 66th Street, Minneapolis, Minnesota 55435

*Mountain Measures*, Junior League of Charleston, Inc., Box 1924, Charleston, West Virginia 25327

*Nutbread and Nostalgia*, Junior League of South Bend, Inc., Box 305, South Bend, Indiana 46624

*Party Potpourri*, Junior League of Memphis, Inc., 2711 Union Extended, Memphis, Tennessee 38112

*Plain & Fancy*, Junior League of Richardson, Inc., Box 835808, Richardson, Texas 75083

*Picnics in the Park*, Brenda Brown and Sharon Mattison, 705 Northway Lane N.E., Atlanta, Georgia 30342

*Pirate's Pantry*, Junior League of Lake Charles, Inc., Box 3066, Lake Charles, Louisiana 70601

*The Pride of Peoria*, Junior League of Peoria, Inc., 256 N.E. Randolph Avenue, Peoria, Illinois 61606

*A Private Collection*, Junior League of Palo Alto, Inc., 555 Ravenwood Avenue, Menlo Park, California 94025

*Private Collections: A Culinary Treasure*, Walters Art Gallery, 600 North Charles Street, Baltimore, Maryland 21201

*Putting on the Grits*, Junior League of Columbia, Inc., 4600 Forest Drive Suite 4, Columbia, South Carolina 29206

*Quail Country*, Junior League of Albany, Inc., 516 Flint Avenue, Albany, Georgia 31701

*Recipe Jubilee*, Junior League of Mobile, Inc., Box 7091, Mobile, Alabama 36607

*Red Checkered Picnics*, Holly Elliott and Betsy Robinson, Box 1826, Vail, Colorado 81658

*River Road Recipes*, Junior League of Baton Rouge, Inc., 4950-E Government Street, Baton Rouge, Louisiana 70806

*Sassafras!*, Junior League of Springfield, Inc., 2574 East Bennett, Springfield, Missouri 65804

*Savoring the Southwest*, Roswell Symphony League, Box 3078, Roswell, New Mexico 88201

*Simply Simpatico*, Junior League of Albuquerque, Inc., Box 8858, Albuquerque, New Mexico 87108

*Soupçon*, Junior League of Chicago, Inc., 1447 North Astor Street, Chicago, Illinois 60610

*Southern Accent*, Junior League of Pine Bluff, Inc., Box 1693, Pine Bluff, Arkansas 71603

*Southern Sideboards*, Junior League of Jackson, Inc., Box 4553, Jackson, Mississippi 39216

*The Stuffed Griffin*, Utility Club, Box 711, Griffin, Georgia 30224

*Talk About Good!*, Junior League of Lafayette, Inc., Box 52387, Oil Center Station, Lafayette, Louisiana 70505

*Tea Time at the Masters*, Junior League of Augusta, Inc., 463 Highland, Surrey Center, Augusta, Georgia 30909

*The Texas Experience*, Richardson Woman's Club, Box 1963, Richardson, Texas 75080

*Thru the Grapevine*, Junior League of Elmira, Inc., 500 Roe Avenue, Elmira, New York 14901

*Tout de Suite I & II*, Jean Durkee, Box 30121, Lafayette, Louisiana 70503

*Vin et Fromage*, Sonoma County Citizen Advocacy, Box 4449, Santa Rosa, California 95402

*Waddad's Kitchen*, Waddad Habeeb Buttross, Box 1506, Natchez, Mississippi 39120

*Well Seasoned*, Les Passees, Inc., 40 South Idlewild, Memphis, Tennessee 38104

*Who's Cooking in Laguna Beach*, Arline Isaacs, 750 Alta Vista Way, Laguna Beach, California 92651

*Winning Seasons*, Junior League of Tuscaloosa, Inc., Box 1071, Tuscaloosa, Alabama 35403

*Winterthur Culinary Collection*, Winterthur Museum and Gardens, Winterthur, Delaware 19735

# BOOK PUBLISHING COMPANIES

There are literally hundreds of publishing companies that are publishing cookbooks. They come in all sizes, shapes, descriptions, etc., and the list changes constantly. Our research in the last few years shows that the companies listed below have been active in the cookbook publishing field. Most of the large publishing houses' names will probably be familiar to you. If you have a certain type of book in mind, and a similar one is already in print, look to see which company published it—there may be an approach there.

When writing one of these companies, the letter should probably be addressed to "Cookbook Editor." Although the company might not have a person with that exact title, the communication will be directed to the appropriate place.

Once again, check with a local bookstore owner when trying to select an appropriate company, or check the LMP in your library for a listing of specialties.

AVI Publishing
Box 831
Westport, CT 06881

A & W Publishers, Inc.
95 Madison Avenue
New York, NY 10016

Alaska Northwest
    Publishing Co.
Box 4-EEE
Anchorage, AL 99509

Alfred Publishing Company
Box 5964
Sherman Oaks, CA 91403

Ancient City Press
Box 5401
Santa Fe, NM 87502

Arco Publishing Company
215 Park Avenue South
New York, NY 10003

Arlis Books/Harris Publishing
1621 Fifth Street
Berkeley, CA 94710

Ashod Press
Box 1147
Madison Square Station
New York, NY 10159

Atheneum Publishers
115 Fifth Avenue
New York, NY 10003

August House
1010 West Third Street
Little Rock, AR 72201

Avery Publishing Group
89 Baldwin Terrace
Wayne, NJ 07470

Ballantine/Fawcett Books
201 East 50th
New York, NY 10022

Banyan Books
Box 431160
Miami, FL 33143

Barron's Educational
  Series, Inc.
113 Crossways Park Drive
Woodbury, NY 11797

Beaufort Books
9 East 40th Street
New York, NY 10016

The Benjamin Company
One Westchester Plaza
Elmsford, NY 10523

Berkley Publishing Group
200 Madison Avenue
New York, NY 10016

Berkshire Traveller Press
Stockbridge, MA 01262

The Bethany Press
Box 179
St. Louis, MO 63166

Better Homes & Garden Books
17 and Locust Streets
Des Moines, IA 50336

Betterway Publications
White Hall, VA 22987

Branch-Smith, Inc.
Box 1868
Ft. Worth, TX 76101

CBI Publishing Company
51 Sleeper Street
Boston, MA 02210

Cachepot
P.O. Box 60158
Palo Alto, CA 94306

Camaro Publishing Co.
90430 World Way Center
Los Angeles, CA 90009

Chicago Review Press
213 W. Institute Place
Chicago, IL 60610

Claitor's Publishing
Box 3333
Baton Rouge, LA 70821

Cloudburst Press of America
Box 147
Point Roberts, WA 98281

Compact Publications
3014 Willow Lane
Hollywood, FL 33021

Consumer Guide/Publications
  International
3841 W. Oakton
Skokie, IL 60076

Consumer Reports Books
256 Washington Street
Mt. Vernon, NY 10550

Contemporary Books, Inc.
180 N. Michigan Avenue
Chicago, IL 60601

David C. Cook Publishing
Book Division
850 N. Grove Avenue
Elgin, IL 60120

Crabtree Publishing
Box 3451
Federal Way, WA 98003

Creative Arts Book Co.
833 Bancroft Way
Berkeley, CA 94710

Crown Publishing Group
One Park Avenue
New York, NY 10016

Cumberland Press, Inc.
Box 296
Freeport, ME 04032

Dembner Books
1841 Broadway
New York, NY 10023

Dharma Publishing
2425 Hillside Avenue
Berkeley, CA 94704

The Dial Press
One Dag Hammarskjold Plaza
245 E. 47th Street
New York, NY 10017

The Dillon Press
500 S. Third Street
Minneapolis, MN 55415

The Donning Company
5659 Virginia Beach Blvd.
Norfolk, VA 23502

Dorison House Publishers
824 Park Square
Boston, MA 02116

Doubleday & Company, Inc.
245 Park Avenue
New York, NY 10167

Dover Publications
31 East 2nd Street
Mineola, NY 11501

Down East Books
Box 679
Camden, ME 04843

E. P. Dutton
2 Park Avenue
New York, NY 10016

EPM Publications
1003 Turkey Run Road
McLean, VA 22101

Farm Journal Books
230 W. Washington Square
Philadelphia, PA 19105

Farragut Publishing
810 18th Street, NW
Washington, DC 20006

Filter Press
Box 5
Palmer Lake, CO 80133

Food & Nutrition Press
One Trinity Square
Westport, CT 06880

Funk & Wagnalls
53 East 77th Street
New York, NY 10021

Garden Way Publishing
Charlotte, VT 05445

Globe Pequot Press
Old Chester Road
Box Q
Chester, CT 06412

Good Books
Main Street
Intercourse, PA 17534

Great Outdoors Publishing
4747 28th Street N.
St. Petersburg, FL 33714

HP Books, Inc.
1019 W. Prince Road
Tucson, AZ 85705

Hammond, Inc.
515 Valley Street
Maplewood, NY 07040

Harian Creative Press-Books
47 Hyde Blvd.
Ballston Spa, NY 12020

Harper & Row, Publishers
10 East 53rd Street
New York, NY 10022

The Harvard Common Press
The Common
Harvard, MA 01451

Harvest House Ltd.
4795 St. Catherine Street
W. Montreal
PQ H3Z 1 S 8 Canada

Hawkes Publishing Co.
3775 S. 5th Street W
Salt Lake City, UT 84115

Hearst Books
224 West 57th Street
New York, NY 10019

Herald Press
616 Walnut Avenue
Scottsdale, PA 15683

Holt, Rinehart & Winston
383 Madison Avenue
New York, NY 10017

Houghton Mifflin Company
Two Park Street
Boston, MA 02108

House of Collectibles, Inc.
1904 Premier Row
Orlando, FL 32809

Ideals Publishing Corp.
11315 Watertown Plank Road
Milwaukee, WI 53226

International Cookbook Ser.
21 Dupont Avenue
White Plains, NY 10605

Irene Chalmers Cookbooks
23 East 92nd Street
New York, NY 10028

Jonathan David Publishers
68–22 Eliot Avenue
Middle Village, NY 11379

The Knapp Press
5455 Wilshire Blvd.
Los Angeles, CA 90036

LaFray Young Publishing Co.
3210 9th Street N.
St. Petersburg, FL 33704

Lakewood Books
1070 Kapp Drive
Clearwater, FL 33515

Lancaster-Miller Publishers
3165 Adeline Street
Berkeley, CA 94703

Lebhar-Friedman Books
425 Park Avenue
New York, NY 10022

Leisure Press
Box 3
West Point, NY 10996

Liberty Publishing Company
50 Scott Adam Road
Cockeysville, MD 21030

Macmillan Publishing
  Company
866 Third Avenue
New York, NY 10022

Madrona Publishing Co.
2116 Western Avenue
Seattle, WA 98121

Marshall Cavendish Corp.
147 W. Merrick Road
Freeport, NY 11520

McGraw–Hill Book Company
1221 Avenue of the Americas
New York, NY 10020

David McKay Company
Two Park Avenue
New York, NY 10016

Meadowbrook Press
18318 Minnetonka Blvd.
Deephaven, MN 55391

Michael Kesend Publishing
1025 Fifth Avenue
New York, NY 10028

Modern Promotions/
  Publishers
155 E. 55th Street
New York, NY 10022

John Muir Publications
Box 613
Santa Fe, NM 87501

New American Library
1633 Broadway
New York, NY 10019

New Castle Publishing Co.
13419 Saticoy Street
N. Hollywood, CA 91605

Nilgiri Press
Box 477
Petaluma, CA 94953

Nitty–Gritty Productions
Box 5457
Concord, CA 94524

101 Productions
834 Mission Street
San Francisco, CA 94103

Orenda Publishing
235 Hoover Road
Santa Cruz, CA 95065

Ortho Books
575 Market Street
San Francisco, CA 94105

The Overlook Press
667 Madison Avenue
New York, NY 10021

Owlswood Productions
1355 Market Street
San Francisco, CA 94103

Oxmoor House, Inc.
P.O. Box 2262
Birmingham, AL 35201

Pacific Search Press
222 Dexter Avenue N.
Seattle, WA 98109

Palisades Publishers
Box 744
Pacific Palisades, CA 90272

Panjandrum Books
11321 Iowa Avenue
Suite One
Los Angeles, CA 90025

Peachtree Publishers, LTD
494 Armour Circle, N.E.
Atlanta, GA 30324

Peanut Butter Publishing
2445 76th Avenue SE
Mercer Island, WA 98040

Peebles Press International
1865 Broadway
New York, NY 10023

Pelican Publishing Company
1101 Monroe Street
P.O. Box 189
Gretna, LA 70053

Penguin Books
40 West 23rd Street
New York, NY 10010

Perigee Books
200 Madison Avenue
New York, NY 10016

Phoenix Publishing
Canaan, NH 03471

Piper Publishing
Box 3205 Traffic Station
Minneapolis, MN 55403

Playmore Inc. Publishers
200 Fifth Avenue
New York, NY 10010

Pocket Books
1230 Avenue of the Americas
New York, NY 10020

Prentice–Hall, Inc.
Route 9W
Englewood Cliffs, NJ 07632

The Putnam Publishing Group
200 Madison Avenue
New York, NY 10016

Quail Ridge Press
Box 123
Brandon, MS 39042

Rainbow Books
675 Dell Road
Carlstadt, NJ 07072

Random House, Inc.
201 East 50th Street
New York, NY 10022

Reader's Digest General Books
750 Third Avenue
New York, NY 10017

Reiman Publications
Box 643
Milwaukee, WI 53201

Richboro Press
Box One
Richboro, PA 18954

Rodale Press, Inc.
33 East Minor Street
Emmaus, PA 18049

Ross Books
Box 4340
Berkeley, CA 94704

Royal Publishing Co.
Box 5027
Beverly Hills, CA 90210

St. Martin's Press
175 Fifth Avenue
New York, NY 10010

Salem Press
1530 Palisade Avenue
Fort Lee, NJ 07024

Sandlapper Publishing
P.O. Box 1932
Orangeburg, SC 29116

Saturday Evening Post
Book Division
Box 528 B
Indianapolis, IN 46206

Schiffer Publishing Ltd.
Box E
Exton, PA 19341

Simon & Schuster, Inc.
1230 Avenue of the Americas
New York, NY 10020

Simply Scrumptious, Inc.
539 Drive
Stone Mountain, GA 30087

The Soyfoods Center
Box 234
Lafayette, CA 94549

Stackpole Books
Box 1831
Harrisburg, PA 17105

The Stephen Green Press
Fessenden Road
Brattleboro, VT 05301

Sterling Publishing
Two Park Avenue
New York, NY 10016

Stewart, Tabori & Chang
    Publishers
300 Park Avenue S.
New York, NY 10010

Stone Wall Press
1241 30 Street NW
Washington, DC 20007

Strawberry Hill Press
2594 15 Avenue
San Francisco, CA 94127

Sunset Books
80 Willow Road
Menlo Park, CA 94025

Tarcher, Inc.
9110 Sunset Blvd.
Los Angeles, CA 90069

Taylor & Ng
400 Valley Drive
Brisbane, CA 94005

Taylor Publishing Co.
1550 W. Mockingbird Lane
Dallas, TX 72535

Ten Speed Press
Celestial Arts
P.O. Box 7123
Berkeley, CA 94707

Time–Life Books, Inc.
777 Duke Street
Alexandria, VA 22314

Tompson & Rutter
Dunbar Hill Road
Grantham, NH 03753

Transatlantic Arts
Box 6086
Albuquerque, NM 87197

Triad Publishing Co.
Box 13906
Gainesville, FL 32604

University Press of Virginia
Box 3608
University Station
Charlottesville, VA 22903

University of the Trees Press
Box 66
Boulder Creek, CA 95006

Wake–Brook House
960 NW 53rd Street
Ft. Lauderdale, FL 33309

Warner Books
666 Fifth Avenue
New York, NY 10103

Warner Press
1200 East Fifth Street
P.O. Box 2499
Anderson, IN 46018

WellBeing Books
Box 735
Brookline Village
Boston, MA 02147

Wide World Publishing
Box 476
San Carlos, CA 94070

William Morrow & Company
105 Madison Avenue
New York, NY 10016

Winston–Derek Publishers
Box 90883
Pennywell Drive
Nashville, TN 37209

Woodbridge Press Publishing
Box 6189
Santa Barbara, CA 93111

Workman Publishing Co.
One West 39th Street
New York, NY 10018

The Writing Works
Box 24947
Seattle, WA 98124

Yankee Books
Dublin, NH 03444

# A GUIDE TO BOOK PEOPLE

*Self-Publisher*—any person, group of persons, organization, or company that personally arranges and controls creation, production, marketing, and distribution of a book. A self-publisher finances, owns, and totally controls the book. He (they) is responsible for all work and costs, and receives 100 percent of the profit.

*Printer*—a company that manufactures books. This usually includes typesetting, printing, binding, and boxing the books. Often, for a fee, extra services are offered. The author owns the book and simply contracts with the printer to produce it.

*Publisher*—this is the term usually associated with the large New York publishing houses (Random House, Simon & Schuster, New American Library, Doubleday, etc.). It is a commercial house that contracts with an author to publish a book. The publisher absorbs the entire cost of manufacturing, promotion, selling, and distribution. The publisher owns and controls the book for a contracted time, even if the copyright is in the author's/organization's name. The author is guaranteed by contract a certain percentage of sales in the form of royalty payments. The publisher utilizes professional editors, designers, public relations and sales people to promote and sell the book. The publisher has complete control from beginning to end, but will often consult with the author on many points.

*Independent Publisher/Small Press*—these are small versions modeled after the large New York companies. There are literally hundreds of them in the United States. Some are very good and are simply "mini" publishers. Many of them specialize in certain subjects.

*Vanity Press*—this is a type of publishing company that does not have a very good reputation. They will publish a book, but the *author* must underwrite all costs. The vanity presses claim to furnish all the services involved in publishing a book, paid for by the author, but many times the services are questionable. This is considered the *least* desirable option in publishing.

*Booksellers*—any retail outlet (bookstores, gift shops, department stores, etc.) that buys books from a publisher to resell to the public. The standard discount offered to booksellers is 40 percent off the retail price, but there are exceptions to this rate. Often booksellers reserve the right to return all unsold books to the publisher in a specified amount of time. This does not hold true for community cookbooks published by nonprofit organizations—these are usually sold to booksellers on a "nonreturnable" basis. Booksellers are billed for the wholesale cost of the book and shipping expenses.

*Distributors/Wholesalers*—these are "middleman" companies in the book industry. They represent many different publishers and sell to booksellers. This system allows a bookseller to buy many titles from one source, offering one order, one shipment, and one bill to pay. Distributors/wholesalers usually buy from the publisher for 50 to 55 percent discount off the retail price, and sell to booksellers at the 40 percent discount (though varied scales exist in this industry, also). This type of company offers a service and there are many different types, both national and regional, with different costs and services.

*Fulfillment Houses/Companies*—a company whose business it is to distribute a publisher's orders. The company usually stores a quantity of the publisher's books. A publisher writes up the orders and invoices, sends these to the fulfillment company, and the fulfillment company puts the order together and ships it to the customer. There is a fee for this service that is usually figured "per book" or "per box."

*Remaindermen*—basically a "sale" company. Remaindermen buy old, out-of-date, unwanted, discontinued, or damaged books and resell them to bookstores, discount stores, or secondhand stores for special sales. The price they offer the publisher for "remaindered" books is very low, usually the actual production cost of the book or less.

*Agent*—a person whose profession it is to negotiate and represent an author with the publishing houses. For a set fee or a percentage of the book contract price, the agent will take on the job of approaching publishers to sell them the idea for a new book, negotiate all terms, and basically oversee the book for the author.

*Book Rep*—a salesperson for the publishing companies. A rep usually travels in a set region or territory, calling on booksellers to promote and sell the books published by his company. He receives a percentage of all sales.

# GLOSSARIES

## Book World Glossary

*AAP*—The Association of American Publishers is the trade association of book publishers in the United States.

*ABA*—the American Booksellers Association is the national association of retail booksellers in the United States.

*ABI*—the Advanced Book Information form that, when filled out and returned, places your book in *Books in Print*.

*ALA*—the American Library Association has both individual and organizational members and is the largest library association in the country.

*Copyright*—the registration of your book with your notice of ownership.

*Discount*—the amount or schedule of the reduced retail price of a book for sale to qualified booksellers; this can vary greatly.

*ISBN*—the International Standard Book Number system.

*LCN*—the Library of Congress Number that allows your book to be cataloged in the library card catalog system.

*OCRA*—one of the widely used type fonts that is readable by both the human eye and computerized scanning devices.

*Out of Print*—notice to a customer or customers that the specified title is no longer sold by that publisher.

## Printing Glossary

*Bid/Quotation*—the offer or proposal from a printing company or publishing company that lists all aspects of work to be done and a price for work and services.

*Bindery*—a company that binds books.

*Binding*—the cover that holds together the pages of a book and the process of attaching it; there are many variations and styles of binding.

*Blow Up*—to have an image (picture or illustration) enlarged photographically.

*Bulk*—a term used to describe the thickness of paper; it is the thickness of the paper in relation to its weight.

*Camera-Ready Copy*—any material to be printed that is ready to be photographed by the printing camera; the resulting printed image will be identical to the copy photographed.

*Clip Art/Pull Art*—art that is available in art or graphic stores and is considered "public domain" for printing use; it is usually available camera-ready, and varies greatly in price.

*Coated Paper*—paper that has a coating on the surface that varies its appearance.

*Collate*—the binding process that gathers printed sheets or signatures of a book, arranges them in the proper order, and prepares them for binding; this can be done manually or mechanically.

*Contract*—in this case, an agreement between a publisher and a printer, or an author and a publisher, for work to be done; it is written and may be enforced by law—a legal document.

*Cover Stock*—the paper or other material that is made specifically for use as the book cover.

*Crop Marks*—guidelines or marks on camera copy that show areas that either will not show or that will be removed from the finished product; the marks designate exact areas to be printed.

*Customer Changes*—changes that a printing customer makes after copy has been typeset; there are substantial charges for these changes.

*Dummy*—an imitation of a real object; in printing it is a model of a proposed book, indicating the general trim size, thickness, shape, and general appearance of the finished product; a preview book.

*Editing*—a process by which a person makes a written work suitable for final printing; subjective decisions concerning style and copy.

*Edition*—all the copies of a single press run on a book, all identical.

    *Revised Edition*—usually a reprint of an original book with changes and alterations in the original copy, layout, or style.

    *Library Edition*—an edition of a book that has been bound either originally or specifically according to library standards.

*Embossed*—raised surface on paper, usually a design or logo.

*Folio*—a page number in a book, especially one assigned to a page during the printing process.

*Format*—a plan or layout of the appearance and organization of a book or publication.

*Four-Color Process*—a printing technique that uses the primary colors plus black, and by photographic and plate process can reproduce an unlimited number of colors.

*Galleys*—a type of proof printed from typeset copy.

*Grain*—the direction or pattern in paper.

*Gutter*—the white space of inside margins between facing pages of a book.

*Illustrations*—any visual material used to clarify by example: photographs, line drawings, graphs, charts, diagrams, etc.

*Layout*—the arrangement, sketch, or proposal for a printed piece; the plan.

*Logo*—the name, symbol, trademark of a product's name, usually in a special design, used in publication and business; an identification symbol or design.

*M*—used often in printing and publishing works, the letter stands for the quantity of 1,000 (i.e., 4M copies).

*Manuscript*—the original handwritten or typed copy for a proposed publication.

*Opacity*—the quality or state of paper that makes it more or less transparent; paper for printing should have more opacity so that printed words do not show through.

*Overrun/Underrun*—terms used in printing runs where either more copies or fewer copies than specified in the contract are actually printed.

*Paperboard*—pasteboard or cardboard.

*Paperbound*—bound or covered in some form of paper.

*Paperweight*—the weight of a certain paper as measured in sheets or reams.

*Paste-Up*—articles to be printed (type, illustrations) affixed to boards in preparation for photography for printing.

*Payment Terms*—the terms or schedule, as specified by contract, under which payment for work or services is made.

*PMS Color*—a standard national code of printing colors and categories called the Pantone Matching System; samples and code numbers are available.

*Press Proof*—instead of a copy, an actual printed piece is run on the press for inspection.

*Proof*—after a manuscript is typeset, a copy is made from which the publisher proofreads for errors and corrections before final printing; may come in several forms (blue line, silverprint, galley, etc.).

*Reprint*—another printing of a book that is exactly like the first run; some books have many reprints.

*Retouching*—to clean up or correct original artwork or photographs by hand before actually photographing for printing.

*Reverse*—a process where, when printed, colors actually reverse from color to white and white to color.

*Score*—to mark or crease paper in order to fold it more easily.

*Signature*—in printing, a large sheet printed with four, or a multiple of four, pages that, when folded, becomes a section of a book.

*Slip Sheet*—a boxing or packing process where a piece of paper is "slipped" between the books to keep them from rubbing or scratching each other in shipment.

*Specifications/Specs*—an exact written description of all details involved in manufacturing a book.

*Stock*—the amount and type of paper to be printed.

*Storage*—stock (books) that is actually stored until used.

*Trim Size*—the actual size of a page or cover after it has been printed and cut.

*Type*—the actual letter as seen after it is printed on a page, with literally hundreds of different styles; the configuration or style (design) of letters.

*Type Face*—the surface of the type that leaves the printed impression in a certain style.

*Bold Face*—a type that is much heavier than the type used in regular text.

*Upper Case*—capital letters.

*Lower Case*—small, lower-case letters.

*Italic*—a type that slants forward.

*Point*—the printed size of the type.

*Verso*—the "back" of a page, always a left-hand page.

## Business Glossary

*Accounts Payable*—the system of recording all purchases you have made and to whom and when you owe money.

*Accounts Receivable*—records or system of goods sold by you, and the customer's name and amount due for collection.

*Balance Due*—the total amount of money due including merchandise, sales tax, shipping and handling, minus any payments or credits.

*Bill To/Ship To*—the "bill to" is the name and address to which invoices or statements for an order should be sent. The "ship to" is the name and address to which the actual order should be sent; these two addresses are often different.

*Book Post Rate*—a special fourth-class rate established by the United States Post Office for use in shipping books.

*Bulk Mail Rate*—several varied and discounted rates for postal mailing, with strict guidelines for marking, sorting, and minimum number of pieces, which must be followed; used for large mailings.

*Consignment*—an arrangement for sale of books to a dealer where payment for books is not made until the books are actually sold.

*Customer*—a person, company, or store that purchases your book.

*Customer Purchase Order/Number*—a written request for the purchase of goods (books), describing the item, cost, method of shipping, etc.; it represents an order and a commitment to pay, and usually has a printed number for identification and bookkeeping.

*Discount*—amount of discount reduced from the suggested retail price, usually figured in percentages, for use in sales for resale or promotional purposes.

*Distribution*—the means or methods by which a book is sent from the publisher to the customer; involves many different methods.

*Inventory*—amount of books still in the publisher's ownership, figured in either number of books or value of books.

*Invoice*—a bill that is a detailed list of books shipped with a list of all costs due.

*Library Rate*—a special discounted rate established by the United States Post Office that can be used to ship books to educational institutions or libraries.

*Net Amount*—the price of sale from the publisher to the customer (price).

*Order Cancellation Date*—a date, usually printed on a customer's purchase order, after which an order should be cancelled if fulfillment is not possible.

*Out of Stock*—a notice to a customer that a book is temporarily out of stock, and a notification date of when it will again be available.

*Packing List*—an itemized list that is shipped with the books, giving the contents of the shipment (a copy of an invoice is often used for this purpose).

*Price Per Book*—the suggested retail price per book or the discounted price per book/unit.

*SASE*—the initials for "self-addressed, stamped envelope."

*SBA*—Small Business Administration.

*Ship On*—a date requested by a customer on which he would like books shipped.

*Shipping & Handling*—any extra charges added to an order besides the cost of books (freight, insurance, etc.).

*Shipped From*—the location and address from which books are shipped.

*Statement*—a written financial account showing an amount or payment due or outstanding.

*Terms*—an amount of time a customer has to pay an amount due.

*UPS*—United Parcel Service.

*USPS*—United States Postal Service

*Vendor*—the person or company that sells goods (books).

*Wage Scale*—the scale of wages (salary) paid to an employee.

*Waiver*—a document that releases a claim voluntarily.

*Wholesale*—the sale of goods in large quantities, at a discounted price, for resale.

# IMPORTANT ADDRESSES

American Booksellers
  Association
122 East 42nd Street
New York, NY 10168
212/867–9060 or 800/637–0037

Cataloging in Publication
CIP Office
Library of Congress
Washington, DC 20540

(Card catalog number available for books not yet
  published)

Register of Copyrights
Library of Congress
Washington, DC 20559
(Request Form TX)

Hays, Rolfes & Associates
Publication Consultants
P.O. Box 11465
Memphis, TN 38111

Independent Literary
  Agents Association (ILAA)
21 West 26th Street
New York, NY 10010

Poets and Writers
  Information Center
201 West 54th Street
New York, NY 10019

R.R. Bowker
205 East 42nd Street
New York, NY 10017

(Write the ABI Department to
  request the assignment of
  a publisher's prefix for an
  International Standard
  Book Number)

Society of Authors'
  Representatives (SAR)
P.O. Box 650
Old Chelsea Station
New York, NY 10113

Small Business
  Administration
Washington, DC 10416

# REFERENCE BOOKS

*AMERICAN BOOKSELLER* (American Bookseller Association) Monthly magazine to the members of the trade association. Directed mainly to the independent bookseller.

*AMERICAN BOOK TRADE DIRECTORY* (R. R. Bowker) Names/addresses/phone numbers of manager/owner of virtually every bookstore in America and Canada. Separate listings for wholesalers and distributors.

*AYER DIRECTORY OF PUBLICATIONS* (Ayer Press, One Bala Ave., Bala Cynwyd, PA 19004) Over 21,000 magazines and newspapers nationally. List of feature editors.

*BACON'S PUBLICITY CHECKER* (Bacon's Publishing Company, 332 So. Michigan Ave., Chicago, IL 60604) Guide to all major trade and consumer magazines, daily and weekly newspapers in the USA and Canada. Lists the types of publicity material.

*BOOKS IN PRINT* (R. R. Bowker) Author and title indexes to some 585,000 books in the USA. Revised each November. International Standard Book Number required for listing.

*DIRECT MARKETING MARKET PLACE* (Gale Research Company, Book Tower, Detroit, MI 48226) Reference book for companies that sell by mail, newspaper, magazine, radio, television, and phone. Advertising agencies, consultants, and artists specializing in direct marketing.

*DIRECTORY OF MAILING LIST HOUSES* (B. Klein Publications, P.O. Box 8593, Coral Springs, FL 33065) Provides alphabetically the names/addresses/phone numbers of more than 3,500 list houses, specialists, and brokers in the country.

*DIRECTORY OF SHORT-RUN BOOK PRINTERS* (Ad-Lib Publications, P.O. Box 1102, Fairfield, Iowa 52556) A nationwide directory of book printers capable of producing from 10 to 10,000 + copies of a book, booklet, directory, or other bound publications.

*DIRECTORY OF SMALL MAGAZINE/PRESS EDITORS AND PUBLISHERS* (Dustbooks, P.O. Box 100, Paradise, CA 95969) Lists editors and publishers of small magazines, presses, and papers by the editor's name alphabetically.

*EDITOR AND PUBLISHER INTERNATIONAL YEARBOOK* (Editor & Publisher Co., 575 Lexington Ave., New York, NY 10022) Comprehensive listing on newspapers in the USA and Canada.

*ENTREE* (7 East 12th St., New York, NY 10003) Tabloid targeted to the gift/gourmet retailer and others in the trade.

*THE FAMILY PAGE DIRECTORY* (Public Relations Plus, Box 327, Washington Depot, CT 06794) Editors of the family section in over 550 newspapers published daily.

*GIFT AND DECORATIVE ACCESSORIES* (51 Madison Ave., New York, NY 10012) The international business magazine of gifts, gourmet, home accessories targeted to the retailer.

*GIFTWARE BUSINESS* (Gralla Publications, 1515 Broadway, New York, NY 10036) Magazine to the gift industry.

*INTERNATIONAL DIRECTORY OF LITTLE MAGAZINES AND SMALL PRESSES* (Dustbooks) Directory listing independent magazines and small presses. Perhaps the most comprehensive listing of self-publishers.

*LITERARY AGENTS: A WRITER'S GUIDE* (Poets and Writers Information Center)

*LITERARY MARKET PLACE* (R. R. Bowker) One of the most valuable reference books available to the self-publisher with sections for distributors, book trade events, agents, book review sources, book manufacturers, associations, services, and suppliers.

*MEDIA GUIDE INTERNATIONAL: BUSINESS/PROFESSIONAL PUBLICATIONS* (Directories International, Inc., 150 Fifth Avenue, New York, NY 10011) Lists business and professional publications across the world.

*PUBLISHERS WEEKLY* (R. R. Bowker) Weekly magazine of the publishing industry. Reviews books and gives current overviews of the industry.

*SMALL PRESS* (R. R. Bowker) A bimonthly magazine addressing the issues and subjects of interest to the independent book publisher.

*TALK SHOW DIRECTORY* (National Research Bureau, Information Products Group, 310 South Michigan Ave., Chicago, IL 60604)   Includes all types of radio and television shows using guest appearances with criteria and subject matter of interest.

*TV PUBLICITY OUTLETS NATIONWIDE* (Public Relations Plus, Box 327, Washington Depot, CT 06794)   Local and network television programs that use outside guests.

*ULRICH'S INTERNATIONAL PERIODICAL DIRECTORY* (R. R. Bowker)   65,000 periodicals classified by subject. Listings from all over the world.

*WHO'S WHO IN CABLE COMMUNICATIONS* (Communications Marketing, Inc., 2326 Tampa Avenue, El Cajon, CA 92020)   Over 1,500 cable stations and the contact person.

*WORKING PRESS OF THE NATION* (National Research Bureau)   A five-volume set covering Vol I-Newspapers/6,900 listings; Vol. II-Magazines/5,000 listings; Vol. III-TV & Radio/ 9,500 listings; Vol. IV-Feature Writer & Photographer/ 2,000 listings; Vol. V-Internal Publications/3,800 listings.

*WRITER'S DIGEST* (9933 Alliance Road, Cincinnati, OH 45242)   Information source about different magazines and newspaper markets.

*WRITER'S GUIDE TO COPYRIGHT* (Poets and Writers Information Center)

# Bibliography

*The American Heritage Cookbook and Illustrated History of American Eating and Drinking.* New York: American Heritage Publishing Company, 1964.

Applebaum, Judith, and Evans, Nancy. *How to Get Happily Published.* New York: New American Library, 1982.

Armstrong, Donald R. *Book Publishing: A Working Guide for Authors, Editors and Small Publishers.* Houston: Bookman House, 1979.

Behr, Marion, and Lazar, Wendy. *Women Working Home.* Edison, N.J.: WWH Press, 1981.

Bourland, Hal. *How to Write and Sell Non-Fiction.* New York: The Ronald Press, 1956.

Brown, Bob, and Eleanor. *Culinary Americana: 100 Years of Cookbooks Published in the United States from 1860 through 1960.* New York: Roving Eye Press, 1961.

Cain, Michael Scott. *Book Marketing: An Intelligent Guide to Distribution.* Paradise, CA: Dustbooks, 1981.

Chickadel, Charles J. *Publish It Yourself.* San Francisco: Trinity Press, 1978.

Daigh, Ralph. *Maybe You Should Write a Book.* Englewood Cliffs, NJ: Prentice-Hall, 1977.

Goulart, Frances Sheridan. *How to Write a Cookbook and Sell It.* Port Washington, NY: Ashley Books, 1980.

McKendry, Maxime. *The Seven Centuries Cookbook: From Richard II to Elizabeth II.* New York: McGraw-Hill, 1973.

Mayer, Debby. *Literary Agents: A Writer's Guide.* New York: Poets and Writers, Inc., 1983.

Meyer, Carol. *The Writer's Survival Manual.* New York: Crown Publishers, 1982.

Neal, Harry Edward. *Nonfiction: From Idea to Published Book.* New York: Wilfred Funk, Inc., 1964.

Nicholas, Ted. *How to Self-Publish Your Own Book and Make It a Best-Seller.* Wilmington, DE: Enterprise Publishing, 1980.

Poynter, Dan. *The Self-Publishing Manual.* Santa Barbara, CA: Parachuting Publications, 1984.

# Index